Compromising Traditions

Scholars in modern languages and literature have enthusiastically embraced the use of the "personal voice," explicitly autobiographical intervention within the act of criticism. However, on both sides of the Atlantic, venerable traditions of classical scholarship have deterred classicists from engaging in such self-reflection as they offer new interpretations of Ancient Greek and Roman texts. Indebted to the insights of feminist and post-structuralist writing, the use of the "personal voice" challenges the traditional notion of the objective critic who analyzes texts from a disinterested perspective.

Compromising Traditions is the first collection of theoretically informed autobiographical writing in the field of classical studies. The contributors represent a wide range of academic areas of specialization and theoretical approaches. All, however, share the goal of creating a more expansive and authoritative form of classical scholarship, which acknowledges distinctive differences amongst its practitioners as vital sources of strength.

Judith P. Hallett is Professor of Classics at the University of Maryland at College Park. She has published widely on Latin literature, women in Greek and Roman antiquity, and the study of classics in the United States.

Thomas Van Nortwick is Professor of Classics at Oberlin College, where he has taught since 1974. He has published a number of autobiographical essays, as well as scholarly articles on Greek and Latin literature, and a book, *Somewhere I Have Never Travelled: the Second Self and the Hero's Journey in Ancient Epic* (1992).

Compromising Traditions

The personal voice in classical scholarship

Edited by Judith P. Hallett and Thomas Van Nortwick

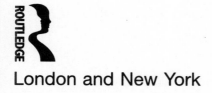

London and New York

First published 1997
by Routledge
11 New Fetter Lane, London EC4P 4EE

Simultaneously published in the USA and Canada
by Routledge
29 West 35th Street, New York, NY 10001

Typeset in Baskerville by Routledge
Printed and bound in Great Britain by
T J Press (Padstow) Ltd, Padstow, Cornwall

British Library Cataloguing in Publication Data
A catalogue record for this book is available from the British Library

Library of Congress Cataloguing in Publication Data
Compromising traditions: the personal voice in classical scholarship
/edited by Judith P. Hallett and Thomas Van Nortwick.
Includes bibliographical references and index.
1. Classical philology.   2. Civilization, Classical.
3. Classicists – Biography.   4. Autobiography.
I. Hallett, Judith P., 1944– .   II. Van Nortwick, Thomas, 1946– .
PA27.C64 1996
480–dc20   96–21412 CIP

ISBN 0–415–14283–0 (hbk)
ISBN 0–415–14284–9 (pbk)

Contents

Contributors

Charles Rowan Beye Distinguished Professor of Classics, Lehman College, City University of New York.

Susanna Morton Braund Professor of Latin, Royal Holloway College, University of London, Egham, Surrey, UK.

Judith de Luce Professor of Classics, Miami University, and Professor and Dean of the School of Interdisciplinary Studies, The Western College Program, Oxford, Ohio.

Judith P. Hallett Professor of Classics, University of Maryland at College Park.

Charles A. Martindale Professor of Latin, Department of Classics, University of Bristol, UK.

Patricia Moyer Visiting Scholar, Department of English, University of North Carolina, Chapel Hill, and Research Fellow, Centre for Women's Studies, University of Exeter, UK.

Thomas Van Nortwick Professor of Classics, Oberlin College, Oberlin, Ohio.

Susan Ford Wiltshire Professor of Classics, Vanderbilt University, Nashville, Tennessee.

Vanda Zajko Lecturer in Classics, Department of Classics, University of Bristol, UK.

Introduction

Judith P. Hallett

The personal voice has been defined by Nancy K. Miller in *Getting Personal: Feminist Occasions and Other Autobiographical Acts* (New York, 1991) as "an explicitly autobiographical performance within the act of criticism." To write or speak about one's research from a personal and autobiographical standpoint acknowledges and explores the unique relationship between the distinctive background of the researcher on the one hand, and the questions which she or he poses and privileges in the course of scholarly investigation on the other. In *Redeeming the Text: Latin Poetry and the Hermeneutics of Reception* (Cambridge, 1993), one of the contributors to this volume, Charles Martindale, suggests a different way of describing our project. If, in Martindale's words, "criticism can be represented as another telling, another story, to explain a text, which thereby enacts a particular closure, or a series of closures, on that text, but which in turn opens itself to further interpretations," then each of the essays in this collection somehow insists on recognizing that the critic's own story is an important component of the act of criticism.

Personal voice criticism may be viewed additionally in the context of a larger movement in literary scholarship, as a further challenge to the traditional notion of the objective critic who analyzes texts from a disinterested and universally relevant perspective. Feminist scholars have for some time now been emphasizing the role played by gender, race and class in the production and reception of knowledge. Post-structuralists have questioned the validity of two paradigms long established within the interpretive community of academic critics: the ideals of the detached scholar and the impartial reader, both of whom absorb and impart knowledge unfiltered by their own political, social or personal circumstances. Both feminist and post-structuralist approaches to literary texts thereby also urge us, implicitly or explicitly, to recognize the person behind the scholarship, and to gauge the effect of that person's own story on his or her efforts to interpret the stories told by others.

This volume is the first collection of theoretically informed "autographic" writing in the field of classical studies, and part of an intellectual conversation involving both American and British classicists. We have entitled it *Compromising Traditions* for several reasons, each related to a different connotation of our English noun and verb "compromise." Most obviously, by revealing something about ourselves and why it is we ask the questions that we do, we contributors have compromised ourselves and our writing in one basic sense: that of exposing ourselves and making our writing liable to suspicion and disrepute. Anxiety that self-revelation in their scholarly writing may compromise their professional reputations as serious and trustworthy scholars surely helps to explain why our fellow classicists have been slow to recognize the validity of "speaking personally" when presenting their research publicly. Indeed, in a paper presented at the 1992 conference on "Feminism and Classics" at the University of Cincinnati, Marilyn Skinner observed that classical studies has traditionally enforced "unusually rigid taboos against speaking of oneself in print."

To be sure, several eminent classicists, all of them British by birth or academic affiliation, have publicly connected their personal circumstances with the ancient literary texts and material data they have chosen to analyze, and with the questions that their analyses have posed. Among the best-known examples of such writing are C. M. Bowra's *Memories 1898–1939*; E. R. Dodds' *Missing Persons*; Bernard Knox's preface to his *Essays Ancient and Modern*; and, most recently, K. J. Dover's widely-discussed *Marginal Comment*. Yet these self-revelatory retrospectives by men in their post-retirement years, elucidating their authors' past scholarly achievements, are not generally classified as serious scholarship. Save for Dover's memoir, they tend to avoid larger theoretical issues. And while the late John Pinsent's idiosyncratic editorial musings at the start of each *Liverpool Classical Monthly* regularly endeavored to link his personal life with his scholarly and professional preoccupations, H. D. Jocelyn's obituary of Pinsent in the *Independent* trivializes these endeavors by asserting that "Many British classicists continued to feel embarrassed by one aspect or another of the enterprise, [although] foreigners . . . found it amusingly British and entirely admirable."

Nevertheless, during the past few years a number of classicists have begun to offer, at much earlier stages of their careers, similar reflections about themselves, and about the links between their personal experiences and their academic research. What is more, they have done so to illuminate ideas that they are presenting in public for the very first time, ideas which stem from serious engagement with innovative analytical and theoretical concerns, and ideas which are meant to be taken seriously. In integrating two different traditions – that of self-revelation with that of intellectual inquiry – in their scholarly writing, they have forged "a compromise" in yet another sense of the word: that of creating something that combines qualities or elements of different things.

Several articles employing the personal voice have come from a group of American scholars seeking to apply feminist theory to the study of classical texts. My own "Feminist Theory, Historical Periods, Literary Canons and the Study of Greco-Roman Antiquity," appears alongside Shelley P. Haley's "Black Feminist Thought and Classics: Re-membering, Re-claiming, Re-empowering" in *Feminist Theory and the Classics*, an essay collection published by Routledge in 1993. Both Haley and I were encouraged to adopt autographic approaches in these essays by one of the volume's editors, Amy Richlin, herself the author of an earlier, prize-winning article on feminist and Foucauldian theorizings of ancient sexuality – "Zeus and Metis: Foucault, Feminism, Classics," *Helios* 18.2 (1991) – which employs the personal voice to haunting effect.

Some of this writing emanates from American literary critics probing their own emotionally-charged relationships with canonical ancient literary texts. Since the mid-1980s my co-editor, Thomas Van Nortwick, has produced a series of pioneering essays which make explicit the close connections between key events in his own life and his evolving analytical and theoretical perspectives on works of classical literature. Another of our contributors, Susan Ford Wiltshire, utilized the personal voice both memorably and evocatively in her 1984 presidential address to the Classical Association of the Middle West and South on Vergilian *labor*. In a 1994 memoir, *Seasons of Grief and Grace: A Sister's Story of AIDS*, she has again availed herself of its puissance, in an affecting account of her brother's death which also incorporates insights derived from her encounters with ancient literary works. It warrants notice that while Van Nortwick's earlier essays were published in journals which specialize in critical studies of modern literary works (such as the *North Dakota Quarterly* and *Plattsburgh Studies in the Humanities*), his newest, entitled "Achilles in Oberlin," has appeared in a mainstream, fairly traditional, American classical period-ical, the *Classical Bulletin*. Like the large and enthusiastic audience attracted by our session on the personal voice in classical scholarship at the 1994 meeting of the American Philological Association, this devel-opment suggests that personal voice criticism holds an interest for a widening segment of classicists, those of conventional as well as those of progressive outlook.

The APA session, which we – Hallett and Van Nortwick – co-organized over a period of nearly two years in accordance with the APA program committee's guidelines for organizer-refereed panels, can trace its genesis to a series of lively interchanges sparked by Skinner's and other papers at the 1992 Cincinnati conference on feminism and classics. But in formulating our intellectual and professional objectives for this panel, we were determined to involve a diverse group of male and female classicists who represent a wide variety of research interests, methodological approaches, and attitudes about the use of the personal voice in classical scholarship. Our original panel proposal to the APA program committee specified our interest in submissions which *adopt, analyze or critique* a personal and autobiographical standpoint in discussing classical texts and artifacts, and in addressing issues of interpretation, which take interdisciplinary and multicultural perspectives into account, and which focus on the benefits *and* dangers of employing the personal voice as a pedagogical technique. What is more, once our proposal had been accepted, we published our call for papers in the *Liverpool Classical Monthly* as well as in the APA and Women's Classical Caucus newsletters, in the hopes of attracting submissions from classicists from outside North America, particularly the UK.

Both of us (and the panel's external referee, W. Ralph Johnson of the University of Chicago) were extremely impressed with the variegated nature and high quality of the abstracts submitted anonymously for our consideration. Later, moreover, when we learned the identity of all the individual authors, we were delighted to discover that they included two members of the classics faculty at the University of Bristol – Susanna Morton Braund and Vanda Zajko – as well as Patricia Moyer, who taught at the University of Exeter for many years before relocating to Chapel Hill, North Carolina. Frustrated by an embarrassment of scholarly riches, in the form of more submissions than our 1994 APA panel could accommodate, we applied to the APA program committee to establish a three-year special topics colloquium on the personal voice in classical scholarship. Happily, this proposal was also accepted, which has enabled us to continue offering opportunities for the exchange of ideas on this topic of lively interest at APA panel sessions in 1995, 1996 and 1997. In addition, owing to the presence of our two British-based colleagues on the 1994 APA panel, and to the concern of my own paper with the ways in which American classicists define and assess themselves relative to their European, and particularly their British, counterparts, we decided to submit the entire APA panel for presentation at the 1995 meeting of the British Classical Association at the University of St Andrews.

The British Classical Association version of our panel turned out to be a somewhat modified version of our APA undertaking. We had originally invited both Wiltshire and Charles Rowan Beye to serve as commentators for, and to provide differing critical perspectives on, the 1994 APA panel. Beye could not join us in Atlanta on that occasion; thus the chance to present the panel a second time in St Andrews made it possible for him to take part in this project at last. The St Andrews version of our panel additionally featured a presentation by Moyer, who also had been unable to attend the APA meeting. Since illness prevented Zajko from traveling to St Andrews, her colleague Charles Martindale not only read her paper, but additionally made a number of important independent remarks about the employment of the personal voice as a literary critical practice.

Furthermore, the 1995 president of the British Classical Association, David West, took an active interest in our panel. He offered comments on some of the individual papers after they were presented; he announced – at the conclusion of his presidential address the following day – that he had, when writing this lecture, decided to criticize the autographic approach to ancient literature exemplified in the "publicity" for our panel "as advertised" in the *Liverpool Classical Monthly*; he read at length from our call for papers; he conceded that, having heard the presentation by Beye, who "has taught the *Iliad* to a class of students who live in a society where murder is a daily occurrence," he was "persuaded that the personal voice could be a useful teaching technique with certain pupils." But after stating that "Charles Beye has taught in the Bronx; David West is in no position to criticize his methods," West decried "a fair amount of modern work with a theoretical basis," stating that "my advice to the young would be to cast out theory, and get down to real work on the texts, the monuments, the surviving objects, the evidence." We regret that Professor West declined our invitation to contribute a revised version of his presidential address to our proposed volume. As should be evident, however, he kindly shared a copy of his text with us, and several of our contributions – most obviously that of Martindale – engage with the ideas he has propounded there and elsewhere about the interpretation of Latin literature.

The essays in this volume amalgamate the APA and British Classical Association "Personal Voice" panels. They appear in approximately the same order which was followed by the panel presentations, although we recognize that other kinds of arrangements might be just as effective. One such possibility would have been a section on issues in the interpretation of Greek and Latin literary texts, which would contain the contributions of Van Nortwick, Judith de Luce, Martindale, Moyer and Wiltshire; a second section on issues pertaining to professional identity within the classics community, which would have contained those of Braund, Zajko and myself; and a third section reflecting on our project to date (and the contributions to this volume) with Beye's paper and Van Nortwick's concluding essay.

Nevertheless, as many of our contributors address issues of literary interpretation *and* issues pertaining to professional identity, and as most of them actively engage with ideas expounded in the essays of their fellow contributors, we ultimately decided against such a restrictive organizational scheme. The interconnections between our various contributions, moreover, testify to a commitment on the part of both co-editors and individual authors to making this volume a collaborative project, an effort expressing our shared hopes for the future of our common calling of classical studies. As such, our volume seeks to further a tradition embodying the literal and etymological, albeit now obsolete, definition of the verb "to compromise," as given in the third (1992) edition of the *American Heritage Dictionary of the English Language*: from the Latin (via Old French and Middle English) *compromittere*, "to promise mutually."

At the same time that it builds on our commonalities, our volume seeks to highlight the diversity among all nine contributors, a diversity which assumes many forms. We are six women and three men, ranging in age from early thirties to mid-sixties and in rank from Lecturer to Distinguished Professor. Some of us write in unmistakably American or British idiomatic prose (and orthography), others adopt a less localized, more transatlantic mode of expressing ourselves. Our places of employment include both private liberal arts colleges and public institutions of higher learning in diverse locales: New York City, metropolitan Washington, DC, Chapel Hill, Nashville and two small towns in Ohio as well as Bristol, Exeter and London, England. While the majority of us work in academic departments which offer the PhD degree in classics, two of us teach in classics departments which cater to an exclusively undergraduate clientele, and another in a classics department which awards the MA as its highest degree. Yet another has spent her entire teaching career as a lecturer not in classics, but in English literature.

We are Latinists and Hellenists, gays and straights, Jews and Christians. We hold advanced degrees from Stanford, Tulane and Big Ten state universities as well as from Ivy League strongholds in the US, and from Nottingham, Exeter and Bristol as well as from Oxford and Cambridge in the UK. Admittedly, our three British-based contributors all hailed from the Department of Classics and Archaeology at the University of Bristol at the time of the APA and St Andrews panels. The contributions of all three, moreover, are the most explicitly theoretical in approach. But they differ from one another in important ways as well: in the goals and scopes of their respective essays, and in the ancient and modern texts with which they have chosen to engage.

What is distinctive about each contribution to this volume is that each, in its own way, tries to tackle difficult problems and tough questions with a forthrightness that is fiercely uncompromising, in the sense of being unwilling to concede to something detrimental or pejorative. Thomas Van Nortwick's "Who Do I Think I Am?" attempts to assess the five of his published essays which take as their starting point a work of Greek or Latin literature that he has seen as representing in some way a dilemma or issue central to his own life. Acknowledging that he originally wrote these essays not as contributions to classical scholarship but as efforts to come to terms with major changes in his personal circumstances, he reflects upon a number of questions which this project has subsequently raised: whether his scholarly engagement with classical literary texts has furnished an escape from serious self-examination; whether his professional career can be integrated with the rest of his life; whether he even has the capability of mastering and adopting innovative theoretical approaches to literary criticism. He focuses upon the figure of Homer's Odysseus, the subject of his first autobiographical essay, and to him a "dark paradigm for his youthful fears of self-disclosure and consequent lack of access to certain truths about [himself]." In so doing, he examines the limitations and strengths of various – modernist, postmodernist and feminist – critical approaches as vehicles for imparting self-knowledge to himself and to his students.

In "Reading and Re-Reading the Story of the Helpful Princess," Judith de Luce also investigates the relationship between changes in her own personal circumstances over the past thirty years and her responses to a group of ancient literary texts. Each of these Greek and Latin poems and plays – among them Apollonius' *Argonautica*, Euripides' *Medea* and Vergil's *Aeneid* – features an archetypal figure whom folklorists have labeled the Helpful Princess, a powerful or influential woman who abandons family or home to aid the hero in his quest. Recalling that as an undergraduate – during the mid-1960s, before the advent of the most recent women's movement – she was taught to admire these female figures for the contributions they made to both the narrative and the hero, de Luce observes that it was not until she had begun her graduate studies, and the women's movement was underway, that she noticed the tremendous costs that each Princess incurred for her helpfulness. She acknowledges that she has now come to regard the Helpful Princess as emblematic of the dilemma faced by women of her own generation: too young to embrace and yet too old to abandon the socialization of their mothers, they are torn between deferring to the ambitions of others and pursuing their own. And she concludes by posing a number of questions: about why the story is so "ruthless," why the hero leaves, and why story-tellers persist in according this figure such a prominent place in their narratives.

Susanna Morton Braund's "Personal Plurals" explores issues related to voices, masks and the person in relation to both classical scholarship and the classics profession. She first considers the process of depersonalization involved in the creation of the impersonal academic voice which has long functioned as the "norm" in classicists' academic discourse: after looking into modes of personal and impersonal pedagogy in the training of graduate students, she laments that Oxford and Cambridge, which have long dominated the classics profession in the UK, "continue to show themselves lamentably incapable of even beginning to diversify the sorts of voices heard." Significantly, she notes, challenges to this normalizing depersonalization in the British classics community have not come from previously under-represented groups (who feel compelled to keep adopting the voice authorized as acceptable to the academy in order to earn a place therein) but from John Henderson, a white, middle-class male who writes from King's College, Cambridge, one of the securest possible positions within the academy.

Yet upon close inspection, Braund contends, Henderson's ostensibly personalizing mode of self-presentation turns out to be as much of an artificial construct as the depersonalized voice validated by the academy. In order to weigh the advantages and disadvantages of using the impersonal and personal voice, and to advocate a strategy of multivocality, she looks at two very different scholarly studies on the topic of ancient obscenity, J. N. Adams' *The Latin Sexual Vocabulary* and Richlin's *The Garden of Priapus: Sexuality and Aggression in Roman Humor.* She also connects her reflections on these matters to wider questions, insisting all the while on the value of the *process* of classical scholarship for fostering personal growth as well as for providing a richer understanding of societies ancient and modern.

Vanda Zajko's "False Things Which Seem Like the Truth" expands upon the paper which she gave at the APA by incorporating portions of the preface to her University of Exeter doctoral thesis (on a group of myths which featured the motif of women resisting sex and marriage); and by discussing both Dover's *Marginal Comment* and some of its reviews in connection with her arguments about status and cultural authority. As she herself recalls, she began to integrate the personal voice into her own scholarly repertoire when writing her thesis several years ago. Inspired by the work of the American feminist psychoanalytic theorist Jane Gallop to "think through autobiography," she found herself able to match the "liminality of these mythic women with what [she] perceived to be [her] own marginal position in regard to mainstream tenured classicists whose concerns had successfully marginalized [her own]."

Yet Zajko admits that the euphoria of discovering personal voice theory was short-lived, and that she now faces several critical questions about the definition, use and potential of autobiographical writing. In pondering these questions she particularly worries about the illusoriness of temporal coherence and authorial credibility; about the difficulties of doing feminist work that fundamentally challenges the assumptions and traditions of classical scholarship; about the validity of gender as an analytical tool in interrogating male-authored texts; about feminism as – like male ideology – both an instrument and an effect of power; about the use of anti-essentialist arguments to deny the intellectual and political validity of feminist thought and action; about the current privileging of previously marginalized voices and the danger of representing "some experiences of life" as "more legitimate than others"; and about the importance of status and cultural authority in validating autobiographical speakers. Observing that "even if we personify the text and pay no attention to the person of the author, we cannot get away from the idea of human agency altogether," she stresses "the need in our day-to-day lives for identifying subject positions for ourselves, however provisional and fragmentary we may feel such identifications to be." And while acknowledging that autobiography enables us to emphasize our affinities with others, she underlines the centrality of reading and writing autobiography to both intellectual and political activity: by making each of us feel unique, they support our individual struggles for self-differentiation.

Charles Martindale has contributed an ambitious and widely-ranging essay entitled "Proper Voices: Writing the Writer," and consisting of three separate parts. In the first he adopts a theoretical (partly deconstructive and postmodern) perspective in looking at some general issues, particularly the rhetoricity and social constructedness of the personal voice, and the contentious response which the mere use of the personal voice elicits among academic classicists. Here he makes use of scholarship providing a rhetorical analysis of various academic discourses: to underline the liberating value ascribed to the personal voice by those who feel constrained by prevailing discursive norms; to note how the distinction between primary literature and secondary criticism can be blurred; to query how we conceptualize the self; to emphasize that explicit appropriation of canonical texts for the concerns of the commentator belongs to a time-honored tradition of interpreting ancient literature; and, much as Rembrandt's Aristotle contemplates the bust of Homer, to contemplate the unorthodox model of autobiography furnished by *Roland Barthes by Roland Barthes*.

In the next portion of his essay, Martindale fleshes out his discussion by reading a major autobiographical text from antiquity, Augustine's *Confessions*, in the process arguing that literariness and truth are not necessarily incompatible, addressing the issue of trust in contrasting Augustine and the autobiography-disparaging Paul de Man, and focusing upon the difficulties and complexities of any autobiographical enterprise. In the final section he has discussed his own recourse to the personal voice, highlighting his essay about ambiguity in Vergil which contains a short autobiographical narrative about his own brief mental collapse and hospitalization in Germany. After reflecting upon the various responses which this paper elicited from three different audiences, he concludes that the experience of presenting this paper has helped him clarify the parameters of what is academically speakable. At the same time, however, he admits that this experience was fraught with both ethical and expository difficulties.

Patricia Moyer's "Getting Personal About Euripides" begins by situating the privileging of the personal voice in the context of postmodern literary theory: contrasting it to "the personal statement that high modernism resisted with its emphasis on objectivity"; characterizing it as "disciplined and aware," and as using "resources of intellect, feeling and experience, without adopting a mask of objective authority"; even comparing its uses in contemporary scholarship and postmodernist poetry. She attributes her own interest in the specific relevance of these issues to classical scholarship in some measure to Marilyn Skinner's paper at the 1992 Cincinnati conference on feminism and classics. Skinner's insistence on the range of voices – traditional, personal and political – available for interpreting classical antiquity, Moyer claims, has heightened her own awareness of how the adaptations of Euripidean tragedies by two major twentieth-century literary figures – the American-born H(ilda) D(oolittle) and the Nigerian-born Wole Soyinka – utilize their authors' personal voices.

This awareness has in turn helped Moyer recognize her own personal reasons for responding as she does to these readings, and for learning Euripides' Greek in order to have her own personal relationship with these Euripidean texts. In the course of analyzing the Euripidean adaptations of both H.D. and Soyinka, she considers how the personal voice can be lost or found in translation, particularly by writers working in the forms of poetry, drama or fiction. Finally, when scrutinizing her own experiences as an academic specialist in English literature and mature student of Greek, she poses a number of key questions: about the challenges of adopting a feminist approach to reading male authors, even those who – like Euripides – frequently create gynocentric texts; about the construction of Hellenism by, and the influence of Hellenism among, twentieth-century modernist writers; about the sheer tactile pleasures of classical philological study; and about the appeal of the Greek language to women of letters during the past two centuries.

The title of my own "Doing What Comes Nationally: Writing as an American in Classical Scholarship," punningly evokes the lyrics and dramatic setting of a humorous song from a popular post-war American musical to articulate a painful perception which I seem to share with a number of other American-educated classical scholars: that we are viewed as comically disadvantaged in academic training and virtually unlettered in our command of the field relative to those trained abroad. By citing numerous remarks, uttered by Americans themselves as well as by scholars from other countries, about Americans' inferior qualifications (and even potential) for scholarly accomplishment in classical studies, I document why this painful perception obtains. I liken these criticisms to disparaging remarks leveled at myself and others because of our gender, and thereby posit an analogy between the situations of feminist and American classical scholars. Furthermore, I take issue with those who, evoking an "international perspective" which supposedly unites all practitioners of classical studies, dismiss as "xenophobic" any effort at acknowledging the major differences between the study and teaching of classics in the generalist and democratic educational system of the United States and in the specialized and more elitist systems of education in European countries; at accounting for these differences; and at questioning US professional practices which privilege colleagues of European training. Expanding upon my analogy between feminist scholarship and classical studies, I note the criticisms often voiced by those resisting the challenges mounted by feminists to the universalizing claims of the "humanistic perspective" – charges that feminists engage in "unscholarly whin[g]ing, white male-bashing, and demands for special treatment by the unqualified." I liken these anti-feminist criticisms to those by which we American classicists fear we will be assailed if we challenge the "international perspective" supposedly common to all classicists by recognizing distinctively American elements in our approaches to scholarship and teaching. After providing a larger American intellectual, historical and political context for my own efforts to think about my own education, teaching and scholarly writing as merely different from, not lesser than, those of non-American classicists, I explain why I have chosen to discuss these emotionally-charged issues in the personal voice.

Charles Rowan Beye proffers an array of autobiographical reminiscences which testify to the high personal costs that he, and other American classicists of his generation, incurred as a result of denying important aspects of their individual identities in order to adopt the generic, anonymous voice of the straight WASP male. He welcomes the personal voice in scholarly studies if "it will allow teacher and student or writer and reader of a scholarly article to isolate, identify and clarify more readily the idiosyncratic aspects of interpretation that hitherto may have been concealed" and "if it will allow a scholar to understand him or herself well enough to recognize the personal elements in what may have initially seemed to be an objective or value-free criticism of a text." Nevertheless, in ruminating about the other contributions to this volume, and about their concern with such aspects of personal identity as gender, race, nationality and age, he wonders why there is so little reference to class. He proceeds to suggest that so much contemporary hostility or indifference to the classics among students "derives from their incapacity to understand what is to them the voice of an entirely alien class and from their teachers' incapacity to speak of antiquity in any other way than as apologists for the ruling class."

Beye's comments upon other contributions to this volume respond to a number of ideas advanced in these essays: by rejecting the notion that figures in ancient literary works merit imitation as models for our own behavior, and by suggesting different ways of interpreting and evaluating the characters of Odysseus and Medea; by finding great danger in the tendency of the "personal voice theoretical approach" to speculate about the critic rather than the text, and by associating this tendency with the roots of personal voice criticism in the feminist movement (and the acculturation of women to analyze other persons, "what dismissive males call 'gossip'"); by protesting against the non-committal voice, arbitrary selection standards and "dreary, unimportant" topics of scholarly publications in classics; by questioning the efficacy of encouraging students in need of acquiring workplace survival skills to write in the personal voice;

and by documenting and deploring the damage inflicted by foreign scholars upon the profession of teaching classics in the US.

Susan Ford Wiltshire's "The Authority of Experience" proposes a framework for the meaning of "authority" in classical scholarship that includes the validity of reference or analogy to personal experience. First, however, she ponders over why, when she completed her first book at the age of forty-six in the fall of 1987, this occasion took so long to come about. After describing her slowly-dawning sense of authorial empowerment, she illustrates her contention that "all writing is personal" by recounting the biographies of her own three books: on themes of public and private in Vergil's *Aeneid*; on Greece, Rome and the Bill of Rights; and on the loss of her younger brother to AIDS.

In the course of her discussion, Wiltshire reminds us that "we write as an act of hospitality to strangers," observing "I see writing as the most public thing I can do because it touches people I will never meet, some of whom will come after me." She closes by listing a number of caveats concerning the personal voice, and by enumerating some advantages of the personal voice. Among these advantages are that "assuming the authority of experience helps keep us connected in ways that make our writing more pointed and vibrant," and that "recognizing and assuming our voice makes us more magnanimous toward our colleagues because we are able to appreciate the fact that unique factors have also shaped their voices."

Thomas Van Nortwick's concluding essay considers what classical scholarship is for, and how classical scholarship written in a personal voice fits into this picture. He observes that earlier generations of classicists, determined to "uncover the world of Greece and Rome undistorted by intervening events and preoccupations," focused on those aspects of classical antiquity that seemed to have mattered most to the ancients themselves. Yet as a result of honoring such priorities, he argues, we classicists have tended to see "the hierarchies implicit in such choices as part of the 'truth' we look for," rather than as the product of our own preoccupations with recovering an antique mentality. He remarks upon our reluctance to examine our own intellectual priorities, to ask "Important to whom?" "Better for what purpose?" "Why is this work of art important to *me*, in my own time and place?" By adopting the role of objective scholars, he emphasizes, "we have been leading an unexamined life."

Pointing out that recent, and more varied, approaches to the study of classical antiquity have drawn attention to the context in which a work of art is created, Van Nortwick observes that postmodernism in particular "marks a major departure" by questioning whether or not any kind of objective truth exists. In this new intellectual climate, he maintains, we cannot hope to achieve any consensus about the goals of classical scholarship without first checking our motives for what it is we do and why we do it. Indeed, he argues that the "subjective aspects" of a personal voice perspective have become "less worrisome in the wake of post-modernism," since

> if finding objective truth seems increasingly problematical, then being open about a personal agenda is only honest. . . . Insofar as we accept that all subject positions are inevitably informed by the author's circumstances, by just so much are we obliged . . . to come clean about our own subjective agency in establishing what is important, interesting, valuable.

Van Nortwick also raises the issue of what classical antiquity has signified in the cultural histories of various western nations. He voices the concern that we classicists – insofar as we are perceived as endorsing the elitist and biased views espoused by certain ancient authors – have been saddled with "cultural baggage we do not want to carry." So, too, in recognizing the impact of feminism on classical scholarship, he provocatively contends that "looking at the assumptions about gender that underlie Greek and Roman thought has shown us that the very idea of objectivity is to some extent 'gendered'." And he additionally associates with traditional notions of masculinity the insistence on maintaining a "detached" analytical position, on engaging in "autonomous inquiry," and on conducting one's self with the dignity befitting a scholar. In that connection, he deplores the way in which classical scholarship has "patrolled" its boundaries "against the intrusion of a private, feminine world."

The *American Heritage Dictionary* first defines (the noun) "compromise" as "a settlement of differences in which each side makes concessions." As several of our contributions have remarked in various contexts, the process of legitimating oneself as a *bona fide* practitioner of our profession has traditionally demanded major concessions: by requiring that those who would call themselves classical scholars consistently write in a manner that suppresses, and even at times denies, the personal qualities which make them distinctive and different thinkers. What is more (to employ a not entirely inapposite analogy with one particular "private, feminine world") such discursive concessions to the conventions of professional acculturation not only loom large during our days as novitiates, but long after we have taken our final vows. By employing the personal voice as part of our classical scholarship – with the goal of creating a more expansive and authoritative form of classical scholarship, one which acknowledges the distinctive differences among its practitioners as vital sources of strength – we are at last seeking concessions from the other side. Classical scholarship and classical scholars both stand to benefit greatly from such compromising traditions.

Chapter 1

Who do I think I am?

Thomas Van Nortwick

I have to admit I was being cute with my title. It could introduce a set of ruminations about identity, selfhood, and so forth, or it could echo my bullying censor, who wants to know how I dare talk to professional classicists about personal issues. The latter fellow, like all bullies, is driven at bottom by fear: that I will appear vulnerable, that I will be revealed as self-indulgent, solipsistic, or − worst of all for the classicist − *mistaken.* I bring all this up partly to deflect criticism, of course, but also because the doubleness in the title leads us to the heart of my topic: I have written and published five autobiographical responses to works of classical literature in the last eight years. These essays all take as their starting point a work of Greek or Latin literature that I have seen as representing in some way a problem or issue central to my own life: my response to Odysseus has changed markedly over the last twenty years. What does this tell me about my own journey from post-adolescence to middle age? The relationship between grief and self-knowledge in the *Iliad* mirror for me my own struggle to integrate my mother's death into my "mid-life crisis." Oedipus' blindness to his own true nature shows me something about the operation of my own denial and my attempts to escape the consequences of a childhood lived with alcoholic parents. Roman ideas of masculine heroism fit uneasily on Aeneas, as did traditional American ones on my father. In the wake of the latter's death, what can I learn about the paternal antecedents for my own unease with heroic masculinity? While I am teaching Thucydides' description of the plague to three advanced Greek students, my nephew, to whom I feel powerful emotional ties, dies of cancer at the age of twenty-one. In the midst of my pain, I feel that my nephew has given me a gift. What is it and what am I to do with it? What can Greek literature tell me about the role of gifts in the life of the spirit?

To classical scholars, and to others absorbed in the knotty questions surrounding the role of personal experience in scholarly analysis, the act of writing these essays may seem full of potentially troublesome questions: what am I offering the reader? Are these essays about literature, or about me? How is such work to be evaluated? Do my discussions of classical texts stand on their own as interpretations that could instruct, say, under-graduates, in the way that traditional "objective" analyses do? Or is the final impact of what I say so implicated in the details of my personal history that the readings are *sui generis*?

The list could be extended, and perhaps what I say here will suggest other questions. But none of these issues were prominent in my mind as I wrote the essays, because I gave myself permission not to worry about what I was doing in a methodological or theoretical sense. The first essay on Odysseus was written at the invitation of the editor of a literary journal, in which analyses of classical literature appear rarely if ever. I thought of these pieces as strictly personal, and as the starting point of each took only the question: what does this work of literature have to do with me? The focal point of this new direction for me was the attempt to come to terms with the enormous and at times painful changes in my own life. People I loved were dying; my first marriage had failed; I had fallen in love and married again; I was entering middle age and feeling alternately adrift and exhilarated by a sense of freedom from my past. Who was I? Had I changed as much as I sometimes thought, or were there continuities in my life that could tell me something about how I had arrived at the threshold of middle age as the person I seemed to be? As far as I could tell, very few if any classicists would ever see the essays (all of which have appeared in the same journal) unless I chose to send them copies.

Looking back after eight years, I see some things I missed or preferred not to address at the time. Tucked away behind the abiding search for my true self was a nagging question: do I really believe that classical literature can tell me something about myself and the world I live in, or am I using all that reading and writing as a way of *not* thinking about myself? Can my professional career be integrated with the rest of my life? Also lurking was the queasy fear that I, trained in the dying idiom of New Criticism, was hopelessly out of date in my approach to literature. Worse yet, was I already an old dog, incapable of learning about newer theories of reading and writing? My veering off (as it felt then) into personal essays offered the hope that I could simply avoid the whole enterprise of deconstruction and the postmodern turn. I would become "a writer!"

It all worked out differently. First of all, I soon noticed that what I was doing, trying to integrate my personal experience into readings of literature, was in fact an area of interest to theorists of the postmodern, and to feminist scholars. In running away from theorists who made me feel inadequate, I had stumbled into their backyard. Working for my state humanities council – another way I thought would help me avoid the cutting edge of theory – brought me to read a book that finally taught me what postmodernism was about, Kenneth Gergen's *The Saturated Self: Dilemmas of Identity in Contemporary Life* (1991). And most delightful of all, it turns out that some classicists at least were not only sympathetic but sometimes even enthusiastic about the value of my work within the context of our profession. So it seems a fruitful thing for me at this point to go back to Odysseus, the subject of my first essay, and re-examine my project within the context of my profession as teacher and scholar of classics. I also hope to explore the implications for my project of three interrelated perspectives on the place of imaginary constructs within the larger cosmos, modernism, postmodernism, and feminism.

Imagine him behind enemy lines. Leaping from behind every rock, exploding from every cave, surfacing from every dark pond, come enemies, ready to annihilate. He must keep his head down, his eyes open; for every threat, a strategy must be at hand. No one must know his true identity; disguise is essential. Sylvester Stallone, you are saying to yourself. No, Odysseus, of course. I ask my students: do you have any friends like Odysseus? Do you want any? Their response is usually that, well, he has to be that way, because he must get home, and the world is full of those who would keep him from it, one-eyed monsters, goddesses with emasculating sexual power, virgins who would weigh him down with devotion. How about his father, I ask? The suitors are all dead, Penelope and Telemachus back in the fold, allies lined up for the final showdown. So now is the time to torture his own father, make him roll in the dirt one more time before finally telling the truth?

I will not play out the classroom scenario any further, as my readers all know the tenacity of young minds and can imagine their own endings. But let me instead push a little further: granting that Odysseus' behavior can be understood as justified, given the aims of the essentially comic narrative he inhabits, are we therefore disallowed from taking him seriously as a paradigm outside the fictional construct? I ask because, you see, I have always done that. My history with the *Odyssey* and especially with its hero goes back twenty-five years or so, to that dark night of the soul, graduate school. Odysseus was for me then an inspiration because he survived, because he let nothing stand in the way of reaching his goal. My own survival as a member of Yale's graduate program in Classics was a dicey thing, as I knew precious little Latin and even less Greek. My only hope was to will my way past the barriers of my own ignorance and inexperience. I was a fraud; that much I knew, so Odysseus' expertise at lying and disguise were inspiring too: I could pretend I was the kind of intellectually serious scholar who really liked answering the question of whether Plautus' meters showed the residual effects of Saturnian verse, and not a lonely, frightened young man in a crumbling marriage, who was hanging on because he did not know what else to do.

Well, I made it (though not without changing graduate schools). I got a PhD and a job; at the age of thirty-six I had tenure and I was still married. I had, in short, survived, and reached the goals I thought would ensure the good life. But I was still lonely, and even more scared because the good life seemed empty. In the next five years I learned, under the pressure of yet more pain, more about why Odysseus exerted such a strong pull on me as a young man. Much of what I learned came to me because I began to explore how growing up in an alcoholic home had affected me. My mother was a practising addict all of my life until eight months before she died of liver cancer in 1987. As I was to discover, children of alcoholics characteristically conceal their feelings from others – when you have an addict at home, you are reluctant to admit it; you are ashamed; you think somehow it is your fault (if only I could have done/said/been...she wouldn't have gotten drunk again). You begin, under the pressure of your secret, to lie: your friend cannot come over after school because you have to go buy shoes, not because your mother is passed out on the living room floor.

The basic urge here is for damage control. Children of alcoholics live in a fearful place. Grown-ups who are supposed to be taking care of things are unable to do so. The response of many children is to pick up the slack. If you cannot keep your parent from drinking, at least you can try to keep yourself safe, by withdrawing into yourself, by controlling the access that scary people and things have to you. In short, you can become a little Odysseus, lying, disguising your true self, keeping your distance from anyone who might discover your secrets and use them against you.

The trouble is that if you invest too heavily in disguises, you can lose track of what is underneath the masks. If you are always looking outward, to see what kind of persona will fit the situation at hand, or please the person standing in front of you, you can lose the habit of checking in with yourself. Do I want to do what this person is asking of me? Am I the kind of person who would do such a thing? Do I believe that this person is telling the truth? One characteristic of children from alcoholic homes is that they begin to feel empty inside, as if there were nobody in there.

This is precisely where I found myself at the age of thirty-six. I felt isolated, but was afraid to reveal myself to anyone, for fear there was nothing to reveal. When I was able to get help and begin to face my problems, I found a renewed interest in Odysseus. I realized that in his hero, Homer had created a profound portrait of precisely those qualities I had come to distrust in myself. Looking again at the man of many turns has prompted me to reflect not only on my own past history with him, but also on how a personal response can offer a perspective rather different from the standard academic portrait. Odysseus' lying, manipulation, and habitual distrust of others would be repellent in us or someone we knew. But once the academic motors are whirring, we take another approach. Because the *Odyssey* is a "classic," we tend not to look at its hero as a paradigm for our own behavior – this is the kind of character Odysseus "must" have to work in the story, and what we are interested in is how the story works, not what the characters might tell us about ourselves. This kind of attitude is one reason why some can feel justified in dismissing classical literature as not addressing concerns relevant to our world. But look at what we can learn about ourselves if we take Odysseus seriously as someone we might see in the mirror one morning.

His behavior is said to be justified by his situation. But how many people do we know who configure the world for themselves so as always to feel behind enemy lines? I certainly did. Though I would have characterized myself as friendly, the fact is that I trusted no one with my secrets, fearing they would be used against me. Once I tried revealing myself to others, I discovered that the world changed to a less scary place. Odysseus also shows us what happens when you never make yourself vulnerable to another: you are triumphantly alone. He has no friends; his companions on the trip home are benighted cannon fodder. And if you keep yourself from others, you keep yourself from yourself. This is one way of understanding why Odysseus' identity is such a central theme throughout the *Odyssey*.

Which brings us to another instructive aspect of the poem, its sanctioning of an extreme form of ends-justifying-means. The narrative of the *Odyssey* is, we might say, goal-oriented. Everything hinges on Odysseus getting home, and nothing that furthers that goal is unacceptable. (Those of us in academic life might feel a slight twinge of recognition here. Substitute "tenure" for "home" . . .) Notice the relationship of goal-seeking to self-alienation. Getting home for Odysseus requires not only that he postpone inhabiting his real self, but that he actively distort that self. To put it another way, any sense of personal authenticity is unavailable to him until he reaches his goal. You might be saying at this point, well, identity in the *Odyssey* is configured according to roles, so getting home for Odysseus means reinhabiting the roles that give him his identity: husband, father, son, king. There you go again. If the inhabiting of roles is sanctioned as the context for establishing identity in the *Odyssey*, are we forbidden to think about whether we want to endorse that view for ourselves?

Take me, for instance. I was so intent on reaching the goal of academic respectability, signaled by the PhD, then a job, then tenure, that I lost track of the difference between me, the guy from Illinois, and a professor of Classics. Like Odysseus, I was alienated from myself to the extent that I played roles, assumed disguises (the avid scholar) in pursuit of a status that I thought would give me personal authenticity. The point here is that I, like Odysseus, saw my entire identity as contained in the performance of certain roles. The trouble was, I wasn't inside the fictive world of the *Odyssey*, where being "a graduate student," "an intellectual," "a professor," would supply an integrated sense of self. I was adrift in a sea of fear and vain hopes, hoping that by playing at being a sober thinker and beacon of light for my students, I could escape facing the parts of myself I disliked or feared, fearing that my disguises would not keep me safe.

The *Odyssey* and its hero have furnished, then, important paradigms for me as a man. We have also reminded ourselves that the *Odyssey* is a poem about the relationships between knowledge, power, and identity. But what about the questions I posed at the beginning of my paper? Does my personal reading of the poem have any legitimate use in the classroom? The objections to such an approach spring to mind immediately. First, matters of propriety: you might embarrass the students, who do not want to be asked either to talk about their lives or to respond to your life. This, I think, is a significant problem. I never ask students to respond to material in class in a way that would force personal revelation. If I talk about my own life, I never ask for comments from them (though I do not discourage them, either). I would add a further qualification. I am in a different place in my life than my students. The kind of reflection I find helpful in mid-life may not be useful for them. Indeed, a characteristic problem for late adolescents in particular is to learn to distance themselves from any issue.

All of this urges caution, forethought, and tact. But let us pass on to other kinds of potential problems, which might be called pedagogical. By offering personal responses to literature, you are encouraging "subjective" responses to the material, rather than the kind of detachment that makes objective appraisal possible. How do you evaluate this kind of work if students pursue it? And what about the risk of distorting the original material by imposing values on it that may not have been shared by the author or audience to which the work was first offered? (There swim before your eyes now the specters of your graduate school professors, gravely warning you of the dangers of "reading in.")

About the issue of evaluation, I see no genuine problem. First of all, I do not assign topics for papers that require any personal revelation, and if I do get some, it must be accompanied by some response to a text. In any event, I judge every piece of writing I see according to the ordinary criteria of clarity, organization, grammar, depth of thought, of whether the writer accomplishes what she or he announces as her/his goal at the beginning of the paper. If the writer argues for an understanding of a poem that is counter-intuitive, he or she must demonstrate the validity of the reading in a way that shows me thoughtful engagement with the material and reflection on the implications of what he or she is saying. What more would I want as a teacher?

And let us acknowledge that behind issues of evaluation lie those of power. The grades we give can be significant sorting devices in the business of handing out the world's goodies to our students. If a student can just tell his or her own story and get an "A", then how can we preserve standards in the practice of – what? Handing out the goodies? Of course the same goes for us. If any Tom, Judith, or Susan can get published by confessing their shameful youth, how can we preserve standards in the practice of promotion, tenure, salary? I am being a little facetious here, but one of the issues that feminists have helped us to see is that the hierarchical, competitive model for doing business in our field need not be the only way to proceed, that anxiety about standards can be a device for hoarding power.

Reflection on the necessity for standards could take us even further, into a controversial area indeed, though one that I consider central to humanistic inquiry. If we conduct our classes in a way that exposes for students the dominant assumptions behind our educational system – that what counts is acquiring accurately measurable skills by which they can compete in the race for money, prestige, and comfort – is that necessarily a bad thing? Are we damaging our students if we encourage them to behave in a way that does not maximize their chances for climbing that ladder? Is winning everything? Do they want to be Odysseus? One thing that encouraging students to use Odysseus as a paradigm for judging their own behavior can show them is the cost of behaving in the ways that our society hails as excellent. If we want them to take the *Odyssey* seriously as a reflection of something important in human life, then we cannot insist that, having acquired some perspective on the competitive, hierarchical assumptions that govern the poem, they must automatically respond in a way that affirms those assumptions.

Now to the issue of "original meaning," about which my views can be stated briefly. We cannot recover exactly what the *Odyssey* meant to an eighth-century audience, and to pretend we can is to distort the actual impact that a work of art has in any given moment. We must try to know a work of art as much as we can on its own terms, learn the language, study the culture, trace the assumptions that seem to be embedded in the story about the nature of the universe and everything in it. But finally, if the work of art is to have any significance beyond the museum, it must engage us now. All we have are the stories, and they must make their way in the present. The practical effect of discouraging personal engagement with classical antiquity is often to ensure that the material will never have any impact on important decisions we make now. That way lies the Dodo bird.

Talk of the cultural context for meaning brings me circling back to the trio of -*isms* I mentioned in my introduction. You may have noticed that my assumptions about myself and Odysseus follow from a modernist point of view. That is, I assumed that there was such a thing as *my self* which could be known, an essential "I" that continued, however beleaguered, under all those masks. Furthermore, I assumed that to be alienated from that essential self was a bad thing, a sign of my ill health. But just as I am beginning to feel better, along comes postmodernism, which tells me that the idea of an essential self is illusory, that my identity is continuously emergent, reformed and redirected as I move through a sea of ever-changing relationships. In other words, my behavior as a young man, constructing contingent selves to fit various communities of assent, was not indicative of moral cowardice or emotional illness. No, I was just doing what comes naturally, as it were, since there was no essential self in there for me to seek. And, far from being a relic from a dead language, Odysseus – remember you heard it here first – was the first postmodern hero!

My third -*ism* fits uneasily amidst the other two. These days, it is dangerous to use the singular form "feminism," because the movement has gone in so many directions. One schism in particular is germane to what I am saying here. By challenging the orthodox patriarchal assumptions that underlie much of the work in our own field, feminist scholars have given impetus to the questioning of what is "natural" that characterizes postmodernist thought. At the same time, this questioning has often been done in the name of correcting injustice, of opening access to traditionally male preserves. And the concern for justice and equitable distribution of resources is one issue that makes people nervous about the ontological relativism of postmodernism – if the "truth" is always contingent, how do we decide what is just?

The connection of my own work with feminist concerns has a peculiar history. Though I like to think of myself as a feminist, I started writing autobiographical essays about classical literature in 1985 without any thought of feminism *per se*. I was trying to move away from academic work altogether, giving myself permission to ignore all *-isms*, at least in their self-consciously academic form. It was only later that I noticed that some feminists were urging personal engagement with the text. I was happy to know this, but also slightly anxious at first in my typically insecure way: what if my writing was not the right kind of personal engagement, not theoretical enough? I had thought at least these essays would not come under scrutiny for correctness, but maybe I was being naive.

Happily, I was wrong. Feminist scholars have been supportive of my work. I would like to think that this reflects their recognition that my intent in writing the essays has been motivated by the desire to make the work flow from who I am, to make my identity a part of the meaning of the stories for me. I say this because this is certainly what I prize most in the work of feminist scholars, who have insisted, in a courageous way, that a certain kind of personal authenticity, which must begin with acknowledging oneself as part of the creation of meaning, is prerequisite to a meaningful life.

This latter reflection takes me back for a final time to the postmodern turn. If I am to take seriously the idea that who I think I am is an integral part of my work as a teacher and writer, and, conversely, that my work can help me to answer my existential question, then I must confront directly the implications of postmodernism for self-knowledge. I have struggled with these issues for some time, and here are my conclusions for the moment. I cannot get comfortable with the idea that I have no essential self to which I must be true. I harbor thoughts that would be considered unclean by a strict postmodernist: I think that there is something called the meaning of my life, and I want to know as much of it as I can; I believe that the deepest essence of it is part of something that transcends my life and is larger than my comprehension; my struggle is to come to trust that what that larger truth gives me, though it is definitely not always what I want or think I need, is what I am supposed to have.

REFERENCES

Gergen, Kenneth (1991) *The Saturated Self*, New York: Basic Books.

Van Nortwick, Thomas (1986) "Travels With Odysseus," *North Dakota Quarterly* 54, 25–35.

—— (1988) "The Double Life of Oedipus," *North Dakota Quarterly* 56, 60–70.

—— (1990) "Aeneas: The Wrong Man in the Right Place," *North Dakota Quarterly* 58, 44–63.

—— (1991) "Remembering Patroclus," *North Dakota Quarterly* 59, 15–32.

—— (1993) "Mike's Gift," *North Dakota Quarterly* 61, 119–128.

Chapter 2

Reading and re-reading the helpful princess

Judith de Luce

In Margaret Atwood's *Circe/Mud Poems*, the famous witch confronts Odysseus and tells him not to lie or pretend that he won't leave her:

> ... you leave in
> the story and the story is ruthless.

(Atwood, 1976: 221)

We know all about this "ruthless" story; the departing hero is not unique to Atwood. In fact, the folktale motif of a princess helping a hero, who then leaves, is a recurring pattern in ancient and modern literature. The motif figures prominently, for instance, in westerns of the 1950s and early 1960s. The schoolmarm, single or widowed with a young son, helps the stranger on the trail of a vicious outlaw. She binds the hero's wounds, hides him, gets him information. Finally, he mounts his horse and rides off into the sunset, alone; or if not alone, then accompanied by a male companion, usually an amusing but unmistakably inferior sidekick.

John Updike works with this motif in "The Journey to the Dead", where he writes about a former classics major who unexpectedly runs into a woman he once knew and who is now dying of cancer. As she gets closer to death, he goes to see her only to discover that all they have in common is their meeting in the hospital room. Finally, he announces that he has to be leaving: "He promised, insincerely, to come again, and, like heroes before him, fled" (Updike, 1994: 73). Well, a classics major ought to know about such departures.

Heroes, especially the folktale hero, cannot go it alone; they often need a fairy or a divine helper, perhaps a sidekick with magical implements, an animal helper, or the aid of the ogre's daughter. I want to look at one such helper, the helpful princess. She is a powerful or influential woman who abandons her family or home to aid the hero in his quest; indeed she often gives up everything of her own to help him. In the end, the hero abandons her, choosing to continue on without her.

As a reasonably well-trained classicist, I could approach this topic in the way peculiar to our discipline. I could catalog every helpful princess in Greco-Roman mythology and folklore, provide a complete list of the primary sources for the stories in which these women appear, review the relevant entries in Pauly–Wissowa, cite the appropriate scholarly work on each princess, and discuss the effect of genre on each version of the story. I would refer at least in passing to the post-classical versions of these traditional stories – Mary Renault's *The King Must Die*, for example, and feminist revisions of classical mythology such as June Rachuy Brindel's *Ariadne* and *Phaedra*.

I am not going to do that here. Instead, this essay is more about my reading and re-reading these "ruthless" stories than about the princesses who appear in them. Thus, I have reserved for another time a close examination of the more refined details of their stories; in fact, those details reveal considerable variety in the accounts of each princess and her role as helper, but my concern here is to paint a broad picture of these helpers as I trace the evolution of my interest in them. I could easily have entitled this essay "Anatomy of a Reading."

My own deeply personal interest in the persistence of the "ruthless" story and its implications drew me to this motif in the first place. Like many women, I have found myself performing the role of the helpful princess too often. I read the "ruthless" story very differently thirty years after I first encountered it, and this difference in my interpretation is nowhere more striking than in my approach to the intertwined stories of Ariadne, Medea, and Dido.[1] I want to look at what it means to be a helpful princess and above all what it costs to be one. In doing so, I will not attempt to formulate a definitive interpretation of the folktale motif. Instead, by tracing my evolving perspective on the princess, I hope to suggest some of the more provocative questions posed by the motif as it appears in Greek and Latin literature, at the same time as I reflect upon those factors which influence how we read literature.

Ariadne, Medea, and Dido share a common story, in spite of individual differences in detail and genre. Theseus requires the aid of Ariadne when he enters the labyrinth to kill the Minotaur. He can get in by himself, but he needs her aid in order to find his way back out. Ariadne provides Theseus with the means for escape, betraying her father in the process. Medea follows Ariadne's example when another hero requires aid. In order to get the golden fleece guarded by the insomniac dragon, Jason must yoke fire-breathing bulls, sow dragon's teeth and then kill the soldiers which spring from the sown teeth. He cannot possibly accomplish any of this without help, so Jason appeals to Medea by citing the *exemplum* of Ariadne, who did not hesitate to aid Theseus (*Argonautica* 3. 960–1001). Failing to mention that Theseus subsequently abandoned Ariadne, Jason succeeds in persuading Medea, who does provide extraordinary help: an asbestos ointment, a strategy to kill the soldiers, a sleeping pill for the dragon, the murder of her brother to delay the pursuit of her father, even the murder of Pelias. Unlike Ariadne and Medea, Dido is not living at home nor is she dependent on her family, but she, too, helps a hero. After escaping from burning Troy, Aeneas has been shipwrecked and washes up on the shores of North Africa. He finds himself in that most vulnerable position, a traveler without connections and resources in a strange land. Dido offers him protection, affection, and opportunity.

In college, I read the stories of the helpful princess very much as I had been taught to and as I have outlined above: that is, for the contributions which the princess makes to the plot. After all, the basic folktale pattern is clear: a hero badly needs help; the daughter of the king (usually a king's daughter but not necessarily so; sometimes she is an independent woman) provides the help, often betraying her father in the process. Carolyn Heilbrun has remarked that Joyce, "interested only in the labyrinth of male questing, did not stop to wonder about Ariadne, did not even mention her" (Heilbrun, 1990: 121). Like Joyce, we were reading the myths of male heroes, and so our discussions focused, not on the helper, but on the help she provided. The hero's quest would have been effectively short-circuited had he not gained the help of such a princess, and our interest did not extend to her as a character. Though poised on the edge of the women's movement of the 1970s which would give rise, among other things, to women's studies as the academic arm of feminism, as students in 1964 we were not encouraged to look beyond the requirements of the male hero to ask about the fate of the princess.

We had, in addition to the princess who is expected to help and to be abandoned, a model of a very different and much less problematic (for the hero at least) kind of helpful woman. Aeneas' Trojan wife, Creusa, presents no threat at all, either to Aeneas or to the Roman foundation story. She has the decency to get out of the way, conveniently disappearing during Aeneas' escape from Troy. When her ghost appears at an appropriate moment later, she frees Aeneas from any responsibility to go back and find her, and sends him on to Italy with her blessing. This is one woman who does not complain about her abandonment but instead urges on the hero to leave her and act on his commitment to the future.

With Creusa as with Dido, however, we asked few questions about these women other than the help they gave the hero.

In graduate school, however, Herbert Howe turned my attention in a new direction, urging me to look at the princess as a character with her own story, rather than as a necessary plot device. That we asked different questions of these stories should reflect the greater sophistication with which we were reading this literature, of course, but there was something more. As an undergraduate, my personal experience with romantic relationships had been non-existent. I had had no occasion myself to offer sacrifices to such a loved one, although I had certainly been raised to assume that such sacrifices and the subsequent abandonment were part of what it meant to be a woman. It was while I was in graduate school that I first became involved in the growing women's movement, however, and began to question that assumption of female sacrifice. So it was then that I began to think seriously about the choices the helpful princess makes and the consequences of her choices.

When my women students consider their own career choices, I warn them to avoid that of the helpful princess because her future prospects with the hero tend to be dim. Literary representations of the princess have sometimes stopped short of finishing the story, although in recent years, feminist scholars have begun to reconsider such traditional tales and have suggested theoretical models for interpreting them (Ostriker, 1982; Zipes, 1986). As Heilbrun notes, Theseus leaves Ariadne's story unfinished even as he abandons her (Heilbrun, 1990: 121). There are indeed a number of different explanations, ancient and modern, for why Theseus left Ariadne and what happened to her after his departure. Plutarch provides a range of possibilities; Renault's is the most lurid and in some ways the most convincing. All versions say that she is left behind.

Medea, like Ariadne, is abandoned. Once they have escaped from Colchis, Jason and Medea make their way to Corinth, where he leaves her and becomes betrothed to the young daughter of the king. Dido, too, is deserted when Aeneas heeds the divine warning delivered by Mercury to leave Carthage and proceed on to Italy. Aeneas nearly manages to escape without facing his helper at all, until Dido confronts him. Aeneas does leave, of course, and Dido commits suicide, but he will see her again in the Underworld where he will attempt to speak to her shade. His justification for his departure – that he didn't leave of his own volition; that he had more compelling obligations and inducements to leave than to stay – does not reflect the slightest interest in or understanding of the position in which he left her, exposed to ridicule and to the hostility of her neighbors. Indeed, doubting that he could have been the cause, Aeneas expresses some surprise that she had committed suicide. It may well be anachronistic to wish that he would at least acknowledge how he had repaid her, but his inability to see beyond himself should not go unnoticed. And like Jason and Theseus, he refuses to be grateful.

It is not enough to remark upon how the hero repays the princess for her help, however. We need to ask yet another question: what did it cost the princess to help the hero? Even when we look at other aspects of her story – the alternative versions of what happened to Ariadne after Theseus left her; why Aeneas fails to be kind as he abandons Dido – we seem reluctant to ask that question. She helps, yes, but at what cost? This is not the same as asking what happened to her; I want to know what price she paid. To be precise, why does she give up so much?

Dido, in fact, had already named the price when she confronted the departing Aeneas:

> Because of you, my honor has been destroyed . . . and my good name.
> $(4.321–322)^2$

This is an extraordinarily high price to pay for the risk she took when she compromised her new home for a hero who was seeking a home himself. In Apollonius, Medea understands that she will lose her family by helping Jason. She dreams of a terrible quarrel between her father and the Argonauts. Since no resolution appears to be in sight, they leave it up to her to choose sides and she chooses Jason, rejecting her parents in the process (3.614–647). When they have escaped from Colchis, Medea reminds Jason of what she has done for him and articulates perhaps more directly than any other princess how high a price she paid: she has lost her parents and her homeland. She has not only betrayed her own integrity but has acted foolishly and in helping him has disgraced all womankind (4.358–370).

When Euripides' Medea confronts Jason, she also reminds him of her help, from coaching him on how to yoke the fire-breathing bulls to drugging the snake guarding the fleece to killing Pelias (476–491). And having done all these things, Medea has nowhere to go now that Jason has deserted her; she can hardly go home, after all, and she certainly cannot expect welcome from the daughters of Pelias (502–511).

Jason's infamous reply reveals a consistent thread in the motif. Aeneas, Theseus, and Jason are all searching for a "home" and position for themselves.[3] Theseus needs to get back to Athens and his birthright; Jason was trying to find his way home when he was set the challenge of obtaining the fleece; and Aeneas, of course, is looking for a new home. It does not seem to cross the minds of any of them that the princess abandons her own home and compromises her identity, which is so bound up with "home," to help the hero find his. Or is that precisely the point? That the ruthless story does not easily allow both hero and helper to be at home? For Jason argues that Medea has indeed gained a great deal more from him than the other way round, because she no longer lives in obscurity among barbarians but now lives among Greeks (535–541). That she is an outcast among those Greeks and actually in peril is lost on him. That she has no "home" any more does not matter within the framework of his heroic tale.

Homelessness dominates Ariadne's story as well. Catullus and Ovid tend to concentrate on the abandoned Ariadne's lamentations over the perfidy of Theseus and her terror at finding herself alone on an uninhabited island. The choice she made to help Theseus and what she gave up to help him, of course, ally her with Medea. Catullus' Ariadne laments the loss of her family in her determination to aid Theseus (64.116–120). Like Medea, Ariadne has no place to go now, even if she can get off the island. After all, she can hardly return to Crete, after betraying her father and enabling Theseus to kill the Minotaur, her own brother. Ovid's Ariadne goes further and equates the danger Jason has exposed her to on the island with his payment for her help (*Heroides* X, 66–72).

In spite of their individual differences, these helpful princesses have much in common. Each abandoned her own home to help a hero in search of a home. For Medea and Ariadne, this meant betraying their father and violating the bonds of kinship which helped define who they were. Dido abandoned the new home which she had been building and the relationships which she had forged with her people. Each was promised or believed she had entered into a marriage with the hero. Each believed that the hero left her either in mortal peril (as on Naxos) or else in so vulnerable a position that her safety was not assured (as with Dido, whose political security had been severely compromised when she stopped construction on the city of Carthage). And each tells us that the price she has paid to help the hero is no less than the loss of her integrity, her very identity. The hero reaches home; the princess helps him get there, but only by losing hers.

But why do I insist now that we ask about the cost to the princess? I cannot settle for interpretations of this motif which recognize only the help the princess provides to move the hero along, or which acknowledge her abandonment but do not ask what she has abandoned herself. These princesses actually tell us what they gave up, but if we pay little attention to that side of the story, then we miss what they are saying and fail to ask the most interesting question, why the story insists that they abandon so much.

I would not ask that question at all, however, had my interest in these stories not evolved as it has; it remains to consider how I have arrived at this point. Were I nineteen, or twenty-nine, or sixty-nine, I might well regard the helpful princess differently, but she reminds me at forty-nine of the dilemma for many of us who came of age at the start of the most recent women's movement. Too young to accept comfortably the socialization of our mothers, but too old to be able to abandon easily that same socialization, we have been torn between the assumption (inculcated since childhood) that we must defer to the male's quest, and the less familiar need to pursue our own. We have attempted an intricate balancing act between the public and the private; we are not always convinced that we can resist *or* play the role of the helpful princess without paying an exorbitant price.

Let me go further. I am a member of the first "baby boomer" cohort. I grew up with "help wanted male/help wanted female" ads and the mixed messages of the media (Douglas, 1995). I am very much the product of a middle-class suburban world which warned that a girl going to college would occupy the place of a man who needed the education in order to support his family. Smart girls were advised to play "dumb" around boys, not to beat boys at games. Dusty Springfield told us how to behave: "You've got to show him that you care, just for him, do the things, he likes to do. Wear your hair just for him; girl, you won't get him, wishin' and a hopin'...". That one needed to "get him" went without question. For many of us who danced to this song literally and metaphorically the helpful princess is uncomfortably familiar. After all, we were raised to accept much of the advice in Mary Wood-Allen's *What a Young Woman Ought to Know,* to practice "feminine constancy, self-abnegation, sweet courtesy" (Wood-Allen, 1905: 260). In college, very much under the influence of this upbringing, we saw in the helpful princess little more than a plot device; her sacrifice was not surprising, neither was her abandonment.

Changes in the United States in the 1970s began to challenge the expectations articulated by Wood-Allen. Girls became explorer scouts and senate pages (1971); Sally Priesand became the first woman rabbi (1972); female tennis players earned equal prize money at the US Open tennis tournament for the first time (1973); women became Episcopal priests (1976); the first women food vendors worked in New York City sports stadiums (1977); Sandra Day O'Connor became the first woman justice on the US Supreme Court (1981); Sally Ride was the first woman selected as an astronaut (1977) and sent into space (1983) (Tavris and Wade, 1984: 22–23). Telephone books included dual listings for married couples; hurricanes were named after men, too; and there were no more "help wanted male/help wanted female" ads.

But the 1970s also saw the publication of Marabel Morgan's *The Total Woman*, a self-help book allegedly intended to enable a woman to improve her marriage. Morgan's book reflected traditional assumptions about the roles of women, regardless of the changes in the 1970s. In *The Total Woman*, the wife is solely responsible for the well-being of her marriage. One must give one's husband admiration first, before he returns love. Morgan distinguishes between men and women: "It's a great strength, not a weakness, to give for the sheer sake of giving. It is [woman's] nature to give" (Morgan, 1973: 65). Indeed, one must adapt to a man's lifestyle; one must admire; one must listen attentively (put the paper down, look at him, don't interrupt, don't be preoccupied). Which is fine, but it is not clear that the husband is required to do anything at all except perhaps breathe. [4]

Why have so many of us played the role of the helpful princess, the lessons of the 1970s notwithstanding? I suspect that while we may have come to realize that our own adventures are worth pursuing, that in the face of the hero's weakness we need not necessarily or automatically give up our own quests, we still share with the story of the princess the lurking suspicion that women above all are supposed to be helpful. Remember Clara Barton, Florence Nightingale. And it is Mother Theresa, not Father. The Republican party, if it has its way, undoubtedly will again require massive private efforts to do the work of providing aid for those in need, and many women will provide that aid – unsalaried or poorly salaried, of course. Yet in the United States, at least, we have never afforded the providing of care much dignity or legitimacy (Wood, 1994).

Self-help books apparently written for the princess (Cowan and Kinder, 1986; Forward and Torres, 1986; Thoele, 1988) join the work of Carol Gilligan and the scholars at Wellesley's Stone Center in their interest in the connection between women and care-giving. Some endorse the role of the helpful princess while others offer strategies for recovering from being one. Some call the pattern which I have associated with the helpful princess, "love addiction."

Consider Norwood's *Women Who Love Too Much*. I will not claim for classical mythology and folktale a facile relevance to modern issues, nor do I propose to apply pop-psychology to these traditional stories. Still, the continuity from antiquity to our own time is not entirely illusory and certainly is provocative. Norwood writes of those who love obsessively as

> full of fear – fear of being ignored or abandoned or destroyed (p. xiv).
> Almost nothing is too much trouble, takes too much time, or is too
> expensive if it will "help" the man you are involved with (p. 19).
>
> (Norwood, 1985)

Norwood's description recalls the desperate acts of Ariadne, of Medea, of Dido, their obsession with the hero, and their willingness to do anything to help him, even at the risk of immense pain to themselves. But if her "obsessive" lovers are motivated in large measure by the fear of abandonment, the painful truth is that by their very act of "loving too much," the Ariadnes and Medeas and Didos guarantee their abandonment.

Recent empirical studies which have suggested that "caring grows out of culturally constructed subordinate status rather than sex-role socialization" (Wood, 1994: 99) reinforce my observations about the assumption that women should provide care. After all, women often find themselves in subordinate positions and may choose to accommodate themselves to the rules and expectations of those in the dominant positions. Women may care for and serve in part because that is how we survive. But in the end we must remember Atwood's Circe; the story is ruthless. It doesn't matter how much we give or for how long, we will be abandoned. That's what the story says.

At this point I need to issue a disclaimer since it is still risky for a woman to question her traditional role as care provider. It is not that helping or caring for others is bad. After all, the hero really does need help. But the role of the helpful princess requires that in order to help the hero she abandon family, friends, and self, and in the end, the princess seldom "gets" anyone and often loses everything. The hero rides off into the sunset without her and without attending to what will happen to her once he has departed.

Why do the helpful princesses from Greek and Roman tradition give up so much? As my reading of these stories has evolved, I have come to think that we need to address this question not to the princess, but to the story and to those who told it. And we may need to ask the question differently: in whose interest is it to tell stories in which women of influence, if not outright power, are reduced to the role of helper and, once helpful, are generally denied the opportunity to accompany the hero or to resume their influence and return to their former lives? Let me suggest just a few directions in which this question might take us. Certainly these "ruthless" stories reflect misogyny and the need of a patriarchal culture to subsume under its own (male) heroes the threatening power of women. Just as heroes must meet, engage in battle, and defeat an Amazon or Amazon-like woman, must the hero also destroy his female helper? The princesses pose a very real sexual threat to the hero; is their abandonment necessary to affirm not only the primacy of patriarchy but the masculinity of the hero? Does Nausicaa survive her experience with Odysseus with little more than mild regret because she is the youngest and least sexually threatening woman he encounters and can therefore be left alone? Or is the point that Odysseus needs her less than he needs the aid of her mother?

Clearly the hero cannot tolerate competition. These stories are about the male hero's quest and do not consider any woman's goals or accomplishments as important as his. More precisely, perhaps the princess must abandon her family, her roots, her own success because the hero cannot tolerate divided loyalties. Not only can there be only one hero, but the princess's loyalty must be to him alone. Yet in the end, the princess cannot abandon enough of herself and so must be left behind. While it might be tempting to claim that these heroes merely suffer from a persistent fear of commitment, making such a claim would slight the political significance of these stories. A woman could learn an important lesson here about her place.

I find Roman marriage practice helpful here. Does the story require the princess to abandon her family because in practice a young woman did "abandon" her family in marriage? In Rome, for example, a bride marrying *cum manu* would literally and legally abandon her natal family, assuming in her husband's family the status of her own children. Even if she were marrying *sine manu*, that bride would in a very real sense leave her own family behind as she joined the household of her husband. Among all the "lessons" contained in these stories, the reality of a woman's experience in marriage should be included.

These stories appear to aim at more than the suppression of individual women's desires for self-definition and for meaningful action. This is certainly not the first time we have seen mythology reflect encounters with other cultures. If the culture that is doing the story telling is to maintain control, then powerful, external threats must be removed or reduced to helplessness in its stories. The three princesses I have been discussing are all foreigners to the heroes: Ariadne is Cretan, not Hellenic, and her name suggests she was originally divine. Medea is a "barbarian" witch from a region famous for its powerful magic. Dido, too, is foreign and represents as formidable a threat to a future Rome as Cleopatra had presented to historical Rome. Moreover, her name suggests that she may originally have been divine. So the abandoning of the princess eliminates a threatening woman and a foreign woman at that.

I could take this even further, however. These stories do more than reflect simple xenophobia; they reflect traditional assumptions which are clarified in mythology about the non-human or liminal status of women. That is, traditional stories generally assume that women are not only the

Other which is not part of the dominant male culture, but that their foreignness extends to their not being fully human either. Women are feared in part because of their liminal status between nature, which always threatens to spin out of control, and male, human culture (Ortner, 1974). Visual representations of women in Greek art, for example, demonstrate this equation of women with the non-human, indeed with the animal, as do the stories of mythological rape victims in Ovid (de Luce, 1993; Reeder, 1995: 299–371, 373–419). If we are going to ask more questions of these traditional stories, then we should also consider whether the abandonment of the helpful princess somehow assures the victory of culture over nature. And that takes us far beyond the original intent of this essay.

EPILOGUE

In graduate school I encountered modern helpful princesses at the same time that I was beginning to reconsider how I read the stories of Ariadne, Medea, Dido, and the others. Similar assumptions underlie the ancient as well as the modern manifestations of the motif I have been discussing. She put her husband through medical school; he left her upon receipt of his degree. She agreed to her husband's insistence that she not work outside of the home. She raised their children, supported him; he divorced her for a younger woman, arguing that while he had developed intellectually and emotionally during their marriage she had not. The story is not unfamiliar to any of us, nor are the underlying assumptions about women's appropriate roles. What is perhaps most remarkable and what demands our attention, is the persistence of the story in literature and in life.

I return to an earlier remark by way of conclusion. I said that I could have called this essay "Anatomy of a Reading." In my exploration of how my perspective on this motif has evolved, I have come to suspect that if we are to understand the motif of the helpful princess in all its complexity[5] we will have to address more carefully a series of assumptions, but above all the question of "who cares?" (*pace* Wood, 1994). As for whether we can do anything to change this persistent and "ruthless story" for ourselves, that remains to be seen.

ACKNOWLEDGEMENTS

I am indebted to Dr Mildred M. Seltzer, Millie, *doctissima amica*, who asked the hardest questions about the hero; to Paula Biren, whose questions helped me look more carefully at the princess; and to Lena de Luce, who read this essay with the vision of a much younger cohort. Tom Van

Nortwick's suggestions have helped me immeasurably as I have sorted out my reading of the motif. And above all, my thanks to Herb Howe who, like all inspired teachers, asked the most challenging question at the most crucial moment.

NOTES

1   The persistence of a simile which ties Nausicaa, Medea, and Dido together underscores the kinship among these women and the dissonance between the princesses' positions before meeting the heroes and after providing help. When Homer describes Nausicaa as the shipwrecked Odysseus first sees her (6. 110–118), the poet likens this self-possessed, energetic young woman to Artemis hunting on the mountains, towering above her nymphs. Apollonius adapts Homer's simile of Nausicaa, but not her good fortune, when he describes Medea as looking like Artemis riding over the hills in her chariot followed by her nymphs and various awe-struck animals (3.876–886). When Aeneas sees Dido for the first time, Vergil's simile comparing the queen to Diana training her dancers in the mountains recalls both Nausicaa and Medea (1.678–692).
2   My translation.
3   I am indebted to Tom Van Nortwick for his perspective on this aspect of the motif.
4   Morgan's disdain for men runs throughout the *Total Woman*, rivaling that of Phyllis Schlafly.
5   It is in fact a complex story which requires that we consider not only the princess but the hero himself. For example, I have suggested that Theseus, Jason, and Aeneas are all trying to get "home" geographically and personally, but it is not necessarily the case that, once home, heroes can stay there.

ACKNOWLEDGEMENT

Excerpt from "Circe/ Mind Poems", *You Are Happy*, SELECTED POEMS 1965–75 by Margaret Atwood. Copyright © 1976 by Margaret Atwood. Reprinted by permission of Houghton Mifflin Co. All rights reserved.

REFERENCES

Atwood, Margaret (1976) *Selected Poems, 1965–75*, Boston, MA.: Houghton Mifflin Company.
Brindel, June Rachuy (1980) *Ariadne*, New York: St Martin's Press.
—— (1985) *Phaedra*, New York: St Martin's Press.
Cowan, Connell and Kinder, Melvyn (1986) *Smart Women / Foolish Choices: Finding the Right Men /Avoiding the Wrong Ones*, New York: Signet Books.
de Luce, Judith (1993) "'O, For a Thousand Tongues to Sing': A Footnote on

Metamorphosis, Silence, and Power," p. 321 in M. DeForest (ed.) *Woman's Power, Man's Game*, Wauconda, IL: Bolchazy-Carducci Publishers.

DeForest, Mary (ed.) (1993) *Woman's Power, Man's Game*, Wauconda, IL: Bolchazy-Carducci Publishers.

Douglas, Susan (1995) *Where the Girls Are*, New York: Times Books.

Forward, Susan and Torres, Joan (1986) *Men Who Hate Women and the Women Who Love Them*, New York: Bantam Books.

Heilbrun, Carolyn G. (1990) "What Was Penelope Unweaving?" in *Hamlet's Mother and Other Women*, New York: Ballantine Books.

Morgan, Marabel (1973) *The Total Woman*, New York: Pocket Books.

Norwood, Robin (1985) *Women Who Love Too Much: When You Keep Wishing and Hoping He'll Change*, New York: Pocket Books.

Ortner, Sherry B. (1974) "Is Female to Male as Nature Is to Culture?" pp. 67–87, in Michelle Zimbalist Rosaldo and Louise Lamphere (eds) *Woman, Culture, and Society*, Stanford, CA: Stanford University Press.

Ostriker, Alicia (1982) "The Thieves of Language: Women Poets and Revisionist Mythmaking," *Signs* 8, 68–80.

Reeder, Ellen D. (ed.) (1995, *Pandora: Women in Classical Greece*, Baltimore, MD: The Walters Art Gallery and Princeton, NJ: Princeton University Press.

Renault, Mary [1958] (1984) *The King Must Die*, New York: Bantam Books.

Tavris, Carol and Wade, Carole [1977] (1984) *The Longest War*, San Diego, CA: Harcourt Brace Jovanovich, Inc.

Thoele, Sue Patton (1988) *The Courage To Be Yourself: A Woman's Guide to Growing Beyond Emotional Dependence*, Berkeley, CA: Conari Press.

Updike, John (1994) *The Afterlife and Other Stories*, New York: Alfred A. Knopf.

Wood, Julia T. (1994) *Who Cares? Women, Care, and Culture*, Carbondale, IL: Southern Illinois University Press.

Wood-Allen, Mary (1905) *What Every Young Woman Should Know*, London: Vir Publishing Company.

Zipes, Jack (1986) *Don't Bet on the Prince*, New York: Routledge.

Chapter 3

Personal plurals

Susanna Morton Braund

I first started thinking consciously about the role of the personal voice in classical scholarship in January 1994, in response to a call for papers for a panel on this theme at the December 1994 meeting of the American Philological Association. I had one of those (what you realise afterwards were) significant conversations with my Bristol colleague Vanda Zajko, who was facing the PhD examination a few days later. As a result of that conversation, I realised that this issue touched a number of chords deep within me. In particular, it set me thinking about my own academic project, much of which to date had been concerned with the concept of the *persona* ("mask") in Roman literature and had been predicated upon the ready separation of autobiography from dramatic performance, or, to put it another way, the personal from the professional. What Vanda said – and what she had written in the preface to her PhD – challenged that separation. She was attempting to elide those categories or, at least, to suggest that there might be a place for the personal within the professional. This might be a strategy familiar from some feminist thought, for example, Nancy K. Miller's *Getting Personal* (1991), but it was new to me at that moment. And as I thought more deeply about it, the idea of some coincidence of the personal and professional appeared to have important implications about the shape, purpose and trajectory of our profession as classicists. On further thought again, it is clear that this idea connects with wider philosophical issues on the nature of person-hood. In this brief essay, then, the fruit of thought-in-process over some twenty months and the very different reactions to two oral deliveries of earlier versions (earlier versions which were joint papers with Vanda Zajko, although in the second version the role of Vanda was taken by her Bristol colleague Charles Martindale), I propose to explore issues relating to voices, masks and the person in relation to classical scholarship and the classical profession.

This chapter will fall into three parts. In the first, I shall explore the process of depersonalisation involved in the creation of the impersonal academic voice which for so long has been the "norm" in classical academic discourse. This question entails an investigation of modes of personal and impersonal pedagogy in the training of graduate students. Second, I shall explore the advantages and disadvantages of use of the impersonal and personal voice. Is personal voice scholarship a reaction against theory or a case of theory run riot? The central issue here is why anyone should want to bother with the non-traditional academic voice. Finally, I shall attempt to relate the above to wider questions about the relationship between the voice and the individual, the voice and personality, the voice and the person. Here I shall insist on the value of the *process* of scholarship. And as part of this process, *my* process, I shall explore different voices for scholarship.

ONE VOICE, ONE STORY

As graduate students and junior lecturers, we tend to be eager to learn the "rules" of the academy in order to gain admission to the hallowed precinct. I was no exception. I rapidly internalised the advice, implicit and explicit, which was offered by people I knew and by people I did not – in the first category my teachers, peers and colleagues, in the second category those scholars with whom I had dealings at a distance, the editors of scholarly journals and the copy-editors at academic presses. The presentation of style-sheets was particularly powerful here, the apparently disembodied advice seeming to have an almost divine authority. The net effect of this advice was the removal of my idiosyncrasies, the individual stylistic variants of my prose, any hint that "I" existed as a real flesh and blood person with feelings. What remained was a depersonalised "academic" voice. And along with it came all the academic apparatus of multitudinous footnotes and hefty bibliographies. This entire process I did not challenge at the time, but accepted, along with my acceptance of the authority of my "elders and betters", above all, that of my *Doktor-vater*, Professor Ted Kenney. (The irony is that the people you owe most to and who know you best are the ones who play the largest part in depersonalising your voice.) I knew, of course, that there was a gulf between this voice and what I might have described as my "real" voice, by which I would have meant (if pressed) my conversational voice, the voice I would use in the classroom or in the common room (which are probably not the same as one another), let alone in the kitchen or in the bedroom, but I accepted that gulf as an inevitable manifestation of professionalism:

there had to be a written voice which differed from my oral voice(s). In retrospect, it seems painfully obvious to me *now* that the depersonalised academic voice which I was encouraged to adopt manifestly bore attributes of gender, race and age: male, white and middle-aged. That I recognised something of this subconsciously at the time is suggested by my choice at that period in my career to be known by my initials only, S. H. Braund, to avoid presenting myself as female to an academy that was almost exclusively male. In the words of the New York philosopher Sidney Morgenbesser, *incognito ergo sum*.

Given my own acceptance, in the early part of my career, of the gulf between how I and people that I know actually talk to one another about the classical texts and ideas which we study on the one hand and how we feel compelled to write about them in publishable form on the other, it now seems highly appropriate (if not predictable) that my approach to my selected field of Roman satire reflected and reiterated that gulf. Profoundly affected by the work of Professor William S. Anderson on *persona* theory, I made one of my projects the explication of the workings of this theory in Roman satire in general and in the satires of Juvenal in particular. Of course, there exists plenty of justification for this approach from Roman culture – especially from Greco-Roman rhetorical theory and practice and also from Hellenistic and Roman philosophy – for example, Cicero's four *persona* theory – and of course the advocation of this approach served the admirable purpose of countering the naïve biographical readings of satirical texts which had previously held the field (and I believe I have made some headway in challenging these views in the UK, although the task has not been an easy one).   ·

But recently I have come to appreciate the limitations of this approach. To posit an author behind the voice in the text, an author of superior detached status who is manipulating the voice/speaker (whatever we call him), runs the risk of containing and thus making safe the potentially explosive and anarchic character created. A more subtle reading now seems appropriate – one perhaps which sees (or should I say hears) multiple voices in any act of artistic communication: author, implied author, internal audience, external audience will do for some of their names. And even this separation of roles will not (necessarily) do justice to the complex dynamics of the performance of narrative. At any rate, it seems to me *now* that for a time I was sucked into a "making safe" of satire and of ancient texts in general.

I can chart this change in my views by speaking of my relationship with my original collaborator on this topic, Dr Vanda Zajko. Some eight years ago, when Vanda was a student of mine at the University of Exeter, making the transition from undergraduate to graduate studies and embarking upon study for the PhD, I gave her the same kind of advice which earlier I had been given and had accepted: internalise the rules of the academy if you want to be admitted. Seven years on, Vanda was holding a junior teaching fellowship at the University of Bristol and was completing her PhD on women's resistance to sex and marriage in Greek myth. She had decided to use the preface to her doctoral dissertation to make a connection between the marginalisation of the women she was studying and her perception of her own marginalisation from the academy. This involved breaking boundaries in certain significant ways. In an academic seminar at Bristol, she delivered a part of this preface in which she spoke frankly of her teenage experience of the development of her body and the awakening of sexuality and linked this to her choice of topic for her PhD and to her treatment of that topic. The challenge that she thus threw down, by this attempt to connect the personal and the professional, was not taken up in discussion at the seminar (perhaps because of the negatively adversarial atmosphere of the Bristol research seminar), and it is my guess that those present who could not believe their ears (that a junior, untenured lecturer was standing up there in front of them and talking about her clitoris) were able to dismiss her paper in a way which in fact precisely re-enacted the marginalisation of which she was complaining. But to me it seemed clear that she was right to challenge conventional ways of thinking about classical texts and classical ideas and that there was every reason to explore connections between the professional and the personal. That there are also profound problems raised by this approach – as Vanda argues in Chapter 4 of this volume – is an issue I shall return to later.

The provocation offered by Vanda's words was insistent. It made me think hard about our discipline. It did not take me long to realise that the "normalising" phenomenon which I described above is deeply rooted in the UK Classics scene, dominated as it is by Oxbridge, a pair of archaic institutions which continue to show themselves lamentably incapable of even beginning to diversify the sorts of voices heard. One readily available means of doing this *might* be to appoint to university posts people who might articulate previously unheard voices, e.g. women or people of colour. On this matter I do not think we in Classics have a good record, and least of all Oxbridge, where the one or two exceptions serve to emphasise how very exceptional they are. But it would be a mistake, of course, to assume that the challenge to the normalising depersonalisation will necessarily come from women academics. In fact, while the gender bias remains so adverse, women may feel themselves compelled to continue to adopt the voice authorised as acceptable to the academy in order to earn a place therein (let alone attain positions of great influence).

Probably the single most striking challenge to the orthodoxy in the UK in published work, in my own field of Latin literature at any rate, has come from Dr John Henderson, who was my undergraduate teacher, though this is a fact which you would probably not be able to glean from a comparison of his and my own writings. In case you are not familiar with John Henderson's approach, which seems designed to shock his readers out of our comfortable assumptions, here is the opening of his essay in the volume *Satire and Society in Ancient Rome,* which I edited in 1989, entitled "Not 'Women in Roman Satire' but 'When Satire writes "Woman"'". He is punning here on the word(s) "Just-if-y".

If I just...

Contemporary feminism makes it impossible to accept what we have been told about Roman Satire or to accept that we know how to get it "right". In return, Roman Satire raises pressing questions for (y)our cultural politics.

To take an example – in fact, as you'll realise, much more than an example – what would it mean to you if I collect together and examine the stretches of Roman Satire where women figure or views about women are featured? After all, that may very well be what you think – maybe guess, maybe take for granted – I am about to try to do. Perhaps it is. It wouldn't be the first time that that sort of project has been attempted. Perhaps it's a familiar proposition, on the way to being "traditional"? But if it once may have seemed obviously *sensible,* too – indeed so obviously and so sensible that the point, purpose or relevance of that project wouldn't need, let alone call for, a justification – I wonder can it seem that way to you right now? *Just* how would you justify it? That is, *if* you would care to try...

You could be anticipating here a neat and tidy chapter on the subject. There would be an unclouded horizon, the prospect of an uncluttered introduction and a plunge into the text. Who would need nagging Nonsense: the baggage that is Theory! Those nuisance False Problems of trend, phase & fashion! And – most important of all from where *I'*m sitting – maybe there wouldn't be any special problems for the writer and just sane, just professional, just expert exegesis and just evaluation would do? (Is that *all*? Does that seem enough to you?)

You would, I suppose we could all agree, be contemplating just one more critical study under the aegis of our Humanist Tradition. I have a point or two to make about this before we get to "Women".

(Henderson, 1989: 89–90)

The ways in which Henderson deviates from the authorised version of the classical scholar's voice are obvious: the presence of the first person; the direct address to the reader – he enters into a dialogue with each of us; the conversational style, whereby he modifies words as he goes along; the emphases, questions and exclamations and such like. And he has remained uncompromising in publications since then, always (I think) utilising the same kind of disconcerting voice, thus engendering (or trying to engender) a politicisation of the academy, even at the level of decisions about what should and should not appear in learned periodicals. For example, when he submitted his recent article on Horace *Satires* 1.7 to *The Classical Quarterly* (published 1994, vol. 44), I hope I'm not betraying any secret when I say that the editors had to consider long and hard whether or not they wished to publish such a piece in which the conventions of the academic article were flouted.

John Henderson's project, then, in his many articles on Latin literature, seems to embrace a challenge to the orthodox ways of writing about Latin literature. But despite first impressions that Henderson's voice is something like a "personal voice", that is not what is going on. His voice is as much a construct as is the depersonalised voice validated by the academy. It is a voice not authenticated by the weight of tradition and hence it lays itself open to the same kind of marginalisation that Vanda Zajko must at times experience. All the more so because Henderson's voice is adopted pretty consistently throughout his writings on ancient texts. It is not, I repeat, a personal voice. But it might be described as a *personalised* voice, in that it acknowledges the existence of writer and reader and the relationship between *actor* and audience, as if part of an ongoing conversation, in a way not done by the depersonalised voice of academe with its authoritarian stance and untroubled assertion of objectivity, which is the equivalent, I suppose, of lecturing to a passively adoring audience or maybe to an empty lecture-hall. Henderson's experimentation with scholarly voice is most welcome. But it is worth observing that this challenge comes from a white, middle-aged, middle-class male who writes from one of the securest possible positions within the academy: from King's College, Cambridge. (And now look at me. I'm writing THIS from a position of (relative) security – a Chair.) How possible is it for someone less secure to adopt such a voice and issue such a challenge? It is not clear that we can with an easy mind commend such an approach to our graduate students who may have to run the gauntlet of unsympathetic traditionalists in order to win "permanent" employment and to get their work published by the established university presses and learned journals.

At this point, then, the question of what constitutes a personal voice still lies open . . .

TWO VOICES/TWO STORIES

Story No. 1

A   Never mind that. What's wrong with the traditional academic voice, anyway?

Z   Because it isn't my own voice. I know that, because it took me quite a long time to learn it. It seems to be an impersonal voice – but now I think about it, it actually sounds like a MALE voice and it likes to assert things more strongly than I think is warranted. It gives the impression that it is AUTHORITY itself.

A   But isn't it a good idea to sound authoritative when you're writing up things that you've studied and thought about hard – when you probably ARE the authority on the subject?

Z   Not necessarily. It depends what you think the whole scholarly enterprise is about. IS it about standing up and coming on as fatherly authority figures? That's not what I think I'm doing. I'd rather see myself as a kind of catalyst, in classical terms a Socratic midwife I suppose, teasing out ideas in people around me by challenging traditional assumptions and patterns of thought. So I don't need the *traditional* voice of authority – but a diploma in intellectual midwifery would be useful! I'd rather open questions up than close them down.

A   And you think that to do that you have to use a personal voice?

Z   Well, maybe. It helps if it's an unconventional or unorthodox voice, I think, or even an unusual STYLE of self-presentation, wacky clothes and so on, because that alerts people to the possibility that what you are saying in that voice is unconventional or unorthodox or somehow challenging. But of course there are other ways of achieving the same effect.

A   For example?

Z   For example, the jargonese used by deconstructionists and the like. That's certainly a challenging way of writing, though it's not one that appeals to me. Far too obscure, parading long, clever words for their own sake and repeating slogans like "Always already".

A OK, so what actually would count as a personal voice? Are you looking for autographics? Or is it enough to reject the conventional, traditional academic voice and find some kind of more natural way of speaking and writing scholarship (whatever that might be)?

Z Here we run into tricky methodological problems. Clearly, the insertion of (apparently) autobiographical details will seem to authenticate a piece of scholarship as written from the personal perspective. But how can we actually ever tell when those details are authentic? Perhaps it doesn't matter, in the end, as long as the act of writing personally provokes more, or different, insights for the reader. And I simply don't know the answer to your question about a natural way of speaking and writing. Is there any such thing as a natural voice or a natural language? I feel that THAT's what I'm using right now, but I can well imagine some people saying, for example, some of my former Bristol colleagues, I can imagine them saying that "all our efforts at communication are so imbued with acculturation that the attempt at recuperation of the genuine becomes irredeemable", or however they'd put it. (*Something* like that.)

A I think you have pinpointed one of the real problems with autographics – speaking personally can so easily seem to be a coercive act which defies and denies contestation. But surely the central difficulty is that so many of what you call traditional scholars will see the personal voice as irrelevant self-indulgence. It could look like theory run riot, couldn't it, feminist theory and psychoanalytical theory and the like. Why should anyone want to bother with it? What's the point? Is it a kind of showing off? Being different for the sake of it? What's wrong with doing it like it's always been done?

Z Lots of issues there. It might just as easily be a reaction AGAINST theory, you know, a feeling that the in-crowds with their theoretic jargon are trying to exclude real people from their discussions and that a more honest representation of expressing oneself is called for. But never mind about that. I think the most important justification for challenging the traditional impersonal voice is this. If you adopt a way of speaking about things that doesn't actually come naturally to you, that you have to learn from your "elders and betters", then there's a risk. The risk is, that by using other people's words, you'll also use their ideas. You might take on their ideas, their ways of looking at the world, without realising it. The whole thing might stop you thinking your own thoughts, or at least make it more difficult. And surely that's one thing scholars don't want to be doing. Making up your own mind about things is really important in what you do. (Although just to say this raises deep questions about what it is to be a scholar.)

A   So what you're saying is that a linguistic straitjacket such as the de-personalised academic voice runs the risk of creating a conceptual straitjacket?

Z   Yes, if you want to put it like that. I'll give you an example.

Story No. 2

Think about the work done by scholars on ancient obscenity. Two impressively learned and wide-ranging books first published in the early 1980s offer contrasting approaches to the subject: J. N. Adams' *The Latin Sexual Vocabulary* (1982) and Amy Richlin's *The Garden of Priapus: Sexuality and Aggression in Roman Humor* (1983, revised edn. 1992). And let me state explicitly and immediately that I have enormous admiration for both these scholars. Obscenity is a topic Adams has to tackle immediately in *The Latin Sexual Vocabulary*, in which he produces a taxonomy of Latin obscenity. His method is to take the comments of Latin authors about the tone of specific words in order to build up a canon of words which he calls "basic obscenities" (Adams, 1982: 1). He acknowledges the difficulties involved in ranking such words in terms of degrees of offensiveness when dealing with a dead language (p. 2; it is not clear to me that it is much easier with a living language, actually, because of the enormous range of contexts), but by examining the different genres to see where these words do and do not occur, he proposes a hierarchy of decency. For example, the word *mentula*, the first entry under the heading "Basic obscenities" and which Adams describes as "the basic obscenity for the male organ" (p. 9), occurs in Pompeian inscriptions and graffiti from the Palatine, in the shorter poems of Catullus, the *Priapea* and Martial (in a quotation from the Emperor Augustus!), but not in satire or elegy, where, to avoid such "basic obscenities", euphemisms and metaphors are brought into use. But what is, perhaps, most remarkable throughout this discussion is Adams' own language. Consider the opening of the chapter devoted to the word:

> The basic obscenity for the male organ was *mentula*. The tone of the word is indicated by a few remarks which Martial makes. At 3.69.1f. he singles out *mentula* as the archetypal obscenity: the epigrams of a certain Cosconius are written *castis uerbis*, in that they contain no *mentula*. At 11.15.8ff. it is implied that *mentula* was the original word for the penis and the direct term *par excellence*. Martial argues that the word was in

use in the time of King Numa: it was therefore akin to English "four letter Anglo-Saxon words", the use of which, at least in dictionaries, is sometimes defended because of their antiquity.

(ibid.: 9)

So where are the "four letter Anglo-Saxon words" which might be so fitting here? Adams resists strongly: he avoids translating *mentula* except with the clinically distancing expressions, "the male organ" and "the penis". (Notice the scholarly and refined register here: one word of Greek origin and one Latin.) In so doing, he mitigates the powerful effect of what was evidently felt to be a crude word which had no place in the mouth of anyone with claims to culture. What is wrong with rendering *mentula* as "cock" or "prick"?

Richlin devotes the first chapter of *The Garden of Priapus* to "Roman Concepts of Obscenity" (Richlin, 1992: 1–31). Her approach is to contextualise obscenity by looking at Roman discussions of the concept. In her discussion of "Four-Letter Words" (pp. 18–26), she subjects Cicero's thoughts on obscenity in *Fam.* 9. 22 to scrutiny. This is a typical example of her writing:

He begins with the originally metaphorical obscenity *anus* ("ring"), then current for a part of the body that he says should not be mentioned at all if it is "foul" or should be called by its own name, *suo nomine*, if it is not foul. By "its own name" he presumably means the obscene word *podex*, "asshole." This illustrates the fact that Latin did not generally turn to medical terminology as an acceptable alternative to either euphemisms or bald obscenities. Parallel with *anus* is the next example, *penis*, an old word for "(animal's) tail," which produced the slang term *penicillus*, "brush," but which was now, from the commonness of its use *sensu obsceno*, itself obscene. Again Cicero says that Paetus [his correspondent] had called the thing denoted by *penis* "by its own name," *suo nomine*, in his letter; presumably he means Paetus had used the word *mentula*, approximately equivalent to the English "prick". Next follow two obscenities hidden in innocent sets of words: *cum nos . . .* ("when we . . .") is pronounced like *cunnos* ("cunts"), *. . . illam dicam* ("shall I say that one . . .") is pronounced *il-landicam* ("th' clitoris"). Returning briefly to his analysis of euphemisms, Cicero cites the phrase *liberis dare operam*, "to work on having children," and observes that no one dares to "say the name of the work," in other words, presumably, to use the verb *futuo* ("fuck").

(ibid.: 22–23)

What is refreshing here, and throughout Richlin's book, is that she does not shirk the relevant "four-letter words". She has broken with tradition in introducing words like asshole, cunt and fuck into her text. And her point about Latin not generally taking over medical terminology illustrates the point about intellectual straitjackets: if we assume that our clinically distancing terms (such as used by Adams) correspond to anything in the Latin language, we run the risk of imposing our linguistic habits in the case of obscenities unwarrantedly (just as we tend to impose our views of sexuality on to antiquity). Of course, there are risks in other strategies too, such as Richlin's choice of using "four-letter words". Perhaps the most important thing is that both these models (and, doubtless, others) are available to us. If we decide to write about Roman obscenity, we can choose between an Adams-type voice and a Richlin-type voice. Or we can even find an intermediate voice. And that, at least, makes me an advocate of pluralism. Let's have lots of different voices – and let there not be an automatic orthodoxy. A faint hope, doubtless, since those who wield power in our profession WILL inevitably set the tone, and maybe the voice too, and they WILL gladly be followed by their acolytes. Such is the academic system within which we work. But that is no reason not to TRY for pluralism.

You might easily object at this point that the contrast between Adams and Richlin is not a contrast between impersonal and personal. That's a valid objection. The contrast would seem to some to be between the more and less discreet, the more and less decorous, the more bland and more graphic expression. Where the personal clearly creeps in is in the reviews of these two books: there we find an unambiguously personal note, as the establishment rallied behind Adams and rounded on Richlin. "Dr Adams possesses a very cool head and very sober judgement," he is "adroit ... and sensitive" and "ideally qualified to tackle ... a subject infested by pitfalls" (Goodyear) – pitfalls into which "Ms Richlin" [sic] is deemed to have fallen in her book which is "disappointingly vague and shapeless as a whole" (Wiseman) and "Richlin is ready to drag in Donald Duck, Burt Reynolds (often 'Priapic'), Woody Allen, Mick Jagger and other pretentious analogies. The book sometimes gives the impression of being out of control" (Adams). I could go on. Suffice it to say that the male reviewers exalt their hero and slam the threatening female; the only ally she finds is another woman. (And let me also say, for the record, that both books have their positive and negative points. But I would not wish to be without either in my study. My friends know only too well how distressing I found the disappearance of Adams from my bookshelves during a recent house-move.) But the trenchant, not to say insulting, academic review does, of course, have a strong tradition in our discipline. Think no further than Housman. A contradiction worth pondering. And, as Nancy Miller says (*Getting Personal*, p. 19), "But what's personal? Who decides?"

Anyway, whatever decision we make about the voice we use in our academic writing, the most important thing is that we should be aware of it. If we are adopting the voice authorised by the academy, we ought to know. And if we decide to do something else, that needs to be a conscious decision too. It seems to me that in the classical academy there is too little self-awareness of the voices we use in our scholarship – and of the ways in which we are all inevitably implicated in political attitudes in the choices we make about which projects to pursue and how we pursue them.

Doubtless you can think of exceptions to this – there ARE exceptions, certainly, more in North America than in Britain. Both sides of the Atlantic, there is a gulf between those who operate or advocate personal-voice scholarship and those who consider it yet another manifestation of fancy theory which is a distraction from the "real" business of studying the ancient world. But how much greater is that gulf in Britain. The difference was clear in the receptions given to the panel on "The Personal Voice in Classical Scholarship" at the American Philological Association in Atlanta, December 1994 and at the annual meeting of the Classical Association at St Andrews, April 1995, where the panel was re-run, with additions. The reaction of the Atlanta audience was warm and receptive and some moving testimonies were offered by individuals from the audience. By contrast, the reaction of the British audience was much more defensive and cautious. This is not to say that personal-voice criticism has yet gained widespread acceptability – let alone orthodoxification – among the US classics community. But the debate is at least a little further advanced in North America than it is in Britain. Still, this venture itself is a start, a welcome start.

MANY PERSONAE/MANY VOICES

So it seems to me now, at this point in my thinking on this subject (which is not the same as twenty-two months ago, when I first started thinking about it, or as it will be twenty-two months hence), that there are profound problems with a choice between the impersonal voice authorised by the academy and the personal voice of each individual scholar. I am suspicious of the baggage that comes with the impersonal voice of classical scholarship. But I might also reject the personal voice as an excessively fragmenting or even self-indulgent device. But is there any way of articulating this question besides a stark choice between (1) a separation of voice and content (the impersonal voice) and (2) a complete congruence of voice and content (the personal voice), or, to restate it even more crudely, between a "natural" voice – the voice labelled (2) above – and an "acculturated" voice – that labelled (1) above?

This question in turn raises wider questions about the relationship between the voice and the individual, the voice and personality, the voice and the person. (These are issues about which Fay Weldon offers some intriguing ideas in her fabulous 1995 novel *Splitting*, which is a must for anyone interested in questions of identity and (split) personality.) How obvious is it that a person has a (distinctive/individual/unique) voice? How separable is a person from the voice(s) s/he uses on different occasions? To what extent is a person responsible for what she says? If we do adopt different voices or masks, *personae*, what does that mean? Is there a voice of a "real person" which "sounds through" (*per-sonare*, whether or not this etymology is valid) the mask, or does the voice belong to the mask? That is, does the term "voice" refer to how I express my ideas or does it encompass the ideas themselves? In other words, how do we separate form from content?

In the choice outlined above, (1) involves separating voice from ourselves as we write and speak, allowing it to hold its own contents, and (2) would seem to involve making our voice *our* vehicle and nothing more. Is there any middle ground, a third and intermediate way? It would have to consist of (3) endowing voice with a content of its own, that is, creating second level persons each of which would have or adopt their own voice(s) with their own content – so that it is perfectly clear that there is an author and her/his characters. (The closest example of this known to me which connects with the world of academe is A. S. Byatt's *Possession* (1990), in which she plausibly creates a breath-taking range of self-possessed voices – voices of scholars and of poets and of lovers, in the past and the present – without relinquishing her hold on the whole.) But would this be an acceptable strategy to the scholarly community? Would it be useful? Would it even be understood? (Confession: I would rather read A. S. Byatt than the *American Journal of Philology* any day of the week.)

It is in this context that I might advocate multivocality: there are other possible voices to be explored, many of them. I invoke the concept inculcated by the Greco-Roman rhetorical system, the concept of *to prepon*, *decorum*, the right voice for the right occasion. I seek the possibility of using many voices and of not being identified with any of them outside of that particular context. This removes the need for you to ask, "Which of these is the real Susanna Morton Braund?" (!!!) There is only the voice (or voices) I choose to present at any particular moment.

To push this a little further, I wonder if the starkness of the debate between the impersonal and the personal voices would have found sympathy in antiquity. I suspect that the ancient concept of personhood was more fluid than ours – and this is borne out, for example, by the free use of literary *personae* in antiquity, as I have tried to show in my own work on Roman satire, for example. My argument for multivocality is, perhaps, supported by consideration of Cicero's four-*persona* theory in *De officiis* 1.107–117. Briefly, the first *persona* is the universal one of the human self and the second *persona* is that of the individual with particular skills and capacities. The third *persona* is that which arises from circumstances and the fourth is the *persona* which consists of our individual choice of role in life. Cicero's analysis clearly envisages that all four of the *personae* he delineates are present in any human being simultaneously. It is not going too far, I think, to suggest that any one or combination of those *personae* might shape the voice used by that person at any particular moment.

So let me try to bridge the gulf between theory and practice by sketching the four *personae* of Susanna Morton Braund, after Cicero, together with her voices.

Persona No. 1

Quote: "I am a human being and I consider nothing human alien to me." Unquote. I believe that, and as I'm a human being as well as a classical scholar, it'll not surprise you that I hate those bits of classical texts where acts of cruelty are described, especially when it's purely for comic entertainment. For example, I'll never forget when I was a first-year undergraduate, reading that young man's *vaunting* description of how he's just raped a virgin in Terence's *Eunuchus*. (Strange, I now think, to find THAT in the same author who penned *homo sum; humani nil a me alienum puto* ... (*H.T.* 25).) The experience left me pretty well gob-smacked, and very upset: voice No. 1.

Persona No. 2

If I have to select individual skills which I possess, in line with those listed by Cicero in his delineation of the second *persona*, I should start by saying that I am a clever and serious person. I use these skills in my professional life to produce scholarship which I hope is lucid and intelligent and lasting. Voice No. 2, then, may be found in my scholarly publications to date (and I'll not bore you with a quotation).

Persona No. 3

I have been fortunate enough to hold positions of modest influence and responsibility within our world of classics – as Head of Department at the University of Exeter and now as Professor of Latin at Royal Holloway, University of London. In these positions, I take the opportunity to do (what I hope is) a good PR job, for my department within its institution and for the subject more widely. For voice No. 3, you need only imagine the bullish and up-beat tone of my representations to the university authorities at Exeter, in my attempt to persuade them to devote more resources to the under-resourced Classics department.

Persona No. 4

This is where my personal choice comes in. I am not interested in the power games played by so many academics (and so acutely analysed by Pierre Bourdieu in his *Homo academicus*, which should be prescribed reading for all ambitious academics). One of my strongest principles is social justice: equal opportunities and self-realisation. To that end, I prefer to use my position in the educational establishment to extend the personal potential of those around me. That's why I'm interested in raising questions like this, about what we are doing as academics. That's voice No. 4. In short, I wish to emphasise and value the PROCESS of scholarship as well as or as opposed to its end. For sure, part of our project is understanding more about ancient societies and our own societies (I use the plural deliberately) by appreciating the analogies and discrepancies between them. But another part of our project is, absolutely legitimately, on the level of personal growth. And understanding and growth are promoted by a continual process of challenging assumptions. That's why the "making strange" of the Formalists is (still) important to me. And that's why the personal voice, whatever that might be, is important. It offers a challenge to convention, which can so blinker us and confine us to well-trodden paths of thought. The most important thing is that some of us, at least, are having this debate.

ACKNOWLEDGEMENTS

My thanks to all who have helped hone my views on this slippery issue: Judy Hallett and Tom Van Nortwick, the organisers of the panel, the other participants on the panel (especially Pat Moyer and Charles Beye), the audiences at Atlanta (especially Dana Miller, with whom I have enjoyed fruitful correspondence since, and Kenneth Reckford) and at St Andrews (especially Chris Stray) and my colleagues and my friends in Bristol, especially Adam Morton and Jonathan Walters. And can I take this opportunity to say what fun it has been to write this footnote-free experimental essay. Some will call it foot-loose and fancy-free, I expect. I don't mind – so long as I can provoke some reaction.

REFERENCES

Adams, J. N. (1982) *The Latin Sexual Vocabulary*, London: Duckworth.

Bourdieu, Pierre (1988) *Homo academicus*, Cambridge: Polity Press.

Byatt, A. S. (1990) *Possession*, New York: Random House.

Henderson, J. K. (1989) "Not 'Women in Roman Satire' but 'When Satire writes "Woman" ' ", in *Satire and Society in Ancient Rome*, Exeter: University of Exeter Press.

Miller, Nancy K. (1991) *Getting Personal*, New York and London: Routledge.

Richlin, Amy (1992) *The Garden of Priapus: Sexuality and Aggression in Roman Humor*, New York: Oxford University Press.

Weldon, Fay (1995) *Splitting*, New York: The Atlantic Monthly Press.

Chapter 4

False things which seem like the truth

Vanda Zajko

> Self-commentary? What a bore! I had no other solution than to rewrite myself
> – at a distance, a great distance – here and now: to add to the books, to the
> themes, to the memories, to the texts, another utterance, without my ever
> knowing whether it is about my past or my present that I am speaking.
> (Barthes, 1977: 142)[1]

I began including the scholarly voice in my own scholarly repertoire six
years ago, inspired by the work of feminist psychoanalytic theorists, in
particular by Jane Gallop. At that time I was working for my PhD thesis on
a group of myths which featured the motif of women resisting sex and
marriage. I had reached something of an impasse and was unhappy with
the lack of theorisation of subjectivity in my work. The woman I had
originally placed at its centre kept sliding to the periphery and I had begun
to think that I did not know what it meant to describe a project as woman-
centred. "Thinking through autobiography", which is one of the ways in
which Gallop describes her project (Gallop, 1988: 4), allowed me to match
the liminality of the mythical women with what I perceived to be my own
marginal position as regards mainstream tenured classicists whose
concerns successfully marginalised mine.

The euphoria of the originary moment of discovering personal voice
theory did not last indefinitely. From where I am speaking now, many
critical questions arise about the definition, use, and potential of
autobiographical writing which did not occur to me six years ago. This
change of perspective in turn makes me speculate about the appearance of
temporal coherence which my current narrative provides, relying as it
does on the subordination of the differences of my historically determined
selves to the authority of the voice which represents itself as me. For which
"I" is represented when today I say "I"? And how is a reader to evaluate
my account of my former self given that in many cases only I can verify
what happened? As Kenneth Dover puts it in his autobiography:

Since my subject-matter is my own experience, I have a uniquely privileged access to it. Here comes danger. What I say about my own thoughts and feelings at a given time in the past, or about what was said by others during an event of which I am the sole surviving witness, cannot be checked against independent evidence. Even if my intentions are honest, it is notoriously true that one may retroject one's present views into the past, and be badly wrong.

(Dover, 1994: 2)

Dover goes on to comment that because he does not want evaluation to obtrude too much on his narrative, he has only occasionally drawn attention to differences between his present and his past feelings. Throughout this chapter I have adopted a different strategy and in the process of reworking old ideas I have deliberately tried to prise apart my past and present selves. The attempt to evaluate the former from the position of the latter has given shape to my narrative, but I have experienced a difficulty similar to the one which Barthes describes above in identifying whether it is about my past or my present that I have been speaking. Autobiography has traditionally relied upon the idea that the representation of one's own self is in certain respects more authoritative than the representation of someone else, precisely because one can be an expert about oneself in a way that one can never be about anyone else. This is the "danger" to which Dover refers but which he then underplays by claiming that his account of his life has been authenticated by the old notes and letters which he has consulted during its writing. It may be that Dover's trust in documentary evidence is the result of a lifetime dedicated to scholarship or it may be that the sustenance of the fiction that one's past is recoverable is necessary to the practice of writing autobiography: in order to offer any kind of coherent narrative my present must construct a past existing prior to my present and offer a representation of a present constructed by the past.

Reading Dover's narrative whilst writing my own led me to consider the relationship between the writing and the reading of autobiography, and my own experience of the fictionality of my graduate student self led me to query the easy equation of the self in Dover's text with the "same" self outside that text. Why should Dover's self-representation be accepted as experientially true simply because he intends the representation to correspond to himself? Reviewers of Dover's book have been troubled by no such questions and a brief survey of its reception forms part of the discussion which follows.

A sense of injustice of one sort or another seems to be what prompts most people to begin to incorporate the autobiographical into their academic work. My body was where it all began for me in terms of engagement with sexual politics. When I was a teenager my body was a constant source of pain to me. I was deeply uncomfortable with the way in which, on the one hand, being a relatively early developer, I was deemed to be attractive by those of the opposite sex, and on the other, there seemed to be no correspondence between their desire and mine. So many things seemed to me to be unfair: the measure of attractiveness which existed for us and not for them, the contortions and manipulations I was expected to put my body through in order to come up to scratch, and, most of all, the extraordinary sexual double standard which caught me in a constant double-bind. The most difficult aspect of all was my complete inability to communicate my dissatisfaction. I had no language in which to express the anxieties I wanted to express.

At this time I was studying Latin and Greek to "O"-level standard at school. The stirrings of discontent about my own body caused me to notice the silence about women's bodies in the ancient world. The absence of women as objects of our study was never remarked upon either by my teachers or by my fellow pupils. Their silence had the effect of silencing me. I was increasingly uncomfortable with my instruction and the absence of women seemed to expand until it was all that was present when I read the set texts, but I did not have a space or a voice in which to express my concerns. My experience within my social context was mirrored by my experience in the classroom, and the connections I was making between the two was my first step towards questioning the distinction between political knowledge and "the mythology of pure knowledge" (Jardine, 1985: 16) which others seemed anxious to preserve.[2]

At university it was different. Fortunately (as I now perceive it) my impotent frustration had metamorphosed into anger and gave me the impetus to start to read, to engage with feminist theory. I remember still the stomach-churning moments when I read *The Second Sex* for the first time and became able to articulate something which I had known in silence for several years, that women are created and not born. I immersed myself in the work of Kate Millet and Germaine Greer and others of those who are now nostalgically referred to as the "first wave" of Anglo-American feminists. Discussions with other women and men, whose experiences and concerns were similar to mine, centred around whether sexual difference was biologically determined or socially constructed, whether women and men are essentially the same, or different but equal. Once I had located it I was able to immerse myself in a language which was there waiting for me to express my feelings about my body.

In the classroom things were different too. It became apparent that it was now acceptable to talk about the patriarchal nature of Greek society and that the silence of women's voices was considered to be something worth commenting upon. It was now legitimate, even praiseworthy, to try to fit women into the picture. Books like Sarah Pomeroy's *Goddesses, Whores, Wives and Slaves* and Mary Lefkowitz's *Women in Greek Myth* were on our reading lists. From these I learned of the Greek male's fear of women and his notion that "a Greek woman's physical beauty conceals from the man who wants her and the son he cannot have without her, her power to do him harm" (Pomeroy, 1975; Lefkowitz, 1986: 37). I positioned myself within that tradition of feminist scholarship which links the depiction of women in literature with women in reality and seeks to assess the validity of that depiction by gauging the level of misogyny it entails. I wrote my undergraduate dissertation on the subject "Is Sappho's Poetry Specifically Female?", and as it was a subject which was of interest to my feminist friends I felt that at last I was achieving some sort of continuity between my social and my academic selves.

When I came to choosing a research topic, I was determined that it should be woman-centred. At the time I did not see that this presented too much of a problem, although the relative dearth of texts written by women made me aware that if I chose a literary topic I would be restricted to what Toril Moi calls "images of women criticism" (Moi, 1985: 42ff). My decision to work on mythological material forced me to think more rigorously about what might constitute such a woman-centred study; the issues concerning the authorship and production of myth are sufficiently tangled to prevent any easy unravelling of threads which might be claimed as originally belonging to women. In order to identify a group of myths which contained the motif of a woman or a group of women resisting sex or marriage I drew on texts by male authors from different times and places over a period of some 1,000 years. Any attempt to analyse their representations of women in terms of their cultural context was bound to be tentative and patchy, or else to depend on the concept of antiquity as a time-free zone in which the status and experience of women did not change sufficiently to invalidate the equation of myths from fifth-century BCE Athens with those of second-century CE Rome. In addition, as each myth survived within a specific literary context, any attempt to interpret the myth rather than the text within which it was contained relied on establishing a reified notion of myth which remained the same throughout antiquity. Only such a reification would make it possible, for example, to separate the myth of the Danaids from the narrative details external to the myth in Aeschylus' *Suppliants*.

These kinds of arguments focus predominantly on myth as a written signifying practice but, prior to the written organisation of material, mythological stories held currency amongst groups of people by being spoken aloud. There are various texts which may be cited as evidence that women as well as men spoke myth. Indeed it may very well have been the case that it was from women that children heard their first mythical stories.[3] So how legitimate is it to claim that the authorship of myth is male? Does this refer to the male speaking or the male writing down of myth? If, as seems reasonable, it might be desirable to claim that some female creative force had a hand in shaping the myths, how might the female elements be separated from the male? Would not what was identified as female and what was identified as male depend on the assumptions that were made about the essential differences between men and women?

My initial decision to compose a structuralist typology of the "resistance" myths may be regarded in part as a pragmatic response to some of the questions outlined above. Structuralism posits the idea that underlying the narrative of any myth there is a structure of binary oppositions which encodes its meanings. The recounting of a myth is significant for its structure in which contradictions are posed and mediated rather than for its specific narrative details. And because it is the structure which is of primary importance and not the time and place of production, the authority of each myth can be treated as equal and the lack of woman as subject ceases to matter. However, once the typology was complete, I remained dissatisfied. The analysis which related the structural stages of life of the women in the myths to the structural stages of life for women historically seemed to me to perpetuate the silence of ancient Greek women as subjects, by defining them solely in terms of their position within the family unit. By focusing on the ways in which the myths articulate tensions surrounding the successful transferral of women from control of the father to control of the husband, it perpetuated a point of view which values women only in terms of their relations to men. Women became sources of anxiety when they did anything other than conform to societal norms. The subversive potential of their resistance to sex and/or marriage was downgraded by a focus on what happened as a result of their resistance, i.e. reintegration or permanent exclusion, and the mediation of the conflict was privileged over the conflict. There was something subversive about those mythical women running away from men which I had not found a way to express in my work thus far. I wanted to find a way to challenge the concepts of centrality and marginality both in terms of the structures of ancient Greek society and in terms of the concerns and approaches traditionally considered to be acceptable to classicists, but I could find a way to do neither. I was so unhappy with my inability to draw together the disparate threads of my work that I put it on one side and spent the next two years working with a theatre company who were devising a project on Helen of Troy.

At that time some of the problems I was experiencing seemed to be particular to my field of study. There are very few voices which can be claimed as authentically talking about women's experiences in the ancient world, and to a greater extent than those working in other disciplines classicists had been forced to rely on the representations of women in texts written by men when trying to reconstruct a picture of women's lives. But it is possible to draw a distinction between women as active, productive, historical beings and women as signs, constructs of culture:

> Imaginatively, she is of the highest importance; practically she is completely insignificant. She pervades poetry from cover to cover; she is all but-absent from history. She dominates the lives of kings and conquerors in fiction; in fact she was the slave of any boy whose parents forced a ring upon her finger. Some of the most inspired words, some of the most profound thoughts in literature fall from her lips; in real life she could hardly read, could hardly spell, and was the property of her husband.
>
> (Woolf, 1929: 43)

The positioning of Latin and Greek as the "quintessential languages of masculine scholarship" (Gilbert and Gubar, 1979: 211) had made the task of criticising the discipline's most fiercely protected orthodoxies seem daunting. Within classics, for the most part, the approaches which had been utilised by feminists elsewhere to expose the fraudulence of the scholarly subject position which claimed gender neutrality, had been kept resolutely at bay. Whilst it was acceptable to piece together fragmentary evidence to examine the representations of women within particular discourses, classics (in Britain at least) had managed to protect itself from the threatening ravages of the disorderly Maenads who would seek to challenge the assumptions and traditions of classical scholarship in a more fundamental way. A feminist piece of work was still regarded as one which placed women at its centre and very little attempt had been made to absorb the work of theorists who question the possibility of such woman-centredness by interrogating traditional concepts of subjectivity.

It was the linking of my specific problems as a classicist with the wider issues of woman's positioning by or in language which eventually provided me with a way out of my impasse which was simultaneously disquieting and exciting.

A breakdown finally occurred with the belated recognition that our sub-field is not merely one more category of specialization within the autonomous and fiercely isolated classical studies profession; by its very nature, it also owes allegiance to the integrative field of women's studies. With that discovery came the realization of a practical need to assimilate feminist methodology: to accomplish its objectives, research on ancient women and gender would have to make use of the innovative techniques of feminist scholarship, which are especially designed to surmount the difficulties of reconstructing truths about women from fragmentary and distorted accounts. Confrontation with women's studies research then evoked, for many of us, a corollary and more disturbing awareness.

(Culham, 1990: 2)[4]

The experience of talking about "my" subject with women who had not been trained as classicists led me to think about what women trained in other disciplines might have to offer me. During my time working for the theatre company, I spent my days off perusing the shelves in the extensive Gender Studies section of the local library. Here for the first time I encountered post-structuralism and psychoanalysis and those women introduced to me as the French Feminists. The fact that I only stumbled upon these vast areas of contemporary critical theory by chance demonstrates the extent to which I had internalised the isolationist tendencies of those who work on material from the ancient world. I had up to that time been unaware that many people in other disciplines were grappling with the kinds of questions which had been concerning me: questions of how to reconstruct a picture of women's lives when explicit information about them is so scanty and so open to the charge of distortion from having been preserved in texts written by men; questions of how to gain acceptance from the academic establishment for imaginative ways of writing which do not necessarily seek to legitimise themselves by claims to objectivity and truth. As so often happens, it was only on discovering these questions in the mouths of others that I had the confidence to articulate them myself.

There were all sorts of ways in which I was repositioned by my encounter with the post-structuralist canon. Confronting assumptions about concepts of self and gender, language, meaning, reading, writing, and desiring inevitably leads to crisis for someone whose self-identity has for all her adult life been bound up with the specificity of being a woman.

From the time when as an undergraduate I had begun to articulate my resistance to biological determinism I had become used to regarding gender as the social construction of sexual difference which overlays biological difference, and the advantages of talking about gender rather than sex had initially seemed irresistible. If gender difference and all the injustice which shelters beneath its roof is a construction rather than a biological given, there is hope that it may be dismantled and rebuilt to a more equitable design. Historical investigations of the ways in which gender has been constructed and of how hierarchical oppositions have been reinforced and perpetuated within particular literary and social contexts may enable the foundations of such a building programme to be laid. Gender, as an analytical tool, seemed a useful concept with which to interrogate the kinds of male-authored texts I was used to working with. However, as time had gone on I had developed some reservations. Observing the ease with which "Gender Studies" replaced "Women's Studies" in book shops and university prospectuses, I became suspicious of the way in which, once again, women's sexual specificity was being eclipsed by a term which professed to be neutral. Gender, as a subject for study, reassured those for whom only the study of women-and-men was broad enough to satisfy scholarly criteria. In addition, the project of replacing the status quo with a less oppressive mode of societal organisa- tion had begun to seem dauntingly complicated. I was already in disagreement with those feminists who looked towards a future where women would be celebrated for and in all their natural biological difference. I had already lost my faith in the creed that patriarchal lies could be replaced with feminist truths. Post-structuralist theories of power encouraged me to cease identifying only male ideology with repression and falsity and to begin to examine the ways in which feminism is itself both an instrument and an effect of power.

In addition I began to think about corporeality in a different way. The acceptance of the fluidity of masculine and feminine positions and of their disconnection from social positions opened up a whole new textual space in which sexuality could be plotted. Contemporary psychoanalytic theorists show that subjectivity is an effect of the ways in which a subject learns to experience her or his body and that experience is different according to whether the body in question is sexed female or male. But the body which is referred to is a body which is produced by the intersection of the psychical projections of individuals and the discursive effects of the dominant systems of representation: as such it is a body located in a particular socio-historical context and not one which must inevitably remain the same forever. At the moment masculinity is the effect of representing the body as masculine and femininity is the effect of representing the body as feminine; but if the dominant systems of representation were to change, then so might the discursive production of the body.

A fruitful agenda for those concerned with the particular forms of oppression inscribed in the female body is then to change modes of representation by pushing existing representations to their limits. Eventually these changes might allow for a new structuring of subjectivity which is not determined by a hierarchical model of sexual difference. Experimenting with writing styles is part of this agenda. The inclusion of fiction and autobiography in a doctoral dissertation was for me a question of "jamming the theoretical machinery itself, of suspending its pretension to the production of a truth and of a meaning that are excessively univocal" (Irigaray, 1985b: 78). It felt bold and exciting but risky. I had to keep in mind the parameters imposed by the PhD and take care to justify my challenge to its pre-set standards of objectivity. Anxious to gain admittance into the academy, I took advice on what was likely to be acceptable to any dissertation committee and agreed to separate the autobiographical material from the main body of the work by delineating it as a "Preface". My observance of scholarly decorum paid off: my examiners did not criticise me for speaking personally, they just ignored the fact that I had done it so.

It was not until I successfully applied for my current job at Bristol University that I found myself amongst colleagues who were prepared to talk to me seriously about the issues of subjectivity in which I had become interested. At the departmental seminars I was able to benefit from lively and informed discussion of my research, and I constantly counted myself fortunate to have ended up working alongside those who had been trained in the same tradition as I but who were also actively engaging with a wide variety of intellectual positions. In addition, for the first time, I was able to incorporate my ideas into my teaching at both undergraduate and postgraduate levels. The experience of communicating with students encouraged me to continue to think about the different status of men and women. It became increasingly apparent to me that one of the results of the students' immersion in "textualist" theories was that what I as a student had been accustomed to call sexual politics was no longer on their intellectual agenda. Whilst they were happy to discuss gender in terms of shifting representation and narrative, any attempt on my part to discuss sexed bodies, or to draw attention to the ways men's and women's bodies have been and are differently culturally inscribed, invariably met with scorn. The charge of essentialism was frequently made as a form of closure and seemed to me to perpetuate the notion that any sustained attention to the body must fall outside the bounds of serious thought. In one third-year seminar I explicitly asked a group of some twenty students whether anyone identified as a feminist: only one affirmed that she did.

Unfortunately it seemed to me that what in the old days would have been called sexism was still observable in the behaviour of both students and colleagues. One example speaks volumes: in the summer term, when facing their final examinations, two students, one male and one female, began to exhibit symptoms of extreme anxiety and seemed to be in danger of complete breakdown. Initially the woman student was described as "hysterical", as was I when I showed my concern for her; the male student meanwhile was suggested to be "having an intellectual crisis". Although subsequently both students were treated respectfully and generously by most people, the initial discrepancy between their categorisations was disturbing and indicated why, in spite of the arguments which problematise subscription to a certain kind of feminism as an intellectual position, I was still prepared to argue that such a position should not be abandoned completely. As long as, in the words of Thomas Lacqueur, "pain and injustice are gendered and correspond to corporeal signs of sex" (Lacquer, 1990: 16), it seems to me that there is a case to be made for continuing to identify as a feminist and for striving to alleviate the pain and injustice.

Such identification does not necessarily involve a commitment to essentialist concepts of the female or the feminine but neither does it involve shying away from such concepts without seriously thinking about the work which they might do. The emphasis of contemporary critical theory on difference has been very challenging to those of us who have in the past relied on feminism as a place of refuge. My own present position as an employed woman with financial independence and intellectual freedom would, in many contexts, make identification with the majority of women in the world seem distasteful. However, by choosing to efface certain differences and investing in a group identity, people the world over have become able to lobby for what they want. As Diana Fuss puts it: "For practitioners of identity politics the link between identity and politics is causally and teleogically defined" (Fuss, 1989: 99). Identifying themselves in the personal stories of others may continue to encourage the disempowered to feel that they too have something to say.

So far I have concentrated on issues concerning autobiography and feminism, in part because, as I have explained, the two have long been entwined with each other in terms of my own intellectual life. In part I chose to set out my arguments in this way because feminism and autobiography have also been linked in most of the other papers submitted to the panel on the "Personal Voice" at the American Philological Association. One of the things which is evident from the establishment of the panel is that the voices which are accepted as being authentically personal are those which, it is argued, have been drowned out in the past because they have not belonged to the white, educated and heterosexual male. Some classical scholars have begun to argue that the non-fictional first-person narrative is a legitimate and useful tool because those voices which historically have been silenced can now be recognised and incorporated into the cultural script. It is worth bearing in mind that there is still a script: although some voices are now shouting loudly and making themselves heard, others are being forced to whisper or not daring to speak at all. It is perfectly possible that in response to social and political change there might be a case at some future date for promoting the adoption of a depersonalised, more uniform voice in order to prevent some experiences of life being represented as more legitimate than others. If those of us who have advocated speaking personally become complacent once our own political agendas have been fulfilled, we shall be guilty of replicating the censorship against which we have fought.

It is interesting to observe that in the case of the marginalised scholar no external evidence is sought to give authority to her text: the intention to represent the self authentically is sufficient grounds for an autobiographical reading. This suggests that the treatment of the narrative is closely linked to the status of the person writing the "autobiography". The question of what is "really" being described is less a demand for more information about the subject matter than a statement about the status of the author. The interpretation of a statement which might be read as autobiographical depends less on its relationship to real life than on the authority its author is perceived to have within the culturally dominant discourses of truth-telling. Hotly debated questions of how to read autobiography frequently support conflicting agendas for how to value the autobiographer. In the words of Leigh Gilmore:

> Some stories are criminalised from the start when the amount of "truth" one can claim devolves from the amount of cultural authority already attached, within a terrain of dominance, to the person speaking and the place from which s/he speaks. This cultural terrain, in which truth represents both a place where some may not stand and a language that some are not authorised to speak, is mapped onto the practice and study of autobiography through publishing practices,

college curricula, community reading programs, and a range of practices through which we are interpolated as readers and writers of autobiography.

(Gilmore, 1994: 26)

Clearly feminism is now a position within the academy from which one is authorised to tell the truth. And it is to the debate about authority and truth-telling that the reception of Dover's *Marginal Comment: A Memoir* is relevant. Published in 1994, this book attracted the kind of attention which the British press normally reserves for the revelations of the former lovers of members of the royal family. In particular a great deal of attention was paid to one chapter in which Dover gives an account of his interaction with a Fellow of the Oxford college of which he was President between 1975 and 1985. Headlines such as "I drove a man to suicide and I'm glad says Oxford don", "Chancellor's death plot" and "Death in the cloister" (*The Times* 30 November 1994, *Sunday Telegraph* 27 November 1994, *The Independent* 28 November 1994) referred to the series of events involving disputes about college property, the renewal of the fellowship and the abuse of college servants which culminated in the suicide of the fellow in question after many years of loneliness, alcoholism and severe depression. The outrage expressed by the reviewers was directed towards the way in which Dover described in detail the thought processes which led him to consult a lawyer to ascertain whether he would be legally responsible should he fail to help in the event of a suicide attempt, so strongly did he desire that the man should be removed from the college. Describing Dover's memoir as "a terrifyingly honest performance" and "brutally frank" and disapproving of its "shocking candour", the reviewers, almost without exception, focused on the parts which could most easily be sensationalised, and took its revelations at face value. Another anecdote which was singled out for the attention of the public concerned an occasion during the war when Dover was so aroused by the beauty of an Italian mountainside that he masturbated on the spot. Although much of the book is concerned with the minutiae of Dover's professional life at Oxford and then at St Andrews where he held the Professorship of Greek for twenty years, it is those incidents concerned with sex and murderous desire which have been the most widely quoted and used to fortify the reviewers' position that the memoir is disturbing because of its truthfulness. Extraordinarily, given the close analysis of the rhetoric of the law-courts which is such a feature of *Greek Popular Morality*, Dover's own rhetoric has not received the attention it deserves. The contemporary belief that "sexuality is the secret within us all, waiting to be revealed" (Foucault 1978, 155) leads to the assumption that some details about a person's life are necessarily more personal than others.

One profile of Dover printed in the *Independent on Sunday* probed further. Commenting on the pride Dover expresses in his detachment from his fellow human beings ("I have found sociability easy enough but firm friendship difficult. I have never yet experienced what could be properly called grief at anybody's death," [Dover, 1994: 15]), Laurence Marks suggests that, far from being dispassionate, objective and truthful, "Privately, Sir Kenneth has a taste for melodrama with himself cast as protagonist." He gives some examples of what he interprets as instances of Dover's self-aggrandisement:

> Sir Kenneth's book is spattered with violent images and rather self-conscious demonstrations of his supposed rational cold-bloodedness.
> ...At Corpus he boasts that he arranged, without consulting the fellows or the undergraduates, for all the stray cats in the college to be shot. The creepiest example is his remark about a professor at Stanford (where Sir Kenneth lectured in the 1980s) who had been eulogised at his funeral for his devotion to his students. The professor had committed suicide when he realised that his persistent abuse of a mentally handicapped boy could no longer be concealed. "That did not falsify the eulogy," Sir Kenneth says. One finds oneself murmuring: "Come off it Ken!" It seems likely that his arresting claim to have mediated homicide was made in the same show-off spirit.
>
> (Marks, 1994)

Martha Nussbaum too queries the apparent contradiction between Dover's assertions of aloofness and the confessional manner in which he has chosen to tell us about his life:

> When a man who until the age of seventy-four has revealed himself very little to others exposes his most private thoughts, wishes, and experiences to the general public, the reader wonders a little about the motive. Is it the love of truth simply, or a longing for that acceptance by others, that knowledge of one's own reality, which the imagined disgust of his peers had previously denied him? One may wonder whether Dover's lifelong assault on customary prudery and reticence – on all that is subsumed by him under the label of "respectability" – is not itself motivated by a wish to sweep away the forces of convention that stood between Dover the boy and bodily acceptance by others. And frequently, as one reads the memoir, one senses that Dover (with his

wife Audrey as, clearly, his approving and loyal partner) is testing his reader's capacity for dispassionate unembarrassed reaction.

(Nussbaum, 1995: 11–12)

Nussbaum then confesses that whilst she was unperturbed by accounts of masturbation, sodomy, hatred and depression, she was disquieted by the chapter in the book which details Dover's problems with sexual impotence in old age. She argues that

> just as most of Dover's life has effaced intimacy by reticence about self, this memoir effaces it just as surely in the opposite way, by refusing to make any distinction at all between what one tells a loved one and what one tells a stranger.

(Nussbaum, 1995: 12)

Nussbaum's reading of *Marginal Comment* is nuanced and subtle and thoughtful about the process of writing autobiography. She insinuates that in practice what is personal is determined not by any particular kind of subject matter but by the value which one places upon the story one is telling. She concludes by commending Dover's account of himself as being that of a "Stoic life, in which the extirpation of emotion goes hand in hand with a ferocious love of truth". It seems to me that the question of why Dover chose to represent himself as he did is at least as interesting as the question of whether or not the events and emotions he describes are true. For classicists should know that self-representation may be a strategy for changing the story of one's life:

> O respected wife of Odysseus, son of Laertes,
> you will not stop asking me about my origin?
> Then I will tell you; but you will give me over to sorrows
> even more than I have; but such is the way of it, when one
> strays away from one's own country as long as I have,
> wandering many cities of men and suffering hardships.
> Even so I will tell you what you ask me and seek for.

Odyssey 19: 165–171
(translated by R. Lattimore)

Odysseus' texts discomfort the reader who tries to read them as autobiography. In the words of Simon Goldhill:

> The fictive personae that Odysseus creates through his tales cannot but in different ways reveal both himself and others in reaction to him. Indeed, it would be difficult to maintain a simple and absolute opposition between the "true representation" of Odysseus and his

fictive personae, but rather the tales construct a series of different shifting levels of representation (in the exchanges of language between polumetis Odysseus and those with whom he converses).

(Goldhill, 1991: 46)

Ideas of what constitutes a person vary according to historical period and methodological persuasion and thus so do the texts which are described as autobiography. A reading of a text as autobiographical accepts the representation of a self in a narrative as a representation of someone who once existed or who exists. This is what might be said to differentiate a reading-as-autobiography from a reading-as-fiction: in the case of the former, the self in the text is accepted as being a representation of the "same" self in real life. The designation of a text as autobiographical is particularly likely when the representation of events and characters within a text may plausibly be connected with the people the author knew and events in which she may have participated or which she may have observed. In the case of such a text, Lejeune's "policing of the autobiographical pact" (Lejeune, 1989: 3–30), the assessment of the accuracy of an autobiographical narrative by the measuring of it alongside relevant "external" texts, is considered good interpretative practice. Indeed, evaluating the plausibility of the connections made between the author of a text and her/his life is the process which commonly decides whether a text is read as fiction or as autobiography, and this applies to both ancient and modern texts. In the case of the *Odyssey* no one would confidently assert that the adventures of Odysseus are representations of the adventures which "Homer" himself had. But the centuries of interest in the "Homeric question" shows how strong has been the urge to make some kind of connection between the life of the author and this text.

At different times the "same" texts have been read both ways and the subject matter of some genres has been considered more realistic than others. Before *persona* theory became the standard mode of interpretation – some thirty years ago – lyric was read as the emergence of a passionate individual voice, satire was read as an expression of authorial anger, and the question of who was Lesbia was on every Latinist's lips. Now there is argued to be a gap between the author and his textual construction of self and the "external" texts are used to gauge when the author is assuming a mask. The project of the scholar who advocates using the personal voice is then at odds with the project of the *persona* theorist who argues that the speaker is not the author's genuine "I". For such theorists, the drawing of a distinction between an author and her text liberates that text from being interpreted as self-revelation. But the reading of a textual self as a "persona" still implies a creative agency responsible for the text. Despite the semantic shift, such readings continue to be grounded in the authorial self.

The way in which studying autobiography highlights the contradictions between the reading and writing practices of some classical scholars is not surprising. For, in addition to the minefield of identity politics, the area which is expanded most by such a study is the space between author and reader which we all must negotiate when confronted by a text. The abandonment of authorial intention as the determinant of how to read a text is easier to achieve when the author is unknown to us than when she or he is one of our colleagues whose foibles, passions and prejudices we know well. It is rare that we know absolutely nothing about an author when we pick up his or her work and the knowledge which we have may very well affect our reading. For example, Nussbaum has noted the difficulty these days of thinking clearly about Foucault: "We know a good deal about Foucault's life – perhaps too much for our own good, in the sense that sensationalising treatment of its events can impair our intellectual confrontation with the work" (Nussbaum, 1995: 1).

Even if we personify the text and pay no explicit attention to the person of the author we cannot get away from the idea of human agency altogether. Similarly, even if we accept the construction of the self through process and relationship we cannot remove the need in our day-to-day lives for identifying subject positions for ourselves, however provisional and fragmentary we may feel such identifications to be. Contradictory as our senses of ourselves frequently are, they are what allow us to engage with and delight in our fellow human beings. Liberating as it is not to have to recount details of Catullus' sex life in order to justify appreciating his poems, the experience of somehow making contact with another human mind is part of what is so fascinating about the process of reading literature. The concept of the voice may prove to be extremely useful in enabling us to reinvigorate debates about human creativity without reverting to the static positionings of passive reader and omniscient author. For it is particular enough to allow us to explore what is distinctive about an author and yet sufficiently flexible to ensure that fluctuations of rhythm and disparities of tone do not have to be dismissed as examples of inconsistency.

When it comes to our own work we are frequently called upon to defend what we have written, so that in practice it is impossible to disassociate ourselves from our own texts in the way in which we disassociate ancient authors from theirs. And because intellectual communities are places where ideas are exchanged and political groupings formed, it is often possible to identify an academic text as the product of a specific period, institution, or ideological position. All writing is certainly analysable under the sign of autobiography whether the author intended that it should be or not. In the following passage from *Homer on Life and Death* Jasper Griffin's descriptions of Circe, Nausicaa and Calypso might easily be argued to be the figurations of woman in the mind of an Oxford don:

> The situation of parting with a woman in love is an emotional and difficult one, which is calculated to bring out the real nature of both parties. . . . The variants on the theme in the *Odyssey* show us three very different women: the hard-boiled Circe, to whom the affair has been one of pleasure which there is no point in trying to prolong; the young Nausicaa, with whom nothing is put into words and yet everything is there, in essence rather than actuality; and the suffering Calypso, retaining her dignity as she loses her love. Each represents a type and offers a different relationship, to which the wandering hero might have abandoned himself, forgetting his wife and home. That he resists them all brings out his unconquerable resolution, the central fact of the *Odyssey*. But we observe also two other things: these women are inscrutable, and they are complex.
>
> (Griffin 1980: 58)

Autobiography is generally analysed through the powerful discursive categories of "identity" and "self" and therefore interpreted as a story about an individual. But the example above shows how autobiography could be described as the story by and within which we are told because it would be possible for all of us to be defined in terms of the attitudes and prejudices which we have in common with others of our age, nationality, education, class, or any other categories we might choose. The struggle for self-differentiation, which can be theorised in various ways, is something which is highlighted by the process of writing about one's own life. For if at times it suits us to identify with others, there are other times when it seems to matter that we feel ourselves to be unique. The reading and writing of autobiography is central to both intellectual and political activity precisely because autobiography continues to be one of the places where the relation between the personal and the plural is constructed and maintained.

NOTES

1 I would like to thank Rachel Alexander for her practical help with this piece and also for the intelligence, compassion and humour she never stints on sharing with her friends. In addition I would like to thank Charles Martindale for his criticism and support.
2 Jardine uses this distinction to point to the historical differences between the concerns of feminists in America and France: "One thing French women are reminding us of is that pure knowledge does not exist."
3 For a wider discussion of the role of gender in oral and literate mythmaking, see Zajko (1995).
4 A comparison between the editorial voices of two collections of essays which were both marketed as "feminist" shows the state of play at that time: "The scholarship displayed in this collection is firmly based in close and critical examination of such sources, rather than in the wholesale application of currently popular theories of analysis such as structuralism or psychoanalysis to images of women in myth-based literature." "The articles are feminist in that women are the centre of each author's enquiry" (Pomeroy (ed.), 1991: xiv and xiv n. 21); "We share the following assumptions. (1) Our work fits into the discipline which is coming to be known as cultural studies. It is a methodological axiom of this volume that text and social context are interrelated, and we all consider issues of audience and conditions of production. (2) With this axiom firmly in place, the application of feminist or other modern theories to ancient material is not inherently problematical" (Richlin (ed.), 1992: xi).

REFERENCES

Barthes, Roland (1977) *Roland Barthes by Roland Barthes*, trans. Richard Howard, New York: Hill and Wang.
Culham, P. (1990) "Ten Years After Pomeroy: Studies of the Image and Reality of Women in Antiquity", in M. Skinner (ed.) Special Issue of *Helios* 13.
De Beauvoir, S. (1968) *The Second Sex*, New York: Modern Library.
Dover, K. (1974) *Greek Popular Morality in the Time of Plato and Aristotle*, London: Duckworth.
—— (1994) *Marginal Comment: A Memoir*, London: Duckworth.
Felman, S. (ed.) (1982) *Literature and Psychoanalysis: The Question of Reading: Otherwise*, Baltimore, MD and London: Johns Hopkins University Press.
Foucault, M. (1978) *The History of Sexuality Vol. 1. An Introduction*, New York: Pantheon Books.
Fuss, D. (1989) *Essentially Speaking*, London and New York: Routledge.
Gallop, J. (1988) *Thinking Through the Body*, New York: Columbia University Press.
Gilbert, S. and Gubar, S. (1979) *The Madwoman in the Attic*, New Haven, CT: Yale University Press.
Gilmore, L. (1994) *Autobiographics: A Feminist Theory of Women's Self-Representation*, Ithaca, NY: Cornell University Press.
Goldhill, S. (1991) *The Poet's Voice*, Cambridge: Cambridge University Press.
Greene, G. and Kahn, C. (eds) (1985) *Making A Difference: Feminist Literary Criticism*, London: Methuen.

Griffin, J. (1980) *Homer on Life and Death*, Oxford: Oxford University Press.

Irigaray, L. (1985a) *Speculum of the Other Woman*, Ithaca, NY: Cornell University Press.

Irigaray, L. (1985b) *This Sex Which Is Not One*, Ithaca, NY: Cornell University Press.

Jardine, A. (1985) *Gynesis: Configurations of Woman and Modernity*, Ithaca, NY: Cornell University Press

Laquer, T. (1990) *Making Sex: Body and Gender from the Greeks to Freud*, Cambridge, MS: Harvard University Press.

Lefkowitz, M. (1986) *Women in Greek Myth*, Baltimore, MD: Johns Hopkins University Press.

Lejeune, P. (1989) *On Autobiography*, Minneapolis, MN.: University of Minnesota Press.

Marks, L. (1994) "Death by Reason: A Profile of Sir Kenneth Dover", *Independent on Sunday*, 4 December.

Miller, N. (1991) *Getting Personal: Feminist Occasions and Other Autobiographical Acts*, London and New York: Routledge.

Moi, T. (1985) *Sexual/Textual Politics*, London: Methuen.

Nussbaum, M. (1995) Review of Dover (1994) in *The New Republic*.

Pomeroy, S. (1975) *Goddesses, Whores, Wives and Slaves*, New York: Schoken Books.

—— (ed.) (1991) *Women's History and Ancient History*, Chapel Hill, NC and London: University of North Carolina Press.

Rabinowitz, N. and Richlin, A. (eds) (1993) *Feminist Theory and the Classics*, London and New York: Routledge.

Richlin, A. (ed.) (1992) *Pornography and Representation in Greece and Rome*, New York: Oxford University Press.

Skinner, M. (ed.) (1990) "Rescuing Creusa: New Methodological Approaches to Women in Antiquity", Special Issue of *Helios* 13.

Tomaselli, S. and Porter, R. (eds) (1986) *Rape*, Oxford: Oxford University Press.

Woolf, V. (1929) *A Room of One's Own*, New York: Harcourt, Brace, and Co.

Zajko, V. (1995) "Speaking Myth", *Arethusa* 28: 21–38.

Chapter 5

Proper voices: writing the writer[1]

Charles Martindale

The highest Criticism, then, is more creative than creation, and the primary aim of the critic is to see the object as in itself it really is not; that is your theory, I believe?

Oscar Wilde, *The Critic as Artist*

I

I'm in words, made of words, others' words

Samuel Beckett, *The Unnamable*

Should classicists follow Nancy K. Miller's example, and get personal?[2] Where is the boundary between the personal and non-personal voice to be drawn, and according to what criteria? Is the distinction of heuristic value, and, if so, what might be its advantages and disadvantages? We may begin (or should that be I will begin?) with some mildly deconstructive moves. When Ben Jonson wrote (*Discoveries* 2515) "Language most shows a man: speak that I may see thee", he was giving lapidary expression to a humanist conviction – humanist both in the sense of a commitment to the Renaissance's programme of *studia humanitatis* and in the sense in which the term is often used today, within literary theory, to denote belief in an essential, transhistorical human nature – that it is in and through the word that we are most fully ourselves.[3] When Erasmus translated the opening of St John's Gospel "In the beginning was the Word" he substituted *sermo*, "discourse", for the Vulgate's *verbum*, thereby underlining the rhetorical function of the Son, the Word made flesh, in a world of disseminated meanings.

Certainly as scholars and critics we seem determined to give ourselves away the moment we speak or write, and not least when we think we are talking about other matters. Here are two scholarly voices, both addressing aspects of Horace's representation of women, in discussions of *Ode* 1.11 and *Epode* 8 respectively:

> Many of Horace's *Odes*, like most of the *Epistles*, derive their special flavour from the scene which Horace sets, and the character he addresses. He leaves his clues, and to catch the special flavour of the poem we must follow them closely and sanely. It is wasteful to forget that these poems are *ad hominem* and *ad rem*. So if Horace says "Don't ask, Leuconoe . . . ", he clearly wants us to suppose, for the reading of this poem, that there was a woman called Leuconoe and that she did ask. The pile of aphorisms then takes on some shape and savour. Horace deals very gently with Leuconoe. There is hardly a trace of his habitual irony. Without teasing or patronising he meets this feminine nonsense with the serious and reasonable insistence that she should accept her human limitations. Then without sentiment, human life is set against the immense power, and size and longevity of the sea. At the end, when Horace says *carpe diem* to a woman, there can be no doubt about what primarily he means. Because Horace does not put his hand on his heart and sigh, his love poetry is usually under-estimated.
>
> (West, 1967: 64)

> Here, from one John to another, is some crude thinking, ill-digested *vaccine*, towards re-siting our reading of Latin 'poetry' within the textual politics of discourse and ideology: in the name of a *carnal* materiality, a body of *human* poetry, Cock an ear to that Artifice of the Orifice, *Horace*; Try to make this poem's transgressive power come alive . . . . **[Layla, you got me on my knees]** *R-e-l-a-x, don't do it.* . . . Stick with *Hässlickkeits Schilderung*, you *need* see no more than a wee slip of a poem, just a bum start from the puerile poet (If you can be *broad*-minded, grin and bear it – try saying "O", niceally with Nil Rudd in *CHCL* ii. 371/ by hygienic quotation of Sellar with Shackleton Bailey 3 / or anyway – with everybody – see Setaioli, 1715, for a survey). Clearly, it's idiomatically *iambic*. . . . So *that's* OK. Besides, it's *literary* – and *about* literature, too, *libelli Stoici* and *illiterati* . . . – so it's *about* 'style' (For the details find Clayman (1), q.v. 55 *a potent combination of obscene insult and literary criticism*, 56 *Callimachus' poetry was a* potent *influence*, e.g. 60 *the opportunity to give* lip-service *at least to the memory of Lucilius himself* . . . or Clayman (2). *My* italicks). *Phew!* There, *that's* better. But . . . O Scholarship, industry of disavowal & deniability! Those *men*! They *would* say that, wouldn't they?
>
> (Henderson 1987, 106–108)

The first "voice" belongs to David West, a sympathetic reader of
Horace who prides himself on giving precise, accurate and historically
convincing accounts of Horace's poems; and the claim that the
Leuconoe ode constitutes an erotic invitation may be felt a persuasive
one (the image of plucking a flower, which perhaps lies within the
phrase *carpe diem*, frequently figures a woman's loss of virginity). But in
calling the ode "a love poem" and in using language like "Horace does
not put his hand on his heart", West moves us to a world of sentiment
and sensibility reminiscent of the bourgeois novel; *amor* is a slippery
signifier indeed, open to innumerable appropriations. And there is the
matter of the "feminine nonsense" to which Horace replies so reasonably (if there is irony here, it is surely of a characteristically collusive,
"Horatian", kind). We may agree with the implication that it is
unobjectionable for a middle-aged man to try to get a young woman
to have sex with him so long as he does it tactfully and his feelings are
"sincere"; and it is true that Roman writers associate astrology
particularly with women. But there is evidence for men too dabbling
in astrology, including Horace's own patron, the pliant Maecenas – but
then he was *mollis*, a notorious effeminate, guilty of torrid affairs with
actors, and moreover an Etruscan.[4] West's comments, while from one
perspective part of a reasonably disinterested pursuit of interpretative
truth, from another become complicit with a particular way of viewing
women today; and in that sense they are as much about West as they are
about Horace.

Part of the trouble may be that scholarship and sex make uneasy
bedfellows. John Henderson, the second voice, invites us to consider
whether modern discussions of the epode may be ways of not talking
about the poem, and he puts this scholarly discourse under pressure, in the
interests of his own very different ideological self-positioning, with his
string of obscene puns. A traditionalist would probably say that we ought
to be talking about the original text, not about current gender battles. But
we can reply that we can't talk about Horace and sex without also taking a
position, consciously or unconsciously, within the sexual politics of our
own day (as do both the cited voices in their different ways). Reading and
interpretation are one significant arena where values are contested, and
there is no way of standing outside the discourses which speak in and
through us. However a scholar chooses to figure herself, his work can
always be situated, seen as the product of a particular time and place and a
particular set of perspectives. We know this about the writings of the past
(where we call the phenomenon history), but we are reluctant to accept its
full implications when we come to our own. We can see such a reluctance

at work, for example, in the continued scholarly anxiety about "anachronistic" interpretation, an anxiety that might be dispelled by the thought that a measure of anachronism is an inevitable concomitant of the very structure of reading, which involves a dialogue between past and present, self and other.

These arguments amount to the familiar point that the distinctions we draw to map our worlds are always capable of being blurred or redrawn. So the most austere scholarly discourse can be represented as reflecting assumptions and values belonging to the writer; on this view their very impersonality becomes an occlusion of the personal in the interests of constructing authority, and so is analysable as a rhetorical strategy, even if an unconscious one. In Paul de Man's words "any book with a readable title page is, to some extent, autobiographical".[5] But equally the personal voice can be subjected to a rhetorical and ideological analysis which would underline the socially constructed and tropical nature of the writing, thereby restoring it to the im- or non-personal. Within such an analysis one could argue that the writings of John Henderson are neither more nor less personal than those of any other classicist, they simply construct a different kind of voice – in this case a transgressive voice – and employ different tropes, with different ideological entailments. This Hendersonian voice can then be easily imitated by followers and admirers and so become as familiar and even (in many circles) orthodox as other, more "traditional" voices.

Since the 1970s much work has been done on the rhetorical analysis of academic discourses (for example, in science, anthropology, sociology, and history) and the writerly procedures by which particular disciplines valorize themselves and their "findings".[6] Clifford Geertz, for example, has explored the difference between Malinowski's official anthropological writings and the diary he produced during his investigations which was not published until 1967. Clearly the former are more authoritative than the latter, but they are not necessarily more truthful. The voice that Malinowski devised for public consumption skilfully blended a sense of sympathy towards natives and native practices with a dispassionate commitment to detailed scientific observation. And this self-construction as simultaneously outsider and insider became the proper, indeed "natural" stance from which to write anthropology thereafter; Malinowski had found a solution to what Geertz calls "the discourse problem" – "how to author an authoritative presentation".[7] Things might have been different if he had told his readers as he did his diary that on the whole his feelings were decidedly tending to "Exterminate the brutes" (Geertz, 1988: 74).[8]

Such rhetorical analyses have been applied to a wide spectrum of discourses which traditionally have seen themselves, not as exercises in social persuasion, but as modes of rationality and explanation in which the content alone concerns us and the language of its inscription is seen as instrumental, technical, or transparent to reality. In historical retrospect it is not difficult to see that the discourses of (say) genetics or gynaecology have been massively rhetorical and ideology-laden and not in the least scientifically "pure". Deconstructive techniques cause disquiet by probing current discourses to try to disclose similar occlusions within various rhetorics of rationality. So, according to J. Hillis Miller, "figure is the battleground between reference and the deconstruction of reference"; with the result that "all good reading is . . . the reading of tropes at the same time that it is the construing of syntactical and grammatical patterns" (Miller, 1991: 108, 188).

Classicists have been comparatively reluctant to examine their own modes of discourse, the "textures of rhetoric" of the profession (Nelson *et al.*, 1987: 5), the ways in which, within the discipline, authority is constructed. Such an examination might produce a greater readiness to query current dispositions and consider what advantages might accrue from changing them; and it might lead to a welcome divergence in professional styles, encouraging scholars to think as hard about how to write as about what to write, or rather to see that decisions about the one are always implicated in decisions about the other. In general a strengthened sense that scholarly practices are constructed culturally and discursively and therefore can be changed ought to lead to a willingness to experiment with those procedures. One classicist who clearly has allowed his reflections on these matters to inform his own writing is Luciano Canfora; his account of the library at Alexandria, *The Vanished Library* (1989), employs passages of fiction-like narration, subtle deformations of scholarly motifs and tropes, flickers of possible irony, and other destabilizing devices to refigure the character and authority of his historical narrative. His successful example might encourage others to do the same – or differently.

In the literary sphere traditionalists frequently make a sharp distinction between artist and critic, between primary texts which are the proper object of scholarly attention (and which display a variety of personal voices) and secondary critical texts which comment, in a completely different impersonal style, on the productions of genius. There could be a desirable humility in this stance; why should a reader of a book about Virgil be interested in the scholar who authors the book? – or so the argument goes (and in many cases this is indeed all too true). But often the humility hides another form of arrogance, as well as ignoring issues of power and authority: the humble critic performs a priestly function for his "God", expounding the truth about Him to the community of the faithful and denouncing the errors and heresies of rivals.

Moreover, in practice, the distinction between (primary) literature and (secondary) criticism blurs or can be blurred, not least in the processes of reception; indeed such blurring always occurs when a great critic is awarded canonical status. Many of us are anyway interested in the personality and views of the critics we most value, and there seems no reason to pretend otherwise. A tendency to deconstruct, or recombine, genres has been a general feature of postmodernism. Geoffrey Hartman argues that criticism can properly aspire to the condition and status of the literature which is its "subject" (Hartman, 1980: 189–213); deconstruction is continually reminding us how text and commentary are implicated in each other, and that implication is frequently instantiated in the textual strategies of the critic.[9] Miller stresses the self-reflexion found in much feminist writing, a self-consciousness about its own metaphoricity and narrative content which "points to the fictional strategies inherent in all theory" (Miller, 1991: xii). It is hard to know how a work like Roland Barthes' *A Lover's Discourse*, which stands at the meeting-point of so many genres, should be categorized; such a text crosses and recrosses the boundaries of literature and criticism, theory and practice, fact and fiction.

Traditional scholars like to think of their own writings as transparent rather than as opaque vehicles. So one of the depositions made against the proposal in 1992 that the University of Cambridge award Jacques Derrida an honorary degree (to which a number of distinguished classicists were signatories, all honourable men) included the following complaint: "It is . . . both absurd and disabling to say that all texts, and all interpretations of texts, are on a par. (The absurdity of this is evident in the vicious regress that results from asking how, on this view, an interpretation of a text should itself be interpreted.)" But if, one might retort, "interpretations" are instantly perspicuous, and do not themselves require interpretation, why are "texts" any different? Within a different discourse "vicious regress" in this statement might translate as "argument", or as "the conversation of mankind" (in Michael Oakshott's phrase), or even as history. Of course texts need interpreting (otherwise academics would all be out of a job); but we cannot expect that our own work will escape the drift of signification that is an inevitable part of the processes of dissemination (though whether anyone will be bothered to devote valuable time and effort to explicating our words is, of course, another question). One of the advantages of adopting·a dialogic model of reading lies precisely in the recognition that no word is ever final, that a reply is always possible.

How far does the stress on the rhetoricity and constructedness of all voices threaten the possibility of getting personal in any meaningful sense? Certainly one could argue that there is a potential fissure, or faultline, within postmodernity, and its commitment to the Other, a potential clash between what we might call its political and its epistemological programmes. On the one hand postmodernism seeks to release as many voices as possible, to empower the disempowered, to let the silent or silenced speak; hence its interest in divergent oral histories, in texts from minority or oppressed racial groupings, and so forth. On the other hand it is determined to undermine, destabilize, all authoritative discourses, including discourses about history, the real, personhood, including any conception of the unified self.[10] Lévi-Strauss put it brutally with his assertion that "the goal of the human sciences is not to constitute man, but to dissolve him" (Burke, 1992: 13). In a sense this is just a version of the central paradox of postmodernity, that its overriding commitment to heterogeneity itself becomes, indeed perhaps must become, a "hegemonic", and to that extent a self-undermining, project (many "soft" versions of liberalism are subject to just such a paradox). But we cannot speak for ourselves, or write ourselves, unless we have selves to speak or write which can be accorded at least some degree of authenticity.[11] Indeed the hunger for authenticity seems to grow stronger as its theoretical underpinning weakens. At all events autobiography, often reconceptualized as a figure of reading rather than a genre (so de Man, 1984: 70), continues to preoccupy postmodern writers, as if the fracturing of subjectivities leaves nothing else "out there", so to say, for us to talk about. As Carolyn Steedman puts it, "autobiography is alluring... *because* it stands at the confluence of many theories that have shaped and continue to shape post-modernist thought" (Steedman, 1995: 323).

It has become something of a defining trope of postmodernism to claim that the self is a constructed fiction.[12] Such a claim has its uses, heuristically; it is always worth reading any apparently autobiographical account under the sign of rhetoric *as if it were a fiction* to see how this would affect one's analysis. It is commonplace also to say that fiction (from *fingere* "to fashion" as well as "to feign") carries no necessary implication of falsity; but if there were no tincture or trace of this common meaning, the phrase "constructed fiction" would become inertly tautologous as well as losing any provocation it might contain. At the very least there seems an insinuation that whether a life is made or made up is undecidable, or may matter less than we care to think. But for many practical purposes we have to distinguish between, say, a story invented for specific personal advantage, one that registers someone's perspective, recorded with a degree of honesty, on a past event, and a fantasy in which the fantasist is persuaded of the truth of an imaginary past. We can call all these three stories fictions if we want, but that won't help us much if we are called on to take some consequent action; for then we shall need such distinctions, however difficult in practice they may be to determine. As with signification in general, undecidability does not mean that we can evade decision.

How we conceptualize the self is obviously likely to have considerable implications for autobiographical writing, and will help to determine which forms of such writing we find most persuasive. Indeed most of what Sidonie Smith calls "the certitudes of traditional autobiography" (Smith, 1993: 184) – not only the concept of a fixed, centred, autonomous self, but orthodox ideas about chronology, causation, origins, reference, and so forth – have, over the last 100 years, been put under considerable pressure. In particular the subject has been regarded as under subjection both to language and to larger discursive formations, themselves of course textualized or at least textualizable, which constitute those "hegemonic determinisms" (R. Smith, 1995: 56), of class, gender, and so forth, which help to decide what we are and which are usually regarded as the province of sociology and politics to attempt a description.[13] Psychology itself has assisted this process of decentring: any concept of the unconscious means that the self cannot know itself or can know itself only imperfectly. Decentred, sentenced to inhabit the prison-house of language, we inscribe ourselves, or are inscribed, within pre-existing subject-positions which constrain as much as they enable.[14] The once sovereign "I" is reduced to a linguistic effect. In the words of Louis Renza, "instead of referring to the writing self, the 'I' (a word authorizing and authenticating the discourse of fictional as well as autobiographical narrative self-references) places this self 'under erasure' as a rhetorico-linguistic shifter, figure, or trope", with the result that "self-reference . . . becomes another illusion of self-presence" (Renza, 1987: 172–173). Barthes, in his inaugural lecture, expresses his sense of frustration with the available range of pronouns which he experiences as a form of coercion:

> Jakobson has shown that a speech-system is defined less by what it permits us to say than by what it compels us to say. In French . . . I am obliged to posit myself first as subject before stating the action which will henceforth be no more than my attribute: what I do is merely the consequence and consecution of what I am. In the same way, I must

always choose between masculine and feminine, for the neuter and the dual are forbidden me. Further, I must indicate my relation to the other person by resorting to either *tu* or *vous*; social or affective suspension is denied me. Thus, by its very structure my language implies an inevitable relation of alienation. To speak, and, with even greater reason, to utter a discourse is not, as is too often repeated, to communicate; it is to subjugate . . . [15]

The linguistic turn, in relation to autobiographical writing, which makes problematic the question of reference (itself readable as a trope),[16] can take either a more pessimistic or a more optimistic form. In the pessimistic version – most strikingly formulated in de Man's classic essay – such writing fails to restore the past, and gives us not a life but a set of tropes whose effect is, in the end, privative. De Man pushes the New Critical concept of the *persona* to an extreme point with the result that the autobiographical subject becomes in effect a death mask evacuated by the person. The master trope of autobiography is, for de Man, *prosopopoeia*, "the fiction of the voice-from-beyond-the-grave", by which "one's name . . . is made as intelligible and memorable as a face".[17] The essay moves, ineluctably, towards its austere and world-weary conclusion: "Death is a displaced name for a linguistic predicament, and the restoration of mortality by autobiography . . . deprives and disfigures to the precise extent that it restores. Autobiography veils a defacement of the mind of which it is itself the cause" (de Man, 1984: 81).

By contrast a more optimistic account of the matter allows us rather to celebrate the way that through language we can continually re-create ourselves. As Drucilla Cornell puts it, "there is always more that can be written through metaphoric substitution and . . . through metonymic displacement" (Cornell, 1993: 6; cf. S. Smith, 1993: 21–22), and she invokes the linguistic theories of the American philosopher Charles Peirce:

> For Peirce, the subject can never be self-identical precisely because it is born into language as an other. Peirce also argues . . . that no form of life or language game can shut itself into a totality that would identify the subject completely with any system of shared norms and deny the possibility of transformative change. A slippage always inheres in the iterability of language that in turn, allows for the transmission of meaning over time . . .

> (Cornell, 1993: 4)

Language then can be construed as a prison-house or as the site where we can transform ourselves and our worlds, the place we go to die or the place where we can be endlessly reborn.

The view that self-writing is a fiction too frequently operates today merely as a gesture of closure, a way of finally framing the text.[18] And in general the decentring of the self and the rhetorical turn in autobiography do not necessarily imply that there are no selves and no lives (Derrida himself has insisted "I don't destroy the subject; I situate it" [Burke, 1992:167]). But they do involve a move away from the lonely, detached, self-present Cartesian *cogito*. Persons may be thought of as constructed socially, interpersonally, within their relationships with other people – which is why it matters so much what these are.[19] Philosophers like Alastair MacIntyre and Charles Taylor develop the notion of making a self in narrative (traditions for MacIntyre are embodied narratives, and it is only within these that useful and fulfilled lives can be led). Selves are dialogic, intertextual, sites of difference. They are the sum total of our *personae*, the masks we wear, rather than real beings "behind" the masks. No voice, on views like these, is best regarded as *essentially* personal or impersonal. Nonetheless, though all voices may be rhetorical and social – there are no private voices in the same sense as there are no private languages – one can argue that, within specific contexts of reception, what is deemed to be a personal voice can be found liberating by those who feel themselves oppressed or constrained by the prevailing discursive norms and who wish to transgress or renegotiate them (and for largely contingent reasons, in recent debates, these protesters have frequently been feminists or members of racial minorities). One should not exaggerate the novelty of the results. One of the most traditional ways of reading canonical texts is to appropriate them for contemporary concerns and for the concerns of the commentator (one thinks, for example, of the moralized Ovids of the Middle Ages). All interpretations can be seen as allegories of the text, and both personal application and moral allegory are long practised modes of exegesis. Moreover what at one point seems a liberation may itself become a mode of oppression, just another way of securing power and rewards for a particular professional group or groups. But here, now, within classics, the personal voice, effectively used (and Miller readily concedes that "like all writing, personal criticism is only as good as its practitioners" [Miller, 1991: 25]) could have a role to play in that process of continuing self-scrutiny without which no subject – the pun is of course intended – is likely to flourish. As Miller puts it, "somewhere in the self-fiction of the personal voice is a belief that the writing is worth the risk".

That there are lives after poststructuralism is shown, for example, by *Roland Barthes by Roland Barthes*. Barthes it was of course who, in 1968, declared the Death of the Author[20] (though maybe, as Séan Burke suggests, you have to be pretty authorist to make such a declaration [Burke, 1992: 27]). But, in his later writings, the dissolution of the self proves consistent with a tradition of intense sceptical self-scrutiny which in France can be traced back to Montaigne.[21] *Roland Barthes by Roland Barthes* explores and critiques the tropes and procedures of autobiographical writing and at the same time is readable as itself an autobiography of unusual persuasiveness.[22] As Susan Sontag puts it "An affirmation of his own idiosyncrasy (which he does not 'decipher') is the main theme of *Roland Barthes*" (Sontag, 1982: xxxiv). At the outset immediately following the title page we are confronted by the injunction "It must all be considered as if spoken by a character in a novel", but we are also teased with a paradox of presence/absence by being given these words in what we presume to be Barthes' own handwriting. It must be doubtful whether many readers have, in this instance, done as they are told, or believe that the writer is wholly in earnest (indeed would it not be naive to do so?). On the contrary the very form and artifice of the book, with its self-reflexiveness, its evasions, obliquities and seeming contingencies, can be taken to disclose what Barthes is "really like";[23] we may even experience this sense of encounter with a unique individual to a greater degree than in the case of more orthodox autobiographies.

In other words, *Roland Barthes* is recuperable, is even hard not to recuperate, for a traditional way of reading autobiography as an act of self-revelation. Paul Jay argues that *Roland Barthes* "seeks to *be* the decon-structed self, and it does so because it wants at every turn to 'attenuate the *risk* of transcendence' " (Jay, 1984: 174). And, if so, this is to concede that at least a residual mimetic impulse persists in the work. Barthes eschews any continuous narrative, and substitutes a series of meditations and biographemes, randomly ordered and fluctuating between first and third person. On the basis that "incoherence is preferable to a distorting order" he uses this structure of diffraction as an attempt to escape the tyranny of binary oppositions: "I am not contradictory, I am dispersed" (Barthes, 1989: 143). But he also acknowledges the overarching rhetoricity from which all his claims to dispersal cannot escape; "by supposing I disperse myself I merely return, quite docilely, to the bed of the imaginary" ("The fragment as illusion" [Barthes, 1989: 95]). We find here both a desire for an authentically non-transcendent mode of utterance and an acknowl-edgement that this cannot be achieved merely by a fragmentation of the discourse, since the fragments are not "outside" rhetoric, "that layer of language which best presents itself to interpretation"; both the desire and the acknowledgement in turn become for the reader part of what Barthes is (and it makes little difference whether or not we put either or both of these last two words inside inverted commas). Autobiography as a figure of reading is not readily evaded; to escape entirely all onto-theology in relation to the self would be as it were to live in a different universe. As an act of deconstruction *Roland Barthes* thus ultimately fails, as perhaps all such attempts must fail, but, precisely in enacting and indeed conceding that failure, it succeeds, as an autobiography, rather triumphantly.[24]

II

> A man's life of any worth is a continual allegory – and very few eyes can see the mystery of his life – a life like the scriptures, figurative.
>
> John Keats, *Letters*

Classicists who favour the adoption of a personal voice could do worse than look to St Augustine as their precursor and model.[25] In the *Confessions* Augustine engages in the exercise of thinking theology (especially the sinfulness of man and the nature of God) by simultaneously thinking his life. That the *Confessions* is the first "genuine" autobiography (and hence that there may be an intimate connection between autobiography and Christianity) has often been affirmed or denied. Critics seem either to be attempting to find at a particular historical moment a validating point of origin that determines the constitution of a (reified) genre, or seeking to show that a universal autobiographical impulse has manifested itself in different forms in every time and place. However that may be, one problem for any reader of the *Confessions* is how to connect the first nine books and their autobiographical narratives with the last four where such narratives are absent and where Augustine engages discursively with the issues of time and memory and the problematics of interpretation.[26] The final book offers a confident, briskly conducted, reading of a text, the first chapter of *Genesis* with its account of the Creation, expounded figurally in relation to human life. Augustine has already defended this mode of reading, and acknowledged the polysemous nature of texts:

> For this reason, although I hear people say "Moses meant this" or "Moses meant that", I think it more truly religious to say "Why should he not have had both meanings in mind, if both are true? And if others see in the same words a third, or a fourth, or any number of true meanings, why should we not believe that Moses saw them all? There is only one God, who caused Moses to write the Holy Scriptures in the way best suited to the minds of great numbers of men who would all see truths in them, though not the same truths in each case." For my part I

declare resolutely and with all my heart that if I were called upon to write a book which was to be vested with the highest authority (*ad culmen auctoritatis*) I should prefer to write it in such a way that a reader could find re-echoed in my words whatever truths he was able to apprehend.[27]

Books and their interpretation, and the right and wrong ways of reading them, play a very large part in the *Confessions*.[28] Augustine tells us that he was first drawn to philosophy by reading Cicero's *Hortensius* (8.7). Latinists find validation for their own responses to the *Aeneid* in the tears the youthful Augustine wept for Dido and for falling Troy (1.13). Just before his conversion Augustine hears a story of lives changed by an encounter with the written Life of St Antony, the Egyptian eremite (8.6). And the climax of that conversion is the moment when Augustine hears a child's voice telling him to take, read, and he opens at random St Paul's *Epistles*, and happens on the text that speaks his condition and its cure (8.12). In this practice of the *sortes*, whose efficacy has been amply confirmed by the historical record, a passage from an authoritative text (whether the Bible or Virgil), arbitrarily chosen and torn from its context, wholly possesses the reader; the appropriation, by which the text's meaning is configured within that reader's value system and personal life-history, has become total. So in turn, in a similar moment of possession (possessing the text and being possessed by it), St Teresa of Avila was to find herself described within the *Confessions*.[29] Just as our lives can be represented as texts which we make, so our selves are inseparable from the texts we read and make our own.

The extreme literariness of the *Confessions*, with the constant presence of Biblical and classical intertexts, has led even traditional scholars to question the literal truth of the narratives and to see them rather as a species of allegory; this is something that happens, sooner or later, in the case of all artful lives by literary artists (Horace, Dante, Petrarch would be other examples). Admittedly an unadorned style may be more effective in inducing belief in some readers (while being just as open as any other style to rhetorical analysis), and there may be a tension between formality and self-revelation (a tension itself representable as rhetorical), but there is no *a priori* reason why literariness and literalness should necessarily be in conflict – minds well furnished with books are likely to produce bookish lives. The presence of the Word, as we shall see, guarantees rather than undermines the stories Augustine has to tell, while the reading of any life, like the reading of any book, requires, for the very facilitation of the reading process, that there are both literal and figurative senses.[30] John

Sturrock claims that "autobiography is not life itself but a certain artful representation of life" (Sturrock, 1993: 25). A Life like Augustine's certainly has a plot and is thus subject to the tropes of narrative, maybe in the form of the sophisticated and self-conscious imitation of previous literary narratives (so in the *Confessions* the theft of the pears recalls, or rather re-enacts, the Fall), but isn't life subject to them too – could there be unstoried life?[31] Thus the tears in the conversion narrative are seen as allusively literary (there is an echo of Virgil as well as of various moments in the Bible) – as Jeremy Tambling puts it, "the tears have been textualised, codified" (Tambling, 1990: 22). No doubt this is so, but could any tears be "untextual"? Tambling – in this like Paul de Man – not infrequently displays a perverse longing (perverse from his own perspective, that is) for a realm of purity, uncontaminated by interpretation or intertextuality.

Augustine then begins by telling his story, and ends by expounding a book. It would be possible to see this as the abandonment, or transcendence, of the personal, as Augustine turns from a previously tormented and divided self to serene contemplation of the world outside and beyond him and of God. But it might be better to regard this final book precisely as the full realization of Augustine's personal voice. Just as the self can only be known in an encounter with an Other, so not until he has made peace with God can Augustine become fully himself. The process has aptly been compared, as "a healing kind of self-analysis", with Freud's talking cure (Jay, 1984: 23). By fashioning a Life Augustine has authored himself, has authorized himself to voice an authoritative discourse – he has become, in the full medieval sense of the word, an *auctor*, at once author and authority. And his work can duly receive the im/personal signature of his name, and become part of the texture of the lives of others. The *Confessions*, in other words, is not only the book of the self but a book about the Birth of the Author. This might seem the opposite stance from that of Barthes, but there is also an underlying similarity – in each case there has to be a death, in preparation for a rebirth, as a Book.

Of all forms of writing autobiography might seem most strongly predicated on a strong notion of "presence". How far, then, can the *Confessions* withstand a deconstructive critique? The whole of Derrida's project is often construed as an unremitting polemic against the metaphysics of presence, the notion that we are present to ourselves and others, and texts to readers; Derrideans are seen as sworn enemies of logocentrism and the "Transcendental Signified". But it can also be argued that deconstruction puts metaphysics firmly back on the literary agenda. Deconstruction, if I understand Derrida's position, is necessarily performed *from within*, so that we are always folded back into the metaphysical systems we are undoing, inescapably. Moreover there is a sense, as Kevin Hart observes, in which, if we speak strictly, we should not speak of the "sign's *failure* to repeat a presence" if dissemination – the generation of new meanings in renewed contexts – is "part of the sign's structure".[32] Metaphysics is inscribed in the sign in so far as the separation of the signifier and the signified can be seen as a metaphysical move, and the distinction between difference and similarity is always becoming a metaphysical one. Derrida thus does not substitute absence for presence (indeed how could he?); rather, within deconstruction, the world is construed in terms of a dialectic of presence and absence. Indeed since identity and difference each contain each other – and here again I quote Hart – "identity and difference are not finally different" (Hart, 1989: 10). In Derrida's own formulation: "Nontruth is the truth. Nonpresence is presence" (ibid.: 122, citing *Dissemination*).

Hart's book begins with a discussion of the twenty-sixth canto of Dante's *Paradiso*, where Dante encounters Adam, who can understand Dante's thoughts without any spoken language-exchange, since they are immediately and fully present to his consciousness. On this view the mobility of the sign is a consequence of the Fall, while Babel is the Bible's principal symbol of the dissemination of language and meaning which results from that mobility. Dante's discourse here is a self-deconstructing one, an attempt, *which must fail*, to go beyond the limits of fallen language, to recover a lost singleness and innocency. Fallen man lives in a world of signs, not presences, and this both necessitates and enables interpretation. So too for Derrida "the sign is always a sign of the Fall" (Hart, 1989: 4, citing *Of Grammatology*). Fallen language involves a movement "from the proper to the figural" (ibid.: 6), its tropical nature at once facilitating, and destabilizing, and deferring meaning; deconstructibility thus becomes, within this discourse, an enabling condition of disseminated meaning.

For believers in "Enlightenment"[33] (including its principal heresy, Marxism) Reason, often refigured as commonsense, reverses the Fall, guaranteeing a full presence by which we can know the meaning of the sign, as Man replaces God. Derridean deconstruction can thus be seen as a return – a welcome return in my eyes – to pre-Enlightenment cognitive modes (though in this respect it is worth remembering that commonsensical and positivistic conceptions of "reality" are being dismantled far more radically in modern physics than anywhere in literary theory). These reflections could serve to close any gap that might be felt to exist between Augustine and Derrida. Just as Augustine does not disguise the metaphoricity of his writing, so he does not regard episodes from his life as transparent to meaning – on the contrary they are surrounded by exegetical paratexts of a metaphysical kind (indeed Augustine writes to particularly telling effect about the way the mind circles and recircles problems of interpretation, in endless mazes lost[34]).

"Pronominal 'I's are historical rather than ontological phenomena": so writes, rather breezily, a recent theorist (S. Smith, 1993: 183) – but the "are" betrays her, in a typical return of the repressed. In Augustine by contrast self-writing and metaphysics necessarily go hand in hand. First there is the very form of the work as a confessional address to God, the ultimate Other; *confessio* like its cognate verb *confiteor* bears the sense of testimony as well as acknowledgement (both *confessio laudis* and *confessio peccati*),[35] and, in Augustine's day, such confession generally took place in public. A discourse addressed to God but also designed for the writer's fellow men and women as over-readers (or perhaps better under-readers) inevitably contains the highest of truth claims; the language of God may be silent, but the invocation of God brings that language to the very threshold of speech. Moreover such confession carries with it the strongest confirmation of self; in Tambling's words "confession always folds back onto the confessant an assurance of self, which is thus validated in the light of the other, here, obviously, though perhaps always in effect, invested with an imaginary plenitude of self-consistent being" (Tambling, 1990: 12).[36]

Second, the notion of conversion enables, underwrites, the representation of life as a narrative. Paradoxically the unified self is discovered precisely in its fissures (an enhanced sense of selfhood is a feature of a divided psyche in the Medeas of Euripides and Seneca, while Augustine continually underlines the weakness of the unaided human will to create a stable personality). One enabling paradox of self-writing is that the self has to be divided into two "I"s, the self who writes and the self who is written, at once subject and object, just as introspection is a paradoxical enterprise – for you to examine your thoughts there have to be two "you"s.[37] There is thus in any autobiographical narrative an assertion of both separation and continuity, difference and identity, for which the idea of conversion, necessarily a narrative process that contains a before and an after, provides both an occasion and a rationale.[38] Augustine can tell his story because he is and is not the same, is and is not different. The deconstructionist Tambling pushes hard to reduce the text to its inevitable self-contradiction. But, as so often, Augustine has been there before him.[39] In books 10–12 Augustine superimposes on his narrative model of a decisive turn in time an a-temporal sense of a self that is always in the process of turning and returning – such are the *aporias* inevitably entailed in spiritual struggle.

Third, and most importantly, the word is guaranteed by the Word. Sturrock shows how in the *Confessions* Augustine seems to start out from the position that individual words have (ostensive) meaning in relation to things but moves to a sentential conception in which meaning only inheres in completed speech acts, which implies that meaning must be deferred before it can be attained (Sturrock, 1993: 24–29). In a meditation on the problematics of conceptualizing time and memory, of explaining the relationship of the present to the past and the future, Augustine teases out the implications of what happens when we sing through a whole psalm, concluding:

> What is true of the whole psalm is . . . true of any longer action in which I may be engaged and of which the recitation of the psalm may only be a small part. It is true of a man's whole life, of which all his actions are parts. It is true of the whole history of mankind, of which each man's life is a part.

$$(11.28)^{40}$$

The Word, which in the Incarnation stands at the intersection of time and eternity, is the sovereign instance of such sentential meaning (Sturrock, 1993: 40–48), which partly explains why Biblical intertexts must inevitably become part of the fabric of Augustine's book.[41]

All this helps to explain why in presenting the self in a text we are necessarily in the realms of figuration. Augustine in creating the *Confessions* combined first-person narratives of self-scrutiny as found, say, in Seneca's *Letters*, with first-person narratives of *acta*, like the *Res Gestae* of the Emperor Augustus. The direction of the discourse is thus simultaneously inwards and outwards, both towards privacy and towards communality, *figura* serving to provide the link between inner and outer. As Sturrock puts it, "Once life has been turned into literature, its 'literal' meaning or 'letter' has been transcended, because autobiography is specifically concerned with rendering a life 'figurative' " (Sturrock, 1993: 30) – I would argue that this is true not only of a Life, but of any life. So it comes as no surprise that Augustine is a master of figuration,[42] of giving his descriptions of life-events an overtly metaphorical cast. Augustine of course believed that the Bible had both a literal sense on which there could be a reasonable measure of agreement and further spiritual senses. Given the polysemous nature of texts there is a need for authority if meaning is not to float uncontrollably – the *Confessions* involves the construction of that authority – just as there is also a need for charity in the reader: Augustine can be trusted because he has merited our trust.

My point all along has been that if the *Confessions* is coherent as a piece of autobiographical writing, it is coherent only in the light of its theology. Augustine can tell his story because the process of doing so is consistent with propositions that can be articulated about confession, conversion, the Word. The view that God and intelligibility go together has obviously been the dominant one in Western culture. Is a secular version of this coherence possible? Or are we left only with solipsism and an inability to make theoretical sense of any distinction between keeping some sort of faith with our own pasts and just making it all up. It is hard to see how we can avoid invoking the concept of trust, which involves its own leap of faith. Certainly in this particular *agon* I would rather side with Augustine than with Paul de Man whose personal hostility to autobiography we now see went deep indeed; the mandarin impersonality of de Man's own academic prose was eventually to collide with other people's narratives of his (hidden) life. And certainly the *Confessions* can help us to think about this whole set of problems, including the coherence of the self, the relationship between writing the self and the practice of confession (including one of its modern forms, consulting a counsellor or analyst), the metaphysical and ethical entailments of autobiography. Those who advocate the personal voice should not forget that, as Nicole Ward Jouve has it, "it is no easier to say I than to make theory" (Jouve, 1991: 10).

III

> And what is the title of the book? asked Don Quixote.
> *The Life of Ginés de Pasamonte.*
> Is it finished?
> How could it be finished, said Ginés, when my life is not finished?
>
> Cervantes, *Don Quixote*

In *Getting Personal* Nancy Miller has an elegant and adroit essay entitled "My father's penis" (Miller, 1991: 143–147). In it she uses reminiscences of her father in order to think through an issue in contemporary feminism, the relationship between the penis and the phallus. She tells us that she would not have written the piece if her father had still been able to read; crossing the boundary between public and private (wherever that boundary may be drawn) is always likely to cause offence or embarrassment, not least with those one is most anxious not to hurt. Any discomfort I feel about the result is less about the breaking of taboos or the revealing of childhood secrets than about the process of transforming human pain into artful writing. The essay ends, in a dazzling passage, with the death of Miller's father, treated as an extended conceit: it begins, "He died, I'm tempted to say, of the penis" (ibid.: 147) – of a urinary infection, in fact. I am tempted to echo Johnson's austere judgement on Milton's "Lycidas", "where there is leisure for fiction, there is little grief". In general we are inclined to grant greater freedom in such matters if a piece of writing is categorized as art, conceived to a degree as being beyond ordinary good and evil; how many readers spare a thought for the poet's wife when reading Yeats on Maude Gonne or Dante on Beatrice?

De me fabula narratur In 1992, I was invited by Karl Galinsky and Christine Perkell to be a member of a panel at the APA in New Orleans; the subject was ambiguity in Virgil. I designed a paper to be called "Reading Ambiguity: Virgil and the Critics" in which ambiguity, normally regarded as a property immanent within a text, would be reconfigured, for heuristic purposes, as a readerly trope, as part of the process of the reception of that text. My plan was to interrogate the use of ambiguity within Virgilian criticism by means of a double process of historicization: I would give both a genealogy for the term and a brief reception-history for Virgil's poetry which would show how differently it has been read, by reason of the different ways it has been framed, the different assumptions within which those readings have taken place. Ambiguity, I wanted to argue, served both to occlude the politics of reading the *Aeneid* and to facilitate various allegorizations by which the poem could be rendered more palatable to critics of a liberal persuasion; a largely unexamined term, it was used as a mode of closure, or to negotiate readerly disagreements.

After I had agreed to write the paper and already had a sense of its likely contents and line of argument, an event occurred which was to have an important impact on my life as a whole. I had for some time suffered from a form of depressive illness, and, while attending a conference on the classical tradition in Tübingen, I experienced a brief physical and mental collapse. During a few hours of torment and "false-consciousness" in a German hospital (with the barrier of language added to the other barriers to effective communication) I gradually became convinced, by a process of interpretation that could be described as "rational" (in so far as interpretation is ever rational), that I was dead and in Hell. Subsequently my "personal" experiences seemed to me so intensely relevant to the public and critical issue I was addressing in my paper that I felt there was no way I could not write about them; and in its final form, retitled "Descent into Hell", it contains a short "autobiographical" narrative, itself surrounded by exegetical commentary, based on those experiences. The writing was also, I would be inclined to say in retrospect, therapy (for myself) and perhaps too a species of punishment or reward (for others). My title was borrowed from Charles Williams, while also obviously alluding to *Aeneid* 6 and Dante's *Inferno*, itself modelled on Virgil. It was only later that I discovered, with a certain frisson, the existence of Doris Lessing's novel about the mental breakdown of a professor of classics: *Briefing for a Descent into Hell*.

I encountered considerable technical difficulty in finding a way to voice this episode from my life. What resulted in the end was a third-person autobiographical narrative, in a style of overwhelming literarity, dense with allusion and quotation, and modelled on the strained depictions of consciousness in the novels of Willam Golding. Ironically this piece of self-writing had two authors, myself and my wife, in addition to the presence of the other intertextual voices. Philip Lejeune has an interesting discussion of the effects of using the third person in autobiography (Lejeune, 1989: 31–51). Since the first person in such writing has usage in its favour, the third person becomes a provocation. As Lejeune puts it:

> It is another way of achieving, in the form of a *splitting*, what the first person achieves in the form of a *confusion*: the inescapable duality of the grammatical "person". Saying "I" is more customary (hence more "natural") than saying "he" when one talks about himself, but it is not simpler.
>
> (ibid.: 33)

At its most extreme it creates a sense of "a disturbing split personality" (ibid.: 40) – hence part of its appropriateness in my case. By using it one holds as it were the self at arm's length, to achieve self-protection or detachment or objectivity or irony or humour or whatever; one may archly tease the reader about whether the narrative is autobiographical or fictional or not (there was some impulse towards that in my case). It reminds us of what Lejeune (ibid.: 36) calls "the tension between impossible unity and intolerable division" that accompanies a sense of self. And in my case, like the intertextualities, it was also designed to highlight the writerliness of the account and raise the issue of the relationship between literature and life. These intertextualities fall into three classes: those quotations which, I believe, occurred to me at the time of the events, particularly the quotation from *Lear* with which I responded to the nurse on coming to myself in the ward; those quotations that I (or my wife) felt appropriate to convey the experience at the time of writing (quotations from Virgil, Dante, Marlowe, Shakespeare, Milton, Hopkins, T. S. Eliot, Plath, the Mass); and allusions that I only became aware of after the narrative was written, most notably the informing presence of the Orpheus-Eurydice myth in its canonical, Virgilian version (which led to my adding further references to this myth elsewhere). The paper also eventually consisted of nine subsections; though not consciously designed, the Dantesque resonances of this number were entirely welcome to me.

As I have already argued in connection with the *Confessions*, this self-conscious literarity has no bearing on the truthfulness or otherwise of the story told, whatever that is taken to mean. The narrative is not designed to be in any degree a complete account (and it has a purpose in the economy of the whole essay), but I tried faithfully to observe two constraints: first, that I would not knowingly make any detail up, and, second, that I would play fair with the reader by including nothing that was intelligible only in the light of information that was not included[43] – the narrative was to be public and readable, while striving to convey, from within as it were, the difficulty of a difficult experience. Whether this personal "testimony" is believed or not is of course a matter for the reader; there is no escape for any of us from the burden of interpretation.

What is such a narrative doing in an academic essay? That was a question asked at the APA. First, it draws attention to the radical contingency of things. Between the writing of the abstract and the writing of the paper certain events happened which could not have been predicted but which affected the results. Second, as I have said, it deconstructs the distinction between literature and life that we use, somewhat glibly, to insulate ourselves from what we do. Academics frequently suppose, or act as if they supposed, that their professional activities have little connection with the way they live their lives; this can be represented as both untrue and irresponsible. Third, it both directly pursues, and raises for the reader in connection with itself, issues about interpretation and polysemy. What is going to count as a text and how are we going to tease meanings out of it? This is no idle question; our very lives may depend on it. The literary, mediated, quality of the narration reminds us that the "literal" text is allegorized always already. For medieval theorists a text had different "senses", contiguous or independent, while the world too was a text from which various meanings could be read off (Barthes' *SZ* could be seen as a modern descendant of this kind of exegesis). In general I myself would argue for a scepticism which also allows for the necessity of interpretation, of living within history, and the politics of that, what another contributor to the seminar, Barbara Weiden Boyd, stigmatized as "a wishy-washy lack of clarity or *democratic* multiplication of meanings".

The varying impact of the delivery of the paper to three different audiences (my own department, the APA seminar, and the Virgil Society in London in whose *Proceedings* it was eventually to be published), its varying "meaning" in those different contexts, illustrated its own emphasis on shifting receptions. And the occasions also brought into focus the issue of what is speakable, and of what should be spoken. Clearly it was more transgressive in a sophisticated academic context to speak one's own mental illness – to use one possible discursive representation of the events – than, say, one's sexuality. And there were obvious ethical problems involved; to write oneself is almost inevitably to write others – and does one have that right?[44] The first delivery, at Bristol, was much the most difficult, the recipients including people involved in what had happened, or aware of the background to it. The atmosphere was highly charged, and many, including myself, found the occasion unpleasant (some evidently reacting with distress, or embarrassment, or anger, or a combination of these). A colleague from a different department (who himself liked, and was moved by, the approach, but was, to an extent, an outsider) commented that, in some people's eyes, it seemed as if I had farted in church. Another colleague later ruefully observed (though not to me) that, while others were struggling to look after me, I was just meditating my next article. When I complained to the seminar about the silence with which my paper was received, someone responded with the argument that, in adopting this particular approach, I had put that paper outside the normal parameters of academic critical debate; by this I suppose she meant that I had removed the protective boundaries between criticizing ideas and criticizing persons, or that I had arrogated to myself a particular form of authority in what could be redescribed as an exercise in power play. Certainly one can argue that some critical distance, some measure of (discursive) impersonality, is necessary for the successful operations of the academy.

The two other deliveries were by contrast comparatively unproblematic, though both were marked by a general determination not to discuss the autobiographical section (there was one reference to it at the APA, but only to query its relevance to the paper, a query accompanied by a murmur of support from others). As I have just argued, one justification for the personal voice in scholarship would be that it reminds us that it matters what we read and how we read it; the academic life can be construed not just as the performance of certain tasks but as a certain way of being-in-the-world, which means that our lives and our work should not become separated. Nonetheless my own experiment with this approach is not one I would necessarily wish to repeat, or recommend to others. We may need to learn to say "I", but we may also need to learn not to say "I".

a shadow seemed to lie across the page. It was a straight dark bar, a shadow shaped something like the letter "I". One began dodging this way and that to catch a glimpse of the landscape behind it. Whether that was indeed a tree or a woman walking I was not quite sure. Back one was was always hailed to the letter "I". One began to be tired of "I". Not but what this "I" was a most respectable "I", honest and logical; as hard as a nut, and polished for centuries by good teaching and good feeding. I respect and admire that "I" from the bottom of my heart. But – here I turned a page or two, looking for something or other – the worst of it is that in the shadow of the letter "I" all is shapeless as mist.

Virginia Woolf, *A Room of One's Own*

ACKNOWLEDGEMENTS

Three persons in particular have helped me to voice this paper: Duncan Kennedy, Irving Vellody, Vanda Zajko. I cannot thank them properly.

NOTES

1   Those with a limited taste for more abstract theorizing might prefer to omit the first part of this chapter and begin on p. 84.
2   Miller (1991: especially Ch. 1, "Getting Personal: Autobiography as Cultural Criticism"). See too Jouve (1991); Marcus (1994: Ch. 7, 273–296, "Auto/biographical Spaces"); Smith (1993: especially 154–182, "Autobiographical Manifestos"). On autobiography in general there is an excellent collection of essays in Olney (1980) and a useful introduction to the issues and bibliographical survey in Marcus (1994); de Man (1984) and Lejeune (1989) are classics; see also Eakin (1992); Fleishman (1983); Jay (1984); Renza (1987); Smith (1995); Sturrock (1993). Two recent works by academics that brilliantly combine theory and self-writing are Alice Kaplan (1993) and Gillian Rose (1995); for two earlier examples see Steedman (1986) and Martha C. Nussbaum, "Love and the Individual: Romantic Rightness and Platonic Aspiration", in Heller *et al.* (1986: 253–277). The term "personal voice" can be used for three distinct phenomena, which may appear independently or together: (i) the presence of an autobiographical narrative or narratives; (ii) the strong expression of the writer's views, with or without the use of the first person; (iii) that combination of stylistic traits and the cognitive vision of things that goes with them that together create the "voice" of any author (whatever form or genre she or he is writing in). With respect to this last it is a remarkable fact (however much we may take it for granted) that, even where an author writes in a variety of genres or in both prose and verse, we can detect a continuity of "voice". This enables us, for example, to identify the author of a piece of writing previously unfamiliar to us.

3   I take Jonson's point to be that speech constitutes an essential part both of our humanness and of our individuality as human beings; but the statement could be read in a more constructivist, or even deconstructionist, way.

4   For these various points see the commentaries (especially Nisbet–Hubbard) on *Odes* 1.1, 1.11 and 2.17.

5   De Man (1984: 70); the problem is, to what extent? Compare too Valéry's *mot* "there is no theory that is not a fragment, carefully prepared, of some autobiography" (quoted in Lejeune (1989: Introduction, vii)), where we could reverse the tenor and rewrite "There is no autobiography that is not a fragment, carefully prepared, of some theory".

6   See the introduction to Clifford and Marcus (1986) and the subsequent essays; also Brown (1977); Nelson *et al.* (1987); Simons (1989). For the turn of rhetoric in general see, e.g., Leith and Myerson (1989), with a full bibliography.

7   Geertz (1988: 73–101, "I-Witnessing: Malinowski's Children", quotation 83).

8   Cf. James Clifford, "On Ethnographic Self-Fashioning: Conrad and Malinowski", in Heller *et al.* (1986: 140–162).

9   So Burke (1992: 151–152) "deconstruction, as criticism, never speaks *in propria persona*, but only with a voice borrowed from the author. Or, put differently, finds its own voice in the hollow of an Other's".

10   Cf. Steedman (1995: 322) "two theoretical and political projects of late twentieth-century feminism coincide, when the rescue and retrieval of real experience is undertaken with theories of language and identity that eschew the real".

11   Smith (1993: 156) quotes Judith Butler: "If oppression is to be defined in terms of a loss of autonomy by the oppressed, as well as a fragmentation or alienation within the psyche of the oppressed, then a theory which insists upon the inevitable fragmentation of the subject appears to reproduce and valorize the very oppression that must be overcome" (from "Gender Trouble, Feminist Theory, and Psychoanalytic Discourse", in Linda J. Nicholson (ed.) *Feminism / Postmodernism*, New York:Routledge, 1990: 327).

12   I have "myself" argued for something like this view in connection with Horace, concluding that the value of Horace's account of events in his life is "not as reconstruction of the past but as part of a construction of the present" (Martindale (1993c: 18). But if we had good reason to suppose, say, that Horace's father died before his son's birth it would surely have an impact on our reading. That there is no alternative, external evidence means that a decision over such issues will depend on our sense of "Horace", and the ways we accord him "trust". Similarly, if we supposed that Milton was not physically blind, for most readers that would make the sonnet on his blindness not necessarily a worse but certainly a different poem.

13   Greenblatt (1980) is an exploration of the "intellectual, social, psychological, and aesthetic structures that govern the generation of identities" (1) in the early modern period.

14   See Martindale (1993a: 30–31).

15   Sontag (1982: 460). For Barthes "literature", where words no longer operate instrumentally, offers some form of escape from this coercion.

16   De Man (1984: 69); Renza (1987: 176).

17 De Man (1984: 76–77). Compare Hillis Miller's view that, in the depiction of a character, catachresis, where words are "transferred from some other realm to name improperly what has no proper name", is the dominant trope (Hillis Miller, 1983: 112) .

18 Cf. Marcus (1994: 245): "the fictionalist reading of psychoanalytic autobiographical narrative is no less enclosing than a representationalist one, and stems from an anxious need to control and contain that which exceeds form and threatens our conceptions of representality"; Burke (1992: 172–173): "far from functioning as an ideal figure . . . the author operates as a principle of uncertainty in the text, like the Heisenbergian scientist whose presence invariably disrupts the scientificity of the observation. . . . Critical theory . . . has shown itself no more capable of accounting for authorial performance, of negotiating the overlap of work and life, since all theory is finally predicated upon an idea of order and systematicity, a reduction of the idea of the text to a clear uncluttered field, to a given whose genealogy is suspended". For a defence of "reference" in autobiography see Eakin (1992).

19 See Altieri (1990 193–223) "Reconstituting Subjects".

20 Barthes (1977: 142–148); for Barthes the death of the Author is the birth of the reader, but the reader too is not precisely a person, but "simply that *someone* who holds together in a single field all the traces by which the written text is constituted".

21 Cf. Sontag (1982: Introduction, xxxiii); Fleishman (1983: 8).

22 So Burke (1992: 58).

23 Cf. Lejeune (1989: 44): "In the end . . . this game of flight from his 'imaginary' turns out simply to become in our eyes his imaginary's essential characteristic." Barthes' own notion of authenticity seems to lie in what he calls "the grain" which he defines as "the body in the voice as it sings, the hand as it writes, the limb as it performs" (see "The Grain of the Voice", Barthes, 1977: 179–189, quotation: 188).

24 Barthes may be said to have done for himself what he desiderates in a biographer: "Were I a writer, and dead, how pleased I would be if my life, through the efforts of some friendly and detached biographer, were to reduce itself to a few details, a few preferences, a few inflections, let us say: to 'biographemes' whose distinction and mobility might travel beyond the limits of any fate, and come to touch, like Epicurean atoms, some future body, destined to the same dispersion" (Sontag, 1982: Introduction, xxxv, quoted from *Sade/Fourier/Loyola*). Cf. Burke (1992: 30).

25 On Augustine I have made particular use of Sturrock (1993) and Tambling (1990); see also Fleishman (1983); John Freccero "Autobiography and Narrative", in Heller (1986: 16–29); Jay (1984); Lionnet (1989); Misch (1973). A good basic introduction is Clark (1993).

26 For an excellent discussion see Lionnet (1989: 31–66); she sees books 11–13 as "allegories of the act of self-creation which had been the narrator's aim in books 1–9" (p. 64).

27 *Confessions* 12.31 (Penguin translation by R. S. Pine-Coffin, Harmondsworth, 1961: 308); all subsequent quotations are from this version.

28 So Elbaz (1988: 22): "the *Confessions* is foremost a study of other texts: it inserts between other lives, within other discourses. In itself it constitutes an intertextual space . . . ".

29   See Barrett J. Mandel, "Full of Life Now", in Olney (1980: 49–72, especially 69).

30   For this argument see Martindale (1993b: 137–139) .

31   For lives as narratives see, e.g., Fleishman (1983: 478): "autobiographies resemble lives not in the sense that they are a close representation of them but because they are stories of that which is itself a story.... We have not only names for portions of life or of text (passage, episode) but also words for special phases of living and for writings about them (romance, adventure). It comes as no surprise, then, that familiar synonyms for autobiography (life, confession) are themselves words of this kind. They are names for books that relate the course of a life, but that life – indeed, the idea of *a life* – is already structured as a narrative".

32   Hart (1989: 13). This whole paragraph derives from my reading of this fine study.

33   I use this word as a shorthand for a particular complex of views after the usage of Alastair MacIntyre who also terms it "encyclopedia"; it is not of course implied that all important eighteenth-century thinkers subscribed to this model.

34   An example would be *Confessions* 7.1.

35   See the entries in Lewis and Short.

36   For Tambling confession is construed as a form of violence, and he has as one of his epigraphs a bleak passage from Derrida: "The narrational voice ... responds to some 'police', a force of law or order. ... In this sense all organized narration is 'a matter of the police', even before its genre ... has been determined." Against this one can argue that the ability to tell a reasonably coherent story is essential for the psychological health and continued existence of both groups and individuals.

37   This is acknowledged in such titles as *Rousseau Juge de Jean Jacques*. Pushed to an extreme it produces an unsettling effect of schizophrenia, as when Richard Nixon in his accounts of Watergate talked about the actions of "the President".

38   Cf. Sturrock (1993: 20): "The *Confessions* record a conversion and in so doing they also effect one: the profound ideological shift within the author which gives to his narrative its finality exemplifies the shift inherent in narrative as such, as a temporal process inescapably transforming of all that it touches". Accordingly, for Sturrock the work serves as "the paradigm of all autobiographical stories".

39   Cf. Tambling (1990: 19).

40   Augustine's position here is very close to that of many modern narratologists, including Paul Ricoeur. See, e.g., Ricoeur (1980: 180): "By reading the end in the beginning and the beginning in the end, we learn also to read time itself backward, as the recapitulating of the initial conditions of a course of action in its terminal consequences. In this way, a plot establishes human action not only within time ... but within memory. Memory, accordingly, *repeats* the course of events, according to an order that is the counterpart of time as "stretching-along" between a beginning and an end."

41   Cf. Jay (1984: 32 n. 21).

42   So Fleishman (1983: 55); for some of the details see his account: 43–69. For the approach see Olney (1972: 34), who rightly insists that such metaphor-

ization does not serve simply to describe a self but to actualize it: "the self expresses itself by the metaphors it creates and projects, and we know it by those metaphors; but it did not exist as it now does and as it now is before creating its metaphors".

43 I am only aware of "cheating" once; there is no way that the reader can identify the "two adults" in the final paragraph.
44 For some of the problems see Malcolm (1993).

REFERENCES

Altieri, Charles (1990) *Canons and Consequences: Reflections on the Ethical Force of Imaginative Ideals*, Evanston, IL: Northwestern University Press.

Barthes, Roland (1977) *Image, Music, Text*, translated by Stephen Heath, London: Fontana.

—— (1989) *Roland Barthes By Roland Barthes*, translated by Richard Howard, New York: Noonday Press.

Bennett, Andrew and Royle, Nicholas (1995) *An Introduction to Literature, Criticism and Theory: Key Critical Concepts*, London: Prentice Hall/Harvester Wheatsheaf.

Brown, Richard H. (1977) *A Poetic for Sociology: Towards a Logic of Discovery for the Human Sciences*, Cambridge: Cambridge University Press.

Burke, Séan (1992) *The Death and Return of the Author: Criticism and Subjectivity in Barthes, Foucault and Derrida*, Edinburgh: Edinburgh University Press.

Canfora, Luciano (1989) *The Vanished Library: A Wonder of the Ancient World*, Berkeley, CA: University of California Press.

Clark, Gillian (1993) *Augustine: The Confessions (Landmarks of World Literature)*, Cambridge: Cambridge University Press.

Clifford, James and Marcus, George E. (eds) (1986) *Writing Culture: The Poetics and Politics of Ethnography*, Berkeley, CA and London: University of California Press.

Cornell, Drucilla (1993) *Transformations: Recollective Imagination and Sexual Difference*, London and New York: Routledge.

de Man, Paul (1984) "Autobiography as De-Facement", in *The Rhetoric of Romanticism*, 67–81, New York: Columbia University Press.

Eakin, Paul John (1992) *Touching the World: Reference in Autobiography*, Princeton, NJ: Princeton University Press.

Elbaz, Robert (1988) *The Changing Nature of the Self: A Critical Study of the Autobiographic Discourse*, London and Sydney: Croom Helm.

Fleishman, Avrom (1983) *Figures of Autobiography: The Language of Self-Writing in Victorian and Modern England*, Berkeley, CA and London: University of California Press.

Geertz, Clifford (1988) *Works and Lives: The Anthropologist as Author*, Cambridge and Oxford: Polity.

Greenblatt, Stephen (1980) *Renaissance Self-Fashioning: From More to Shakespeare*, Chicago and London: University of Chicago Press.

Hart, Kevin (1989) *The Trespass of the Sign: Deconstruction, Theology, and Philosophy*, Cambridge: Cambridge University Press.

Hartman, Geoffrey (1980) *Criticism in the Wilderness: The Study of Literature Today*, New Haven, CT and London: Yale University Press.

Heller, Thomas C., Sosna, Morton, and Wellbery, David E. (eds) (1986)

Reconstructing Individualism: Autonomy, Individuality, and the Self in Western Thought, Stanford, CA: Stanford University Press.

Henderson, John (1987) "Suck it and See (Horace, *Epode* 8)", in Michael Whitby, Philip Hardie, Mary Whitby (eds) *Homo Viator: Classical Essays for John Bramble*, 105–118, Bristol: Bristol Classical Press.

Jay, Paul (1984) *Being In The Text: Self-Representation from Wordsworth to Roland Barthes*, Ithaca, NY and London: Cornell University Press.

Jouve, Nicole Ward (1991) *White Woman Speaks With Forked Tongue: Criticism as Autobiography*, London: Routledge.

Kaplan, Alice (1993) *French Lessons: A Memoir*, Chicago and London: University of Chicago Press.

Leith, Dick, and Myerson, George (eds) (1989) *The Power of Address: Explorations in Rhetoric*, London and New York: Routledge.

Lejeune, Philippe (1989) *On Autobiography*, translated by Katherine Leary, foreword by Paul John Eakin, Minneapolis, MN: University of Minnesota Press.

Lessing, Doris (1971) *Briefing For A Descent Into Hell*, New York: Knopf.

Lionnet, Françoise (1989) *Autobiographical Voices: Race, Gender, Self-Portraiture*, Ithaca, NY and London: Cornell University Press.

Malcolm, Janet (1993) *The Silent Woman: Sylvia Plath and Ted Hughes*, New York: Alfred Knopf.

Marcus, Laura (1994) *Auto/biographical Discourses: Theory, Criticism, Practice*, Manchester and New York: Manchester University Press.

Martindale, Charles (1993a) *Redeeming the Text: Latin Poetry and the Hermeneutics of Reception*, Cambridge: Cambridge University Press.

—— (1993b) "Descent into Hell: Reading Ambiguity, or Virgil and the Critics", *Proceedings of the Virgil Society*, 21, 111–150.

—— (1993c) "Introduction", in Charles Martindale and David Hopkins (eds) *Horace Made New: Horatian Influences on British Writing from the Renaissance to the Twentieth Century*, 105–118, Cambridge: Cambridge University Press.

Miller, J. Hillis (1983) " 'Herself Against Herself': The Clarification of Clara Middleton", in Carolyn G. Heilbrun and Margaret R. Higgonet (eds) *The Representation of Women in Fiction: Selected Papers from the English Institute 1981*, 98–123, Baltimore, MD and London: Johns Hopkins University Press.

—— (1991) *Theory Then and Now*, New York and London: Harvester Wheatsheaf.

Miller, Nancy K. (1991) *Getting Personal: Feminist Occasions and Other Autobiographical Acts*, New York and London: Routledge.

Misch, Georg (1973) *A History of Autobiography in Antiquity*, vols. 1 and II, Westport, CT: Greenwood Press.

Nelson, John S., Megill, Allan, and McCloskey, Donald N. (eds) (1987) *The Rhetoric of the Human Sciences: Language and Argument in Scholarship and Public Affairs*, Madison, WI: University of Wisconsin Press.

Olney, James (1972) *Metaphors of Self: The Meaning of Autobiography*, Princeton, NJ: Princeton University Press.

—— (ed.) (1980) *Autobiography: Essays Theoretical and Critical*, Princeton, NJ: Princeton University Press.

Renza, Louis A. (1987) Review of Fleishman (1983) in *Comparative Literature* 39, 172–176.

Ricoeur, Paul (1980) "Narrative Time", in *Critical Enquiry*, 169–190.

Rose, Gillian (1995) *Love's Work*, London: Chatto and Windus.

Simons, Herbert W. (ed.) (1989) *Rhetoric in the Human Sciences*, London: Sage.

Smith, Robert (1995) *Derrida and Autobiography*, Cambridge: Cambridge University Press.

Smith, Sidonie (1993) *Subjectivity, Identity, and the Body: Women's Autobiographical Practices in the Twentieth Century*, Bloomington and Indianapolis, IN.: Indiana University Press.

Sontag, Susan (ed.) (1982) *A Barthes Reader*, London: Cape.

Steedman, Carolyn (1986) *Landscape for a Good Woman*, London: Virago.

—— (1995) "Difficult Stories: Feminist Auto/biography", in *Gender and History*, 7, 321–326.

Sturrock, John (1993) *The Language of Autobiography: Studies in the First Person Singular*, Cambridge: Cambridge University Press.

Tambling, Jeremy (1990) *Confession: Sexuality, Sin, the Subject*, Manchester and London: Manchester University Press.

Taylor, Charles (1989) *Sources of the Self: The Making of the Modern Identity*, Cambridge: Cambridge University Press.

Vance, Eugene (1978) "Augustine's *Confessions* and the Poetics of the Law", *Modern Language Notes* 93, 618–634.

West, David (1967) *Reading Horace*, Edinburgh: Edinburgh University Press.

Chapter 6

Getting personal about Euripides

Patricia Moyer

Postmodern theory's most enlivening contribution to literary scholarship
could easily prove to be the privileging of just that personal voice which
this collection of essays invites us to explore. We are now quite distant from
those earlier twentieth-century critical practices which accepted clear
distinctions between objective and subjective discourses. We, indeed I, no
longer believe such distinctions are valid or even possible. Even poets in
that period of high modernism sought to cultivate the extinction of the
personality and the use of "objective correlatives," terms that later
became an embarrassment for T. S. Eliot, who formed and used them in
his critical essays. In "Tradition and the Individual Talent," Eliot argues
that "the progress of an artist is a continual self-sacrificing, a continued
extinction of personality." Here, too, he claims "Poetry is ... an escape
from emotion; it is not the expression of personality but the extinction of
personality," expanding on his assertion that "It is in this depersonalization that art may be said to approach the condition of science" (Eliot,
1950: 7, 10). In this last decade of the twentieth century, we find all
manner of writers – poets, critics, linguists and generalists – who use the
personal voice and the personal pronouns.

Over the years, those of us trained in the methods of the then-New
Criticism derived from modernism have performed numerous dedicated
exercises in critical analysis grounded in these illusory goals of objectivity.
Not only did we marginalize our own personal responses to literature, but
we also prided ourselves on not taking a gossipy interest in the "private"
lives of the authors whose works we studied. Our watchword was "The
text's the thing wherein we catch the knowledge of the work." When a
newer formalism proclaimed the death of the author, we simply focused
more intensely on the text, its patterns of imagery, its linguistic structures,
its intricate polarities and monisms, convinced that this textually-based
mode of discourse communicated, or at least seemed to communicate,

with our colleagues and peers. Under our pedagogical influence, several later generations of students adopted similar critical methods. Even now, in numerous conservative departments of literary studies in both the USA and the UK, students are encouraged to aim for both objectivity and originality, twin illusions fostered during that period of criticism when literary specialists aimed for pseudo-scientific precision.

Yet today we and our students are asking different questions of ourselves, of each other, and of the texts we still try to inhabit. The complexities of the social, educational and cultural changes which have made us get personal are thoughtfully presented in the excellent introduction and widely discussed in the essays comprising this volume. My particular emphasis in this essay is on the personal voices used by two very different twentieth-century writers in their readings and rewritings of Euripides. The works of concern to me are in fact translations of Euripidean texts: one, by H(ilda) D(oolittle), comes directly from the Greek; the other, by Wole Soyinka, relies more upon previous translations. Both authors, however, know the ancient Greek language and are familiar with a range of Euripidean adaptations. Both also adhere closely enough to Euripides' texts to give us significant new translations. Their personal voices are expressed indirectly, in the form of elaborate insertions, character development, stage directions, narrative emphases, and – in Soyinka's version – radical additions to the Euripidean original. The results are outstanding works of literature in their own right, a memorable form of dramatic representation which challenges conventional modes of performance.

My main point in this discussion is that each of these writers uses a Euripidean text not only to create a contemporarily-resonant translation but also, and inextricably, to speak in a personal voice about contemporary situations. H. D.'s version of Euripides contains a puissant subtext about the new, twentieth-century modernist woman, her diverse personae in relation to her sexuality, and the radical choices demanded of women by both ancient and modern social conditioning. Soyinka writes out of and within the conflicts about the political regime in his native Nigeria, particularly its efforts to separate from Biafra. He shatters and expands Eurocentrically-imposed national boundaries by fusing Greek, Yoruban and Christian rituals while exploring the themes of slavery and liberation. This multiplicity of functions served by a single literary text may seem obvious to those of us who have taught and read translations, and in and of itself necessitates that each new era produce new translations. Nevertheless, I have a different reason for suggesting that a translated and adapted re-vision of a Greek text can be valued for its personal statements.

When applied to translation, personal voice theory shifts attention from the question of whether or not a translation is "dated" or "outmoded" to what it offers us as a text located in a particular time related to the author's/translator's larger body of work.

For example, we used to read T. S. Eliot's *The Waste Land* as a radical modernist text about the fragmentation of twentieth-century society, a text which drew upon a wide range of cultural, anthropological and linguistic references. We now realize that *The Waste Land* is not only a stylistically powerful collage of historical fragments, but also a subjective statement by Eliot. We read it as personal testimony about his own life in England and Europe in the volatile period between the two world wars. We also insist upon reading the sections of the early manuscript, deleted later, dealing with Eliot's birthplace, the United States. We now can find in the poem various insights into Eliot's own private poetry workshop, as he later described it. Similar additional readings open up for us when we apply personal voice theory to the study of translations.

H(ilda) D(oolittle), who lived from 1886–1961, began her translation of Euripides' *Ion* when living in England from 1915–1917. She continued to work on the project over the next twenty years – most notably while travelling in Greece (Athens in 1920 and Delphi in 1932) and while staying in Switzerland in 1935 – and published a translation along with a commentary in 1937. After a 1954 radio broadcast of the play from London, H. D., then residing in Switzerland, made further emendations, which were incorporated in her *Ion: a play after Euripides* (Doolittle, 1986).

Like H. D., Wole Soyinka, who was born in 1934, availed himself of the personal voice in choosing the title of his Euripidean adaptation. His *The Bacchae of Euripides: A Communion Rite,* was produced at London's Old Vic by the National Theatre in 1973, during one of Soyinka's periods at a series of British universities and theatres, and after his release from detention in Nigeria because of his active opposition to the separation of Biafra. In late 1994, after his United Nations passport had been withdrawn, Soyinka escaped from Nigeria to Paris to avoid another arrest for his continuous protests against the repressive Nigerian regime. As I write this essay, we are mourning the hangings in November 1995 of nine activists, including the writer Ken Saro Wiwa, who were arguing against the regime in Nigeria with arguments similar to those of Soyinka. Soyinka himself is alive in England with a new play under production in London. The personal voice takes risks.

In their personal lives and in the writings in several literary genres, both H. D. and Soyinka challenge modernist/postmodernist dichotomies, particularly in their subversions of gender and national stereotypes. They cross a range of boundaries: textually, politically, biographically as well as sexually and nationally. I am not suggesting that both writers cross the same boundaries. In many ways they are radically different: in gender, in nationality, in terms of active political engagement, in methods of work, and of course in time. For each of them the use of the personal voice marks a stylistic development which reconciles numerous disparate and frag- mented lived experiences. H. D. – female, white, expatriate, an American living in England/Paris, Switzerland, travelled in Egypt and Greece, and used her Anglo-American hellenism centrally in all of her work. She is international in the high modernist sense which we now often perceive as apolitical. Wole Soyinka – male, black, a Nigerian who spends periods of time studying and working in England, the United States, and France, has developed a pan-African version of hellenism important in both his drama and prose writing. He has an active commitment to Nigerian politics which has continuously taken him back to residence there in spite of the dangers. Notwithstanding their differences, though, H. D. and Soyinka share a profound interest in Euripides and a conviction about the contemporary relevance of tensions and polarities articulated in these texts from the fifth century BC. To deconstruct this boundary of twenty- five centuries is itself a radical crossing over.

In an elaborate prose introduction to the appearance of Athene in the last scene of her version of Euripides' *Ion*, H. D. praises Ionian architecture and sculpture as embodying:

> that high water-mark of human achievement, the welding of strength and delicacy, the valiant yet totally unself-conscious withdrawal of the personality of the artist, who traced on marble, for all time, that thing never to be repeated, faintly to be imitated, at its highest in the Italian quattrocento, that thing and that thing alone that we mean when we say, Ionian.

> (Doolittle, 1986: 113)

This prose of sixty years ago sounds datedly humanist, indeed subjective, to our end-of-the-century ears. Yet it extols the disappearance of the individual, the "withdrawal of the personality of the artist." This is one version of that high modernist desire for objectivity that we now recognize as illusory. This passage is also representative of the borderline area between late Victorian and modernist hellenism or classicism. Even its editorial first person plural pronoun, which lingers on in my own essay for this collection on the personal voice, signals a now-suspect elite omniscience. The most relevant point for this discussion is, however, that in her aesthetic descriptions H. D. takes for granted a negation of the personal and the particular as a corollary to her version of the Ionian artist.

We have begun to distrust the denial of the personal, to find danger lurking in elegant abstractions. In a lecture of 1986, presented when he accepted the Nobel Prize for Literature, Wole Soyinka writes of the comments made by the German ethnologist and explorer Leo Frobenius (1873–1938) when Frobenius visited the Nigerian center of Yoruban culture at Ile-Ife. Describing Frobenius as "one of a long line of European archaeological raiders," Soyinka quotes him as saying:

> Before us stood a head of marvellous beauty, wonderfully cast in antique bronze, true to the life, encrusted with a patina of glorious dark green. This was, in very deed, the Olokun, Atlantic Africa's Poseidon.
> (Soyinka, 1988: 16)

Then Soyinka goes on to state: "Yet listen to what he had to write about the very people whose handiwork had lifted him into these realms of universal sublimity":

> Profoundly stirred, I stood for many minutes before the remnant of the erstwhile Lord and Ruler of the Empire of Atlantis. My companions were no less astounded. As though we had agreed to do so, we held our peace. Then I looked around and saw – the blacks – the circle of the sons of the "venerable priest", his Holiness the Oni's friends, and his intelligent officials. I was moved to silent melancholy at the thought that this assembly of degenerate and feeble minded posterity should be the legitimate guardians of so much loveliness.
> (Soyinka, 1988: 16–17)

Soyinka compares this particular form of racist condescension and dispossession to other, more lethal, examples of the denigration of black races. It is indeed just these spectres of racism, misogyny, and homophobia among others that we so often find lurking in the opaque folds of so-called objective or universal statement, or, to use Soyinka's phrase, "the realms of universal sublimity."

The Euripidean adaptations of H. D. and Soyinka make it clear that to attempt to try out the range of personal voices available to us is neither a self-indulgent experiment nor a casual bit of autobiographical repartee. Writing in this way is a serious, even crucial, effort to situate our beliefs in a context with principled integrity. It permits us to undertake the key responsibility to which we must attend in our current writing, speaking and teaching practices. What is more, the personal voice of the 1990s is radically distinct from the personal statement that high modernism resisted with its emphasis on objectivity. There are, of course, a multiplicity of personal voices available to each of us; we no longer search for the essentialist single voice. Yet each of our voices is informed by the conviction that not only is the personal the political but also that "the personal is also the theoretical: the personal is part of theory's material." This quotation from Nancy Miller's *Getting Personal* (Miller, 1991) is one which several of us contributing to this collection of essays have found particularly relevant to the discourse, and of course the title of my paper echoes Miller's title. One of the most illuminating aspects of working on this project was my excitement in discovering that my friend and colleague of many years, Susanna Morton Braund, who was my first Greek teacher and remains my valued mentor, also invokes Miller's book in her essay. I can assure you, dear reader, that I am not going to conclude my paper as Nancy Miller does her book, with an essay on "My Father's Penis." I should say, however, that I find the misreadings of Miller's chapter on her father's penis – which interpret it as merely representational and neglect its skillful combination of elegiac tone and Lacanian perspective – all too typical of the reductionism which is applied as soon as a personal pronoun, particularly the first person singular, appears in a scholarly or critical context.

In critical essays, in specific seminars, in some classrooms, in small and large group meetings often of minority scholars, in conferences in numerous countries, we are hearing the new personal voice, a voice as disciplined and aware as any scholarly voice has ever been, but a voice which uses resources of intellect, feeling and experience, without adopting a mask of objective authority. This voice accepts and includes its gender, race, nationality, age, sexuality, family/professional roles, the private/public spheres – the very aspects of our lives this collection encourages us to consider – in its critical discussions. The immense range of topics associated with interdisciplinary and multicultural approaches are also related to the multiplicity of personal voices.

I find certain analogies here with the revaluation of the personal pronoun in postmodernist poetry. Its foremost practitioners challenged modernist literary conventions by adopting the "I" as part of their narrative stance, and by incorporating personal experience directly as subject matter. Robert Lowell's *Life Studies* (Lowell, 1959) marked a change in the style of poetry written in the English language comparable to the innovations by Wordsworth and Coleridge in *Lyrical Ballads* (1798), itself a late eighteenth-century effort to reassert "the ordinary language of real men" as well as to present the heightened treatment of more supernatural subjects. Lowell, long a crafter of classical verse forms, a translator of Latin poetry, skilled in a variety of English rhymed metrics, made a radical shift to write about his own family, his difficult marriages, and his mental problems. His poetry workshops in Boston included both Sylvia Plath and Anne Sexton. This new poetry was called "confessional" verse; praised for its bold subject matter and skilled techniques, it was attacked as too subjective and merely personal. Many of the reductionist ripostes currently thrust at practitioners of personal voice criticism were used to discredit these postmodernist poets. That the "I" of these writers was often of astonishingly disciplined austerity was frequently overlooked in the initial reaction to the mere presence of personal narrative or anecdote.

The specific relevance of these issues to classical scholarship is increasingly apparent in the thinking, writing and teaching done by many of us who attended the important conference on Feminism and the Classics held at the University of Cincinnati in November 1992. The presence at the conference of, and the contributions by, outstanding feminist classicists have encouraged us to re-read and re-assess much earlier scholarly writing. Judith Hallett, whose paper at the conference and whose challenging questions during the discussions formed one of these contributions, follows through in this collection with an exploration of the relationship between feminist and nationalist scholarly identity. Marilyn Skinner's excellent paper at that 1992 conference suggested that we can choose among a range of voices – the traditional, the personal and the political, for example. One of the objections to Skinner's paper questioned such multifariousness as not genuine, positing yet again the essentialist single voice. Another objector resisted the idea that minority scholars actually have the luxury of making such a choice about how they are to be perceived.

Providing answers to these objections and undertaking explorations of the areas that they open up are two main concerns of the essays in this volume. We contributors represent a wide range of views, and possibly the entire spectrum of degrees constituting the personal. Some of us speak comfortably in the "I" of our own voice in a tone which combines the personal with the traditional or public voice. Others of us still distrust the first person singular as perhaps too singular, even limiting; we want to speak personally but in the Emily Dickinson style of "Tell all the truth but tell it slant." Yet others of us want to try all of the above: to use the first person plural with a new non-royal, non-elitist, and ideally egalitarian tone, then cross over to the first person singular whenever it seems appropriate. Many scholars are now writing autobiographically-grounded literary criticism and analysis. The Modern Language Association is taking cognizance of this interest by requesting letters that examine the place, nature, or limits (if any exist) of the personal in literary scholarship, which it plans to publish in the October 1996 issue of its journal. I am also eager to see what reflections of the personal voice panels from the 1994 and 1995 meetings of the American Philological Association surface during the next major research conference on "Feminism and Classics: Framing the Research Agenda," to be held at Princeton University in November 1996.

One way of approaching the personal voice in the criticism of ancient Greek and Roman literature is through translations and the multiple versions of texts which translations engender. A personal voice can be lost or found in translation, particularly by writers who are also working in the forms of poetry, drama, fiction, journals, diaries, letters and combinations of these different discursive modes of literature. An aspect of high modernism which classicists have yet to assimilate is its emphasis on the poet-critic. As we liberate ourselves from overly rigid expectations of scientific objectivity in our scholarly writings, we are freer not only to accept the mixing, merging, and transfusing of the devices of poetry and non-academic prose but also to recognize the merits of the interpretative translation. The two texts I have selected for discussion both adhere to a classical original with great fidelity and boldly integrate personal and political interpretations which are not so much additions to Euripides as they are emphases on gender and race in particular, culturally-specific contexts. Both H. D. and Wole Soyinka get personal about Euripides.

H. D. was especially tenacious about her involvement with Euripides. Indeed, during the time when her work on the *Ion* was her main contact with writing, there were periods of personal difficulty, of sexual transformation and geographical change. We can obtain a glimpse of the profoundly personal approach she took to her Greek studies in this eloquent passage from her *Notes on Euripides, Pausanias and Greek Lyric Poets*:

> the lines of this Greek poet (and all Greek poets if we have but the clue) are today as vivid and fresh as they ever were, but vivid and fresh not as literature (though they are that too) but as portals, as windows, as portholes I am tempted to say that look out from our ship, our world, our restricted lives, on to a sea that moves and changes and bears us up, and is friendly and vicious in turn. These words are to me portals, gates.
>
> I know that we need scholars to decipher and interpret the Greek, but that we also need poets and mystics and children to re-discover this Hellenic world, to see through the words: the word being but the outline, the architectural structure of that door or window, through which we are all free, scholar and unlettered alike, to pass. We emerge

from our restricted minds (with all due reverence to them, of course) into a free, large, clear, vibrant, limitless realm, sky and sea and distant islands, and a shore-line such as this in Egypt and another along the coast in Asia Minor or further toward the Bosphorus, and again Greece, Hellas, the thousand intimate bays, the foaming straits.

(Doolittle, n.d.)

This sort of personal voice is from a particularly elusive notebook, a text which evades us partially because it is still unprinted (although it is being edited for publication) and thus only available for reading at Yale University's Beinecke Library, but also because it crosses genre boundaries between travel writing, philosophy and polemic. Like other modernist women writers, including Virginia Woolf and Natalie Barney, H. D. and her female partner Bryher (a name constructed for Winifred Ellerman from a Scilly Island place name) worked consistently on the precisions of learning Greek. These women were resistant to the elitist classical brotherhood, its misogyny, its control of educational possibilities for both women and men. Yet they were determined to learn Greek. Indeed, during the earliest period of her work on the *Ion*, H. D. was still married to Richard Aldington; she was staying with him in Devon before his conscription and later re-located to Dorset to be near his army camp. Aldington and H. D. were both in turn assistant editors of *The Egoist*, each involved in *The Poet's Translation* series. They had worked together at the British Museum when Aldington was still too young to obtain a reading card. There H. D. copied out the Greek texts of Anyte, Meleager and other poets from the *Anthology* for his translation work and presumably certain of Sappho's fragments for her own.

H. D.'s initial efforts on the *Ion* significantly took place during the same years in which she was writing and revising her extended versions of Sappho's fragments. These verses sometimes take the form of heterosexual love poems, sometimes that of lesbian love poems, and at yet other times are sexually ambiguous or express bisexual passion. The same poem can assume all three erotic modes in various drafts. In a letter of 24 November 1934, H. D. wrote to Bryher, "what I write commits me – to one sex, or the other, I no longer HIDE" (Edmunds, 1994: 190). Her selection of a personal voice, in other words, defines her sexuality in connection with her choice of the relevant pronoun system. So, too, H. D. would appear to have employed this Greek connection with the *Ion* in particular as an anchor of continuity through an emotionally-stressful period, one which witnessed in turn intense involvement in her marriage to Aldington, a series of miscarriages, marital separation, the death of her brother in the First World War, pregnancy by Cecil Gray, the birth of her daughter Perdita, a new and lengthy relationship with a woman (Bryher), alienation from several strong friendships with male writers, an abortion, and the exchange of paternal and maternal roles in child-rearing – a multiplicity of crises. Euripides' *Ion*, which centers on crises of identity undergone by both Kreousa and Ion, was a focus of interest for H. D. during her trips to Greece, first with Bryher, and later with Perdita. H. D. adds an abundance of interpretative prose commentary to her version.

One of the most fully developed threads in H. D.'s additions to the Euripidean texts involves her varied representations of women. These are linked with the portrayal of Kreousa as experiencing a series of transformations in her own thinking about her past sexual encounter with Apollo, and her abandonment of their son: although initially resistant to the mere idea of Apollo, she eventually accepts him when it is revealed that he has cared for their child. Kreousa's rage at Xouthos' seemingly recovered child, the same Ion, is also transformed from murderous violence into joy at the recovery of her own child. H. D.'s prose introduction to the passage in which Kreousa appears treats her as a female archetype:

> She has always been standing there. She seems, simply, a temple property that we have so far neglected. [and later, after Ion speaks] A woman is about to step out of stone, in the manner of a later Rodin. It is impossible, at this moment, not to swing forward into a – to fifth-century Greece – distant future. This poetry rises clean cut today, as it did at the time of its writing. And today, we may again wonder at this method and manner of portraiture, for the abstract welded with human implication is, in its way, ultra-modern.

> A woman is about to break out of an abstraction and the effect is terrible. We wish she would go back to our preconceived ideas of what classic characterization should be. It seems this queen of Athens had leapt forward that odd 450 years that separates this classic age from our own. She is mother of sorrows, indeed (Doolittle, 1986: 29–31).

We need to remember that by the time H. D. completed this version of her text she had also completed the two series of sessions with Freud in Vienna during 1933 and 1934, which led to a renewed involvement with her writing in both prose and poetry. Her treatment of Kreousa in this passage signals an expansion of H. D.'s long fascination with female figures and their relationship to her own life in the wider context of the twentieth century. She is certainly interested in Greek male figures as well, but it is in her original revisions of Eurydice, Demeter, and most fully, Helen, that H. D. most fully rediscovers character. Her version of Kreousa is connected to her view of Euripides as "ultra-modern," of particular significance for H. D.'s modernist world. As she says:

> The poet Euripides, one of that glorious trio of Athens' great dramatic period – the world's greatest – predicts the figure of the new-world woman; tenderness and gallantry merge in this Kreousa, who yearns in neurotic abandon for a child she has lost, yet at the same time retains a perfectly abstract sense of justice, of judgment toward the highest aesthetic religious symbol of the then known world. She questions the god, and she questions him with emotional fervour and with intellect. Her personality, her unity was violated by this god, by inspirations. She has accepted her defeat, yet has retained her integrity.
>
> (Doolittle, 1986: 61)

We have here an indication of why H. D. remained focused on the *Ion* for so long a period of time. As late as 1954, when she listened to the London radio broadcast of her English version of this play in a room in Switzerland, she was continuing to revise and amend what she had written. This particular passage prefaces the scene between Kreousa and the old man who was her father's teacher. Numerous prose descriptions of this sort function as a subtext to the modernist poetry of the verse translation. Although the alternation of prose and poetry is a stylistic technique which H. D. would eventually use to great effect in her triumphant (and classically-derived) long poem, *Helen in Egypt*, here the device is related to the vogue for reading editions of plays made familiar to us by G. B. Shaw and James Barrie.

At the beginning of the scene H. D. characterizes Kreousa as "the figure of the noble woman," "the very embodiment of that Virgin Mother of her city, Athene." Yet later in the scene, when Kreousa agrees to killing Ion with, in H. D.'s words, "suspicious alacrity," she is perceived as becoming "the queen" instead of "the woman":

> Kreousa, the queen, stands shoulder to shoulder with the sword-bearer of the Acropolis. She, too, holds a weapon; she, too, strikes infallibly at the enemy of her city. Kreousa, the queen, standing shoulder to shoulder with Pallas Athene, becomes Kreousa the goddess. The price? Kreousa, the woman.
>
> (Doolittle, 1986: 73)

This polarity between the functions of the feminine – as goddess vs mortal woman – was also articulated by H. D. elsewhere, in connection with both female objectification and female subjectivity. She later portrays Helen, for example, as both object and subject, character and writer/reader, as simultaneously at Troy and in Egypt, unified and plural, both an eidolon and a hieroglyph. The Helens in H. D.'s text continually rewrite, reinterpret their own histories and narratives, giving us new versions of the story and its characters, especially that of Achilles. These representations of female self-retrieval were, I believe, crafted by H. D. during the long years when she was absorbed in the translation of the *Ion*. H. D.'s Kreousa questions the god and her relationship to him, and in this way survives; similarly, H. D.'s Helen is a skilled and active narrator, who revises her entire story.

The transformation of Ion from a state of surprise when he initially recognizes Kreousa as a powerful woman, to a feeling of hatred for his poisoner and desire to kill her, to a revealed and joyous acceptance of her as his mother involves a spectrum of experience which also was of great significance to H. D. herself. Her interest in the figures of both Ion and Hippolytus is articulated in one of her 1950 notes, in which she states that her drama *Hippolytus Temporizes* had "for theme and centre, the portrait or projection of the intellectualised, crystalline youth, whose prototype is again found or first found in the actual Greek drama" (Doolittle, 1986: 122). I would argue that H. D.'s acceptance of the modernist male within herself as well as within her relationships with others is partially worked out through her characterization of Ion. Her bisexuality is at an early stage indicated, for example, in the alteration of "the love of my lover for his mistress" to "the love of my lover for her mistress" in her adaptation of Sappho fr. 131 L(obel)–P(age), which H. D., following Bergk's numeration, identifies as fr. 41. This brief fragment – which Mary Barnard renders as "After all this/Atthis, you hate/even the thought/of me. You dart/off to Andromeda" (Barnard, 1958) is expanded by H. D. into a much longer poem, with various versions, each involving a range of sexual ambiguities. The sexual complexities she describes, let me emphasize, cannot simply be resolved in lived human experiences, even those of H. D., Bryher and their numerous friends, who were continuously engaging in complex, sexually-charged, inter-relationships. When H. D. writes about the conflict in writing things down which forced her to adopt one sex or the other, she is expressing that tension between the abstract longings of the personal voice and their concrete realisation within particular literary genres. In the genre of drama the author can realize these gendered potencies by identifying with a multiplicity of characters. She can be both Kreousa and Ion.

As I noted earlier, Wole Soyinka wrote his adaptation of a Euripidean play – *The Bacchae of Euripides: A Communion Rite* – as a commissioned presentation for the National Theatre of Great Britain in 1973, following his release from detention in Nigeria. He had initially been arrested in 1965, in connection with pirate radio broadcasts from the Nigerian Broadcasting Company subsequent to the disputed Western Region elections. Soyinka has also been vocal in his support for Swahili as the common language of the African continent, most prominently in a lecture which he presented at an international festival of Negro arts and culture. Nevertheless, like other Nigerian writers, including Chinua Achebe, Soyinka has reached a world-wide audience through his brilliant poetry, drama and critical writing in English. His subjects range widely: from "The Critic and Society: Barthes, Leftocracy and Other Mythologies" to "Shakespeare and the Living Dramatist" to "The Fourth Stage: Through the Mysteries of Ogun to the Origin of Yoruba Tragedy" to "The *Lysistrata* of Aristophanes." Soyinka's hellenism is politicized and personalized through its location in contemporary Nigeria; it is also highly theorized, indeed postmodernist.

Soyinka's other works related directly to the political situation in his native Nigeria include *The Man Died* (Soyinka, 1972) a book written after his two years in prison, in which he analyzes the massacres, the repression of trade unionists, and the alliance between a corrupt generation of politicians and the army. It is an uncompromisingly personal statement addressed to "the people to whom I belong" (p. 15). Soyinka hopes to begin to deconstruct the "power group"; his prefatory letter to his compatriots says "a first step towards the dethronement of terror is the deflation of its hypocritical self-righteousness" (pp. 15–16). These words could almost read as a stage direction for his version of the *Bacchae*, and particularly for his interpretation and deflation of the character of Pentheus. In his function as scapegoat in Soyinka's version, Teiresias, too, is repeatedly mocked and diminished. Soyinka boldly presents specific evidence of the Nigerian government's complicity in terror and cruelty in *The Man Died*, employing a direct-action mode of political discourse which he still practices and for which he is still at great risk. As early as 1994, during an appearance on British television, Soyinka predicted the latest government interventions. And certainly Soyinka's own statement about the Nigerian struggle for independence in conflict with a terrorist government – published in November 1994 in the *Guardian Weekly* – resonates powerfully with his version of the *Bacchae*, whose parallels with the current Nigerian situation are even more forceful since the recent, deplorable hangings.

In a prefatory acknowledgment, Soyinka credits the translations of

Euripides by Gilbert Murray – whose translations were also used by H. D. – and William Arrowsmith. T. S. Eliot offers an interesting comparison between H. D.'s and Gilbert Murray's translations (Eliot, 1950: 50): "The choruses from Euripides by H. D. are, allowing for errors and even occasional omissions of difficult passages, much nearer to both Greek and English than Mr Murray's." Eliot is here eager to give recognition to the personal voice used by H. D. in her translations: he is writing merely of her renditions of the choral sections, not her full version of the *Ion*, but even so he is responsive to the distinctive aspects of her writing style. Soyinka's language has a similar vitality, whatever the stylistic differences between himself and H. D. He infuses his version of Asian and Greek cultic rituals with Nigerian mythology. In addition to acknowledging the translations of Murray and Arrowsmith, Soyinka also credits his own work *Idanre*, "a Passion poem of Ogun, elder brother to Dionysos. From this long poem I have also lifted entire lines, especially in the praise chants" (Soyinka, 1973: 234).

The first time I truly began to understand what the term "Eurocentric" meant to contemporary artists working within a postcolonial tradition was in reading the essays of Wole Soyinka. His brilliant parallels between the Yoruban god Ogun and the Greek Dionysos enrich by association. There is no effort to universalize these gods. Rather, there is a fine exploration of similar divine forces. The parallels with the present-day Nigerian political situation are there; in some ways Soyinka's *Bacchae* is as personal a statement as *The Man Died*.

Although he adheres to Euripides' texts quite precisely, Soyinka makes radical additions. His opening stage direction establishes the centrality of slavery to his version of the story:

To one side, a road dips steeply into lower background, lined by the bodies of crucified slaves mostly in the skeletal stage. The procession that comes later along this road appears to rise almost from the bowels of earth. The tomb of Semele, smoking slightly, is to one side, behind the shoulder of this rise. Green vines cling to its charred ruins.

In the foreground, the main gate to the palace of Pentheus. Further down and into the wings, a lean-to built against the wall, a threshing floor. A cloud of chaff, and through it, dim figures of slaves flailing and treading. A smell and sweat of harvest. Ripeness. A spotlight reveals Dionysos just behind the rise, within the tomb of Semele. He is a being of calm rugged strength, of a rugged beauty, not of effeminate prettiness. Relaxed, as becomes divine self-assurance

but equally tensed as if for action, an arrow drawn in readiness for
flight.

(Soyinka, 1973: 235)

Here we have a Dionysos familiar to us from Greek tragedy but in an
historical dimension including the crucifix icon, with not just one
sacrificial victim but many slaves. When Dionysos lists the range of places
throughout Asia Minor and Arabia where his rituals have been
established, Soyinka's Dionysos specifically adds Afghanistan, Ethiopia
and Crete. Some of these additions give contemporary relevance to the
text, but others are more racially inclusive. It is as if Soyinka is anticipating
Martin Bernal's emphases in *Black Athena* (alternatively, Bernal may be
influenced by Soyinka) on the close connections between Dionysos, Osiris
and Attis, and on the importance of Ethiopia in the ancient classical
world. Bernal also argues for the origin of the name Semele (Dionysos'
mother, destroyed at his birth by a flash of lightning wielded by his father
Zeus) in an Egyptian word for "wild cow" (we could easily divert ourselves
with many gender speculations on this matter!). Soyinka's stage direction
for a Chorus of Slaves stresses racial complexity:

> The Slaves, and the Bacchantes, should be as mixed a cast as possible,
> testifying to their varied origins. Solely because of the "hollering" style
> suggested for the Slave Leader's solo in the play it is recommended that
> this character be fully negroid.

(Soyinka, 1973: 234)

Soyinka's *Bacchae* is a post-Frazerian text, where – in accordance with the
assumptions informing *The Golden Bough* – Attis/Adonis rituals are taken
for granted as part of agrarian societies. Teiresias is treated quite roughly
as the annual scapegoat sacrificial victim until he is recognized by
Dionysos, whom Teiresias immediately recognizes as the god. Soyinka
handles the rituals so that we are more fully initiates than we are in the
Euripidean original, although there too we perceive Pentheus' illusions. In
the Greek version, however, we do not have this sense of Dionysos and
Teiresias as co-participants in a recurrent annual ritual, paralleled by
Yoruban rituals of renewal and vegetative reflourishing, the slaughter of
winter with rebirth in the spring. Soyinka also has a procession to Eleusis
with a Master of Revels, Vestals, Priests and Floggers. Soyinka uses the
drama to emphasize the dependence of a slave culture on the ruling class
and the need to organize a resistance for revolutionary political
transformation. Thus the slaves and women are the supporters of
Dionysos, the transformer.

When Teiresias and Cadmus participate in the cross-dressing scenes we are prepared for the later feminization of Pentheus. The sexual borderlines experienced as the *Bacchae* is performed are gender-specific to men. That is, we perceive men voluntarily transformed by wearing the costumes of women. At times, this is done with gleeful celebration – as in the episode with Teiresias and Cadmus, in which the change is very much under control – and analyzed, at times, with ominous intensity, as in Pentheus' cross-dressing, when another boundary, a psychic one, is crossed. Control is lost even before we see Pentheus swaying from the exposed heights of the tree-limb.

The women enact a wide and wild range of activities which cross extreme boundaries. But they do not change sexes, even as Maenads. The humorous side of the cross-dressing with Teiresias and Cadmus is stressed in Soyinka's addition of the collapsible thyrsus which Cadmus has had designed and which keeps collapsing, full of phallic fun and games. We do not find Cadmus and Agave wandering off as exiles at the end, when Cadmus cries, "Why us?" Agave simply answers, with a postmodernist twist, "Why not?" (Soyinka, 1973: 307).

The tragic intensity of the conclusion is further modified by Soyinka with a stress on the inevitability of the ritual and on the freedom enacted in the transformations. This freedom is signalled by the blood–wine transformation at the end when Cadmus thinks that blood is flowing from Pentheus' head and Teiresias recognizes the spurting liquid as wine. The play ends there. Soyinka writes: "I see the *Bacchae*, finally, as a prodigious, barbaric banquet, an insightful manifestation of the universal need of man to match himself against Nature . . . he is in turn replenished for the cyclic drain in his fragile individual potency" (Soyinka, 1974: Introduction, x–xi) He argues that Agave recognizes and accepts the "cosmic forces for which the chorus is custodian and vessel in the potency of ritual enactment" (ibid.: x). There is a rich field, indeed the familiar minefield, of gendered concepts in these statements by Soyinka about the accepting Agave and the renewed "man." Whatever the limitations of his thinking about gender, Soyinka does powerfully resist a Eurocentric hegemony of myth.

Ironically, H. D., who in her more austere exploration of transformation in the *Ion* stresses the crises of identity in the characters of Ion and Kreousa, at the same time foregrounds national issues in her treatment of Delphi and Athens. Somewhat surprisingly, the Nigerian activist Soyinka has created a *Bacchae* which is centered on Thebes alone, and – with its Dionysian/Apollonian polarities – is largely focused on ritual rather than national and political change. In so doing, each reminds us of the complexity and multiplicity of their personal voices, of how they function as instruments capable of both revealing and downplaying an array of unpredictable concerns.

A challenge of our essays in the personal voice is to locate, to write in, and to define our own personal voices. My mode of writing here has been oblique, slanted. By directing my attention to uncovering glimpses and hints of H. D.'s and Soyinka's personal voices in their versions of Euripides, I have given indirect pointers to my own convictions. Some questions I ask myself have a few tentative (and parenthetical) answers, which in themselves open up further questions:

What is an English Lit. specialist like me doing in the world of classics anyway?

(A flight from social realism and representationalism? A desire for a limited number of texts whose female figures intrigue through elusiveness, a sort of patriarchal doom which forces a feminist in the 1990s to return to male-written texts to understand what our own conditioning is?)

Why have I spent an astounding number of hours in the last seven years learning Greek, working on translations of Sappho, Anyte, Euripides, Homer, Sophocles, Stesichorus, Plato, Theocritus – this in no chronological order?

(In order to understand the hellenism of modernist writers in the first half of the twentieth century? In order to work with words and phrases individually again, to work with the texture of language and not the intensely theorized vocabulary with which I also work? To retrieve space for my own poetry writing? To follow the paths of Mary Ann Evans, Virginia Woolf, H. D., Natalie Barney and other women writers who wanted to learn Greek? Certainly not for any careerist reasons, nor for any admission into the patriarchy, but for actually being with the words themselves.)

Can the personal voice unite, untie, relate, create a voice which is both critically alert and creatively vital?

My personal voice is a question.

REFERENCES

Barnard, Mary (1958) *Sappho: A New Translation*, Berkeley and Los Angeles, CA: University of California Press.

Doolittle, Hilda (1986) *Ion: a play after Euripides*, Redding Ridge, CT: Black Swan Books.

—— (n.d.) "Notes On Euripides, Pausanias, and Greek Lyric Poets," typescript, H. D. papers, New Haven, CT: Beinecke Library, Yale University.

Edmunds, Susan (1994) *Out of Line: History, Psychoanalysis, and Montage in H. D.'s Longer Poems*, Stanford, CA: Stanford University Press.

Eliot, T. S. (1950) *Selected Essays*, New York: Harcourt, Brace, and Company.

Gibbs, James ed. (1980) *Critical Perspectives on Wole Soyinka*, Washington DC: Three Continents Press Inc.,

Jones, Eldred Durosimi (1973) *The Writing of Wole Soyinka*, London: James Currey, and Portsmouth NH: Heinemann 1988.

Lowell, Robert (1959) *Life Studies*, New York: Farra, Straus, and Cudahy.

Miller, Nancy (1991) *Getting Personal*, New York: Routledge.

Soyinka, Wole (1972) *The Man Died: Prison Notes of Wole Soyinka*, New York: Harper & Row.

—— (1973) *Collected Plays I*, New York: Oxford University Press.

—— (1974) *The Bacchae of Euripides: A Communion Rite*, New York: W. W. Norton & Co.

—— (1988) "This Past Must Address Its Present," Nobel Lecture, New York: Anson Phelps Institute for African, Afro-American, and American Indian Affairs.

Chapter 7

Writing as an American in classical scholarship

Judith P. Hallett

For Ronald Mellor

Nineteen ninety-five was an *annus memorabilis* for me, marking the thirtieth anniversary of my professional vocation. During the course of 1965, I ceased to be merely a passive participant in the academic study of classical languages and cultures: for the first time I assumed the active roles of classics teacher and scholar. In June of that year I became a teaching assistant in classics at the summer session of Phillips Academy in Andover, Massachusetts (a prestigious secondary school whose alumni include President George Bush and Professor Charles Rowan Beye). Three months later, when I returned for my final undergraduate year at Wellesley College (then as now an all-female institution), I began an independent research project on golden age myths in Ovid: asking my own questions of the texts; making my own connections with previously published scholarship. These two experiences convinced me that both of these activities, classics teaching and classical scholarship, were gratifying, productive pursuits which I wanted to continue for the rest of my life.

Yet both experiences also afforded me the impression that I was congenitally unworthy of undertaking these pursuits. Before applying to teach at Andover, I had to be reassured that its best-known classics master, Alston Hurd Chase, fled the campus each June when it was transformed from an all-male to a coeducational academic environment. Chase's beginning Greek textbook had prompted my fears: he introduced the noun *gyne* with the sentence "woman, silence brings adornment to women"; the noun *hydor* with "I write the oaths of women on water"; and the perfect tense with "Two days are sweetest of a woman's life, when someone marries her and buries her dead body." Remarks in Chase's autobiography – published a few months after his death in 1993, although first drafted after Phillips Andover admitted women students in the 1970s – have since proven my worries well-founded. I have quoted some of the most troubling in the appendix at the end of this chapter: my own favorite is his assertion that the women of his youth were "too busy by day and too weary by night to agitate for liberation: the thousand electrical devices which make some idle and discontented today were scarcely thought of."

Fortunately, my direct supervisor at Andover, in what turned out to be an all-male class reviewing Latin grammar and striding into Caesar, was immensely supportive and helpful. He shared myriad pedagogical devices which I still plug into my Latin classes today (such as calling the third conjugation the Right Guard Future – after a popular American brand of deodorant – because it, unlike the first and second conjugations, has no BOs). But another classics master on campus pronounced "these women's colleges" disgracefully negligent for failing to provide me with the requisite year of Xenophon. He insisted that I meet with him twice weekly to march through the *Anabasis*. He indicated his satisfaction with my performance at these sessions by musing, "I suppose, though, you'll be a matron rather than a pedagogue." After returning to Wellesley that fall, I had similar experiences with male classics professors from other institutions when I tried to describe my research project to them. One sniffily dismissed all such endeavors by female undergraduates, commenting that we would, "if lucky, soon be changing diapers (a.k.a. nappies) anyway."

In retrospect I suppose I am thankful for those initial, and rationally groundless, expressions of little-to-no confidence in my professional "promise." They toughened me to survive various criticisms and dismissals of my pedagogy and scholarship in years to come. My appendix contains some excerpts from a 1980 report by my department chair at Boston University evaluating me for tenure and promotion. Among other things, he faulted me for "conduct[ing myself] more like a teacher of early elementary school children than a college professor"; for exhibiting a manner "of condescension towards [my] students"; for "insisting on terminology inappropriate for ancient Rome (e.g. 'feminism' . . .)"; for "typical . . . unenlightened attempts to make scholarly studies somehow more readable by inserting 'cute,' trivial allusions"; and for "the intellectual poverty of [my] work." Soon after this report was written, I attended a reception given by the classics department at my graduate alma mater for its new students and local alumni. As I was chatting with a senior professor there who had helped me immeasurably with my research, and who had so far been extremely supportive to me during my Boston University tenure ordeal, he welcomed a young man to our conversation. He introduced the young man to me as a new classics graduate student; he introduced me merely as "Judy Hallett, a prominent hostess."

Because many of these expressions of little-to-no-confidence in me as a future and present classicist have devalued me as an individual owing to my gender, they, in combination with other non-academic experiences, spurred me to become and to remain a committed feminist. By this term I mean that I – in my capacities as citizen, teacher and scholar – have devoted much time and energy to working with others, men as well as women, in order to address inequities which disproportionally affect members of my own gender, and to create a more inclusive as well as a more equitable environment for us all. No less importantly, because the expressions of little-to-no confidence in me I have related so far came from classicists born (or at least employed) in my own country, they, in combination with my feminist identity, have helped me to think about as well as to survive other criticisms: criticisms levelled not only at me as a classicist but also at all of us classicists trained in the United States.

Now these other criticisms are often of the subtle, "a prominent hostess" variety. My graduate school professors, the American- as well as the European-trained, would indirectly indicate that those students who had at some point attended institutions abroad were generically superior to those of us who had not: by exempting such students from required courses; by awarding them the most generous fellowships and the best teaching assignments; even by voicing gratitude that they had deigned to enroll in the program, when calling the roll at the first meeting of a graduate seminar. This conduct sent the rest of us the message that such students were bound to have a better command of the ancient languages, and to have developed more refined philological sensibilities, because they had been exposed to a higher caliber of teaching and scholarship (some, it is true, had a philological edge over us home-grown products, but others did not). During a post-doctoral year in England, I was once interrupted, in the midst of delivering a paper, by a German-born British scholar offended by my pronunciation of Latin, specifically my American habit of pronouncing v's as w's. This man, a refugee from the Nazis who had benefited from the largesse of American higher education during several sabbaticals in the United States, routinely mispronounced numerous English words (including my own name): yet no one ever corrected him. Furthermore, he never publicly interrupted Europeans, even those a decade younger than myself, to correct their English or Latin mispro-nunciations.

Such criticisms of American classical education as by its very nature inferior to its European counterparts are, however, at times voiced openly and directly. Sir Hugh Lloyd Jones has written that

Classical scholarship in the United States has suffered greatly from the failure of most schools to teach languages; it is hard to learn Greek and Latin really well if one starts late, and although America makes a vast contribution to classical scholarship, not many Americans are experts in these languages. One result is that the enemies of exact scholarship can easily find an audience there, and gifted rhetoricians find it possible to set themselves up as local gurus, teaching a method which rapidly produces fashionable results.

In the fall of 1994 a foreign-trained, Canadian-based colleague fulminated on the University of Pennsylvania classics graduate education e-mail list:

> I am not even going to [interview job candidates at the meeting of the APA and AIA – American Philological Association and Archaeological Institute of America] . . . because Grad Ed in the US doesn't produce [Roman historians and Greek archaeologists able to teach Latin and Greek] . . . I should be happy to close down about half of the [graduate programs] in the States tomorrow, because they do not provide or require a coherent education. . . . We have hired three US PhDs, and all have been disasters; in all cases the programme they took was so open-ended they didn't know anything well, and their thesis was minimal.

More often, though, these criticisms are uttered in contexts protected by "confidentiality": letters of recommendation and evaluation; discussions about hiring and promotion.

Furthermore, while I may have regarded my former chair's remarks about me as outrageous misrepresentations and lies, I confess to having accorded such general criticisms about American education in classics the status of truth. I have long struggled to overcome deep feelings of inferiority, or at least perceived inferiority, about my own training and command of our field relative to those of classicist colleagues from abroad.

In the original title of this chapter, I planned upon the title of a popular American comic song, "Doin' What Comes Natur'lly," from Irving Berlin's 1946 musical *Annie Get Your Gun*. In presenting oral versions of this paper at the Ancient Mediterranean Culture research seminar sponsored by the George Washington University, at the 1994 American Philological Association meeting, and at the 1995 meeting of the British Classical Association, I invited the audience to sing the opening lyrics with me (in their best Bill Clinton accent): "Folks are dumb where I come from, They ain't had any learnin'. Still they're happy as can be, Doin' What Comes

Natur'lly" (as a matter of historical record, my American audiences responded with substantially more enthusiasm and vocal vigor than did their British counterparts).

These lyrics, I should note, date from early in the post-war era, at a time when the US was asserting herself in a leadership role throughout Europe. Sung by the eponymous Annie, an unlettered woman from the back-woods, the song describes and defends her intellectually disadvantaged background. I invoke these lyrics (and, when delivering the paper orally, also outfitted myself in American flag colors and motifs) because I perceive that I am perceived by classicist colleagues from other countries as comparably and indeed comically disadvantaged in academic training, and as similarly unlettered in my command of the field relative to those who have studied in Europe – simply by virtue of my American nationality and education. What is more, I see the low regard in which classicists apparently hold American relative to European classical training affecting my fellow Americans as well as myself: as internalized by many of us, and as incorporated into our professional sense, or non-sense, of self-worth.

Let me focus now upon this internalization: first providing some evidence that I am not alone in feeling that I am often regarded as comically inadequate merely because of my all-American education; then describing how I myself have started to exorcize this feeling, and how this exorcism has transformed my view of my own, personal, scholarly work and worth. As recently as 1993, exorcism was not in my repertoire. In honor of President Clinton's inauguration, I cobbled together various Vergilian and other Latin phrases in some dactylic hexameter verses, and sent these Vergilian verses to the American journal *Vergilius*. Expecting my efforts to be warmly welcomed, I was taken aback by the anonymous reader's report, which I have quoted at some length in my appendix, and which I assume was written by an American. Criticizing one phrase as "having the appearance of the ridiculous," this reader insisted, "this should be repaired. There are a lot of mean-spirited British classicists out there who will just take it as one more proof that Americans don't know anything about classics."

Now my first reaction to this report was: Who the hell cares? I wrote these Vergilian verses for an American journal about an American president! Let those mean-spirited British classicists write some Ovidian verses about their leaders – elegiacs about the lunchtime *amores* of Tory MPs, or hexameters on Prince Charles' wished-for metamorphosis into a paper product for feminine hygienic use! Nevertheless, I proceeded to make that repair, worrying that not only I, but all of my fellow Americans, would suffer adversely if I alone were to corroborate British (and general European) prejudices about us.

Since that time, though, I have refused to be complicit in this self-abasement process. Early in 1992 I published an article in a volume of essays about the classicist Werner Jaeger, who left Nazi Germany to teach in the United States, first at the University of Chicago and then at Harvard. After investigating some previously overlooked details about Jaeger's arrival, and about his thwarted efforts to achieve a prominent national professional role in the US, I concluded that Jaeger withdrew from professional activities as a result of losing the presidency of the APA in 1942 to a candidate nominated by petition. While I did not offer any comparisons between the (Swiss and) German academic environment in which Jaeger had flourished and the environment in which he functioned on our own shores, other essays in the volume did (by, *inter alia*, quoting Jaeger's renowned remark that "Without the continuing prestige of the ancient idea of Man in human culture, classical scholarship is just a waste of time. Anyone who does not see this ought to come to America and let himself learn from the way classical studies have developed there.").

Later in 1992 I gave a paper at a conference on feminism and the classics: it pondered why classics departments at American research universities, in comparison to departments in other humanities fields, have appointed relatively few women, especially those doing feminist work, to senior positions. I considered concerns voiced by Thomas Figueira of Rutgers University about the relatively high number of classicists from abroad appointed to such positions, although I was ultimately unable to come to any conclusion about the relationship between these appointments of foreign scholars and the relative paucity of women and/or feminist scholars in these posts.

Shortly thereafter, Z. Philip Ambrose of the University of Vermont responded to both my article and paper. In so doing, he suggested that he, too, finds American classicists wanting in comparison with their European counterparts, especially when they appear to pass judgment on their European counterparts. Reviewing the Jaeger volume in the May 1993 issue of the *New England Classical Newsletter*, Ambrose not only says outright that I perhaps overrate "how significant [Jaeger] considered the APA presidency." He also cites another, earlier, review of the Jaeger volume by Charles Rowan Beye, to applaud Beye for "properly" suggesting that Jaeger's "withdrawal" from professional activities after leaving Germany for America in the 1930s may signify Jaeger's "discouragement at the 'shallowness' (Beye's term) of his American colleagues." Yet while Ambrose agrees with what he perceives as Beye's

low assessment of mid-century American classicists, he also criticizes
Beye's call for "more research on the possibly negative European
influence in American classical studies."

What is more, Ambrose takes issue with Beye's complaint that some of
the articles in this volume are in German, by saying:

> this, not the only expression of xenophobia I have recently heard from
> American classicists, is a betrayal of a unique resource of our
> profession: that we have learned not only to study the languages and
> culture of antiquity, but that we have taught ourselves to do so with an
> international perspective.

Now, Ambrose attended my presentation at the conference on feminism
and classics (where several people made known their discomfort at my
decision merely to discuss the topic of foreign scholars in American
classics departments). Thus I have good reason to assume that one
expression of xenophobia Ambrose heard was my paper there (and he has
yet to reassure me that I am wrong).

I was disconcerted by Ambrose's unwillingness to consider how
European classical studies may differ from, even have a negative effect
upon, classics in the United States. Had he not read Lee Pearcy's call – in
an article Pearcy and I co-authored back in 1991 – for Americans to define
what is distinctive about classics in our country? There Pearcy concludes
by observing: "Our relation to our society cannot be an unimaginative or
timid reproduction of European experience." This time, though, I
decided to take some professional action. I was intrigued by Ambrose's
invocation of an "international perspective" as a unique professional
resource shared by American classicists. It prompted me to start asking
myself a number of questions. Have we American classicists in fact taught
ourselves to study the languages and cultures of antiquity from an
international perspective? If so, how has that perspective been defined
and justified? Has it been imparted to classicists elsewhere? Do American
classicists express xenophobia if, like myself, we acknowledge some major
differences between the study and teaching of classics in the United States
and in European countries, if we attempt to account for such differences,
and if we question professional practices in our country which privilege
colleagues of European training?

I must admit that I had a difficult time conceptualizing any of my own –
undergraduate, graduate or post-graduate, formal or informal – training
as fostering an "international perspective." Rather, it has been my
experience that classicists demolish or lionize scholarship in other
languages and/or by foreign scholars largely on nationalistic grounds:

because a given study is thought to typify, rather than to transcend, a distinctive national approach. But – in my capacity as chair of a task force organized by the classics graduate education group at the University of Pennsylvania – I decided to send a questionnaire about my task force's own bailiwick, the professional socialization of graduate students, to a diverse group including several foreigners as well as Americans. I did so on the assumption that many American graduate students study abroad, many foreigners come to teach on our shores – and that consequently professional socialization of American graduate students is not merely the province of American-based classicists. In addition to including questions on whether respondents believed that American classicists shared an "international perspective" on classical antiquity, and if they thought American classicists were regarded as products of inferior academic training relative to those elsewhere, I enclosed the abstract of this paper (to contextualize Ambrose's invocation of an "international perspective" and to acknowledge my own sense of my professional qualifications as inferior).

This questionnaire yielded a rich and thought-provoking array of responses, a representative selection of which I have quoted in the appendix. Yet these responses did not alter my skepticism about an "international perspective": even classicists believing in its existence merely talked about the multilingual character of their scholarly reading or the multinational composition of the graduate department in which they studied. A number of American respondents shared my sense that they were inferior to their British and German counterparts, and admitted to having internalized a low assessment of their relative scholarly worth. Respondents from abroad denied that American-trained classicists were so viewed all that much any more.

Regrettably, I did not hear anything which had not occurred to me already about the differences between American and European education in classics. Yet it is precisely these differences between me and my European counterparts which have caused me to harbor feelings of scholarly inadequacy. Ours is a generalist rather than a specialist system, one which prides itself on giving rather than foreclosing academic options. Not only did I start the classical languages late by foreign standards (Latin at thirteen, Greek at nineteen). I also did not concentrate totally on classical languages and culture as an under-graduate because American liberal arts degrees (the only kind which allow an undergraduate to concentrate in classics) require their recipients to fill numerous "distribution requirements" by taking courses in areas outside their majors. I did not focus exclusively on one area of research in graduate school until I reached the dissertation stage because American PhD training also requires extensive course work on various aspects of classical studies. My teaching responsibilities since receiving the doctorate involve far more courses outside my area of research specialization than inside (and even so I am fairly specialized for an American classics teacher, as I do not teach any courses in the Greek language). Although I teach many courses in my specialty of classical Latin literature, most do not enroll advanced students or demand much engagement with scholarship.

But these responses to my questionnaire have encouraged me to think about my education, and about the kind of teaching that I do, as merely different from, not lesser than, those of non-American classicists. Some of my academic experiences specifically reflect institutional demographics. At the University of Maryland, College Park, for example, I am almost never the oldest person in my classes. So, too, I increasingly teach students who spoke other languages – often non-European languages – before they learned English and for whom the Western cultural tradition is something with which they are still seeking to become familiar. Most of my academic experiences, however, are shared by other American classicists, regardless of where they teach. And I now see more clearly that these experiences significantly influence my approach to research, the way I pursue and write classical scholarship.

Most obviously, the American insistence that undergraduates fill various "distribution requirements," making it impossible to devote one's self exclusively to classical studies on the undergraduate level, enabled me – and makes it possible for my students – to become acquainted with other, related fields. My own undergraduate course work in English literature and sociology, for example, familiarized me with texts, contexts and concepts which have figured prominently in my research in classics (particularly my recent projects on the history of American classical studies). Teaching undergraduates, some of them excellent students, who are not necessarily classics concentrators has forced me – and many of my colleagues nationwide – to focus on larger cultural issues, on the "big pictures" of classical antiquity, in our scholarly writing as well as in the classroom. Since colleagues from other fields are often expected to approve the courses we American classicists offer, and to assess both our scholarship and teaching, we have been encouraged to adopt a wider social perspective (and thus make issues like race, class and age as well as gender, categories of analysis); to present material in a more accessible way (and thus to translate everything in any foreign language!); and to connect the questions that we ask of this material with those asked in other academic disciplines (and thus to draw and draw on modern and cross-cultural analogies to ancient Greek and Roman phenomena).

I was helped in my efforts to think about and deal with these differences by the publication of the fall 1993 issue of *Tulsa Studies in Women's Literature*. It features a spirited discussion of "Is There An Anglo-American Feminist Criticism?" by a diverse group of English and American feminist critics widely ranging in ethnic and cultural background, age, theoretical approach and political stance. These critics speak frankly about the differences between the general cultural and specific academic environments nurturing feminist literary criticism in the United Kingdom and the United States. Furthermore, acknowledging, as I do, similarities between feminist criticism and classical studies – as modes of interdisciplinary academic inquiry taking different forms on opposite sides of the Atlantic – may aid in formulating an answer to a further question: why is recognition by American classicists of distinctively American elements in their approaches to scholarship and teaching customarily muted if not problematized? Despite Lee Pearcy's clarion call, I do not see much written about how we classicists do things differently from colleagues abroad. *Classics: A Discipline and Profession in Crisis?*, a 1989 collection of essays on our profession edited by Phyllis Culham and Lowell Edmunds, contains excellent discussions of foreign scholars and American classical education, and of the plight of classics in Margaret Thatcher's Britain. But neither dwells on the differences between teaching environments and scholarly interests in the United States and abroad. Strikingly, other essays in the volume pay much attention to differences on both scores between those American classics departments offering the PhD and those which do not. By the same token, a lively debate about the hiring of foreign-born and trained scholars in modern languages and literatures which appeared in the 1994 and 1995 issues of the Modern Language Association's journal *Profession* largely avoids the issue of how American training in these areas differs from that abroad.

Thinking as a feminist as well as a classicist, however, I found a striking parallel between what we feminists have done already and what I am surprised that classicists have not done yet. That is, since the 1970s, scholarship initially focused upon the issue of gender, and subsequently embracing the related issues of race and social class, has challenged the universalizing claims of the "humanistic perspective": for implicitly assuming that all human beings share the experiences of privileged white males, and for thereby erasing important differences among the ways that the human condition may be experienced. These challenges, however, have been assailed in reactionary quarters as unscholarly "whining," "white-male-bashing," and demands for special treatment by the inadequately schooled and resentfully self-absorbed. Might the negative response to these feminist scholarly challenges illuminate why we American classicists hesitate to pose similar challenges to what Ambrose idealistically views as the "international perspective" enshrined in our own profession – and what I, more cynically, might term instead our unwillingness to acknowledge national differences?

That is, given the conservative nature of our national – and our international – classics community, do we American classicists fear that such challenges will be viewed as trivializing the goals and achievements of our common calling, classical scholarship itself (that is, as unscholarly whining)? Do we American classicists worry about being perceived as unjustly attacking foreign colleagues for having – as males have traditionally had relative to females – academic training and credentials superior to our own, for enjoying advantages historically unavailable to those educated solely or largely in our country (that is, as "white-European-bashing")? Are we afraid of appearing to valorize our difference, our mere exclusion from the classical traditions of countries imbued with strong physical and cultural memories of an ancient Greek and Roman presence (that is, of appearing to make ignorant and resentfully self-absorbed demands for special treatment)? Are we hesitant to celebrate the accomplishments of classical studies in our country, with its elective (rather than inherited) ties to Greco-Roman antiquity, because this "pride of the Yankees" may strike foreign colleagues as either naively "provincial" or smugly self-congratulatory?

Since submitting my abstract to the APA Program Committee I came across a 1994 issue of the *Boston Review* edited by the classicist Martha Nussbaum. It responds to the call, by Sheldon Hackney, chair of our country's federally-funded National Endowment for the Humanities, to initiate a national conversation to discuss American identity, especially where education and the humanities are concerned. In her opening essay, Nussbaum rejects Hackney's assumption that we Americans need to focus on what makes us distinctive as Americans. Rather, she defends a cosmopolitan outlook that places allegiance to the community of human beings in the entire world before any group or country.

Curiously, Nussbaum's cosmopolitan model of *Weltanschauung*, which draws heavily on examples from the Greek Hellenistic world, has much in common with the idealized international perspective on classical studies invoked by Ambrose. I was gratified to see that most of the twenty-nine replies to Nussbaum challenge her universalizing notions, defending aspects of nationalism on various grounds. I was, though, surprised that even the feminist critics responding to her essay, such as Judith Butler, did not draw the analogy between Nussbaum's cosmopolitanism and the academic humanism which has erased perspectives grounded in difference of gender, race and class. Nevertheless, I am hopeful that debates such as these, which demonstrate that this issue has larger ramifications beyond the field of classics, will spark American and non-American classicists to think more, publicly and privately, about national differences.

Since submitting my abstract, too, I have also discovered that these questions about how we define and celebrate our distinctively American achievements as classicists were asked long before Lee Pearcy voiced them: in 1919, on the fiftieth anniversary of the APA, by Paul Shorey. Curiously, Shorey worries "equally" about "the brag of provincial chauvinism and the undue self-deprecation of... the anti-patriotic bias." But he promptly segues into the Nya-nya-nya-nya-nya-mode of American self-validation: generalizing about the inability of "the German philological mind... to weigh arguments"; listing trivial mistakes by German scholars (such as a long *e* in *negotia*!). A companion essay on the history of the APA relates that at the first APA meeting in Washington the members were presented to President Theodore Roosevelt in the East Room of the White House, where they heard him "commend scholarship and its achievements," and speak of his recent interest in a new French book on the *Odyssey*, which he "hoped all would read." Yet Shorey faults Teddy Roosevelt for "sneer[ing] at the man who spends his youth in a German University" and for not "compar[ing] the last twenty volumes of the AJP or of Classical Philology, or the fifty best American doctoral dissertations with similar products in Germany."

In the words of our current US President, the British-educated William Jefferson Clinton, I've chosen to speak in the personal voice so that you might "feel my pain": pain caused by my feelings, by no means unique feelings, of inadequacy relative to non-American classicists, as well as pain inflicted on me by other American classicists. I've done so to emphasize that we American classicists inflict enough, needless, pain on one another: we have no need to injure ourselves further by regarding our differences from Europeans as proof of our inferiority to them. Nor do we need to hurt our European colleagues, as Shorey would have had us do, by spotlighting their scholarly shortcomings. But by coming together nationally – by trying to understand the commonalities we Americans share as classicists, especially the commonalities we do not necessarily share with colleagues abroad – we may all become better informed and more assured practitioners of doing what comes nationally, and goes internationally, as classical scholars.

AFTERWORD

In raising these issues about how we American classicists come to terms with our distinctive national identity within the global community of classicists, did I need to use the personal voice, to share so many personal experiences and reflections from my three decades in our profession, to write autobiographically as well as autographically? By adopting this self-centered approach, by emphasizing my own feminist perspective, by acknowledging my own emotional stake and baring my own emotional scars in the matter of how American-trained classicists are perceived (albeit with some attempts at leavening humor), am I not guilty of unseemly "whining"? Of constructing myself as a victim in the way that all of us so-called "gender feminists" are accused of doing? Why couldn't I say the same things in a more distanced and impersonal way? I certainly managed to do so in the original abstract of this paper, which I submitted to the program committees of the APA and the British Classical Association.

I would begin responding to these questions by arguing that my topic lends itself to personal reflection because much of what I have to say (although by no means all of it) is based on personal experience rather than published material. But why didn't I merely rely on what published material is available and leave my own experiences and feelings out? Well, my main reason for speaking in the first person about my own experiences and feelings in this essay is that I am writing about insensitive and even cruel attitudes and behavior that have caused me (and others) substantial emotional pain. Mindful that – as the essays in this volume by Susanna Morton Braund, Charles Martindale and Vanda Zajko observe – recollections such as mine are likely to engender self-fictionalizing as well as self-scrutiny, I hasten to admit that I may be mis-remembering or altering or oversimplifying "what actually happened." But without detailing these incidents, however "inaccurate" my recollections may be, I could not have intelligibly explained the deep-rooted and painful feelings of inadequacy which such insensitive and cruel treatment has instilled in me. Had I taken a detached stance when discussing professional conduct capable of causing such pain, had I refused to recognize the human costs of such conduct, I would have erased the powerful emotions that are involved and thereby seriously misrepresented my subject matter.

A more practical reason for employing the personal voice in this essay is that the published material available on this topic is meager, far less helpful to the argument that I am trying to make than evidence which is not only from me personally but also about me personally. Admittedly, I could rely more heavily upon the personal experiences of fellow classicists which I have witnessed or they have shared with me over the years. But I am reluctant to speak for and about others, at least not without acknowledging my own stake in and my own spin on their experiences: that is, how their experiences affect me personally, and how my own interpretation of their experiences may not be the only valid one. Unless I am citing their published work, or they have given me permission to use their names, most classicists who figure in this essay are either nameless or dead.

Indeed, my reluctance to speak for and about others has increased as a result of delivering oral versions of this paper, and of encountering various listeners who have queried my own pained reactions to my own personal experiences. The characterization of me, by that Andover classics master, as a prospective matron rather than a pedagogue, remains vividly in my mind because much was made of this remark at the time to my fellow, female and male, teaching assistants by the other participant in those Xenophon sessions. An Andover "old boy" employed that summer as a teaching assistant in American history, he was completing the equivalent of an undergraduate classics major at a coeducational institution, Stanford University. Yet he, too, was judged in need of remedial work on Xenophon by his former Latin and Greek teacher (despite the fact that his Stanford professors included another Andover graduate, Charles Rowan Beye). And even in those days, several years before the second wave of feminism had launched the term (and concept) of "sexism," he – and ultimately all of my fellow teaching assistants – found the classics master's questioning of my academic seriousness laughable, and hypocritical on an institutional level as well as personally insulting. After all, the Andover summer session took visible pride in its coeducational faculty and student body, and claimed to apply the same standards to both sexes in its hiring and admissions procedures.

Nevertheless, several of those who have heard me recount this story, including avowed and publicly identified feminists, have suggested that I and my fellow teaching assistants should not have taken umbrage at the classics master's remark. They have argued that both laughter at the institutional hypocrisy and pain at the insulting trivialization of my commitment to classics teaching were highly inappropriate reactions. Some of them have accused me of judging the Andover academic environment in 1965 by anachronistic and unrealistic feminist criteria. Others have interpreted the expectation that I would become a "matron" rather than a "pedagogue" as an aristocratic-style compliment: proof of the classics master's faith in my ability to attract a wealthy husband rather than have to earn a living by teaching, and of his hope that I would enjoy material circumstances which would enable me to promote the study of classics as a patron.

Similar challenges have been posed to my interpretation of the incident in which a senior professor and mentor introduced me – to a male classics graduate student in the department from which I had received my PhD nearly a decade previously – merely as a "prominent hostess." I was deeply hurt at the time that nothing was said about my academic credentials, or my special areas of scholarly expertise, or my current academic position (especially as I was struggling so hard to hold on to it). But I have been told repeatedly that the phrase "prominent hostess" was a compliment too: that it paid tribute to my success at entertaining and simultaneously signalled to the young man that I was worth cultivating socially if he wished to prosper professionally. My response to those who would disagree with my personal reactions to situations in the past is first to contextualize those situations more fully, to help illuminate my reactions by providing further information which explains why I reacted as I did. Ultimately, though (and as Susan Ford Wiltshire has reminded us), I can only justify my personal reactions by invoking the authority which accrues to me from having experienced these situations myself. Concomitantly, my unwillingness to draw upon incidents experienced by others without obtaining their permission to do so, and without also eliciting their own, personal, interpretations of these incidents accords respect to their, individual, authority.

My final reason for employing the personal voice, in other venues as well as in this essay, is that it allows me to be more honest – or at least more explicit and forthcoming – about why I do what I do in my writing and in the classroom. Here, for example, I have explained why I am a committed feminist who regards gender as a matter of major importance, and why I consider that my identity as a feminist scholar enriches and elucidates my identity as a classicist. I appreciate similar efforts at honesty from colleagues, direct acknowledgments of where they are "coming from," because such efforts in turn help me assess those colleagues' criteria for assessing others.

But are such efforts at honesty likely to become accepted professional practice? As the associate editor of a scholarly journal, I am frustrated by the reports of referees who find no fault with the argumentation or the documentation of a submission, but dismiss its approach or choice of topic on the grounds that they are not "important" or "interesting." More often than not, such referees rely upon – and make no effort to justify – personal, and indeed highly subjective, criteria of judgment in reaching their decisions. But the fact that these referees do not find the project chosen or the questions asked by the author of importance or interest should not in and of itself disqualify the author from choosing that project or asking those questions.

In such cases justice obviously demands that the author state explicitly why s/he has chosen this project and asked these questions, and that the referee provide the author with a personal justification of why s/he regards the submission as having, or lacking in, importance or interest. Yet it is difficult to see how this can be done in an anonymous system of "objective" assessment where authors and referees are not supposed to be cognizant of or concerned with one another's identity. The issue for me, consequently, has become how we classicists may best employ the personal voice in circumstances when it can be employed – and how we can do so in a way that is fair to our subject matter, our colleagues and students, and above all to ourselves.

APPENDIX OF SELECTED QUOTES

On Alston Hurd Chase, see *A New Introduction to Greek*, third edn, revised and enlarged, by Alston Hurd Chase and Henry Phillips, Jr (Cambridge, Mass., 1962: esp. 22) (6. γύναι, γυναιξὶ κόσμον ἡ σιγὴ φέρει.); p. 34 (6. ὅρκους γυναικὸς εἰς ὕδωρ γράφω); and p. 115 (C. Δύ ἡμέραι γυναικός εἰσιν ἥδισται, ὅταν γαμῇ τις κάκφέρῃ τεθνηκῖαν).

Time Remembered, by Alston Hurd Chase (Parker Publishing, Inc., San Antonio TX/Odyssey Press, Dover NH, 1994: especially 50–51):

> The women of that age were too busy by day and too weary at night to agitate for liberation. The thousand electrical devices which make some idle and discontented today were scarcely thought of.... Surrounded as I was by females, I have quite a clear memory of the feminine costume of the time which made seduction a major achievement and rape well-nigh impossible.

and p. 59:

> Captain Jack's emphasis upon manly comradeship in sports added fuel to my desire for the friendship of my own sex. Franklin Park did provide me with one such friend.... He, too, was branded a sissy and, like myself, was so ill-coordinated as to be barred from most of the informal games which most boys enjoy. Intelligent, decent, wryly humorous, he

was a good companion, but not what my femininity-sated soul desired. He and I were virtually condemned to one another's company or that of girls.

Boston University Tenure and Promotion Form: Judith P. Hallett Part IIIa: Chairman's Evaluation, September 26, 1980:

Hallett . . . seems to be more admired by the younger students, who treasure her congeniality. Other students, especially some of the more mature ones, find her "shallow" and deplore the quantity of trivia she injects into classroom lectures. [The] comment on her "low pressure and entertaining pedagogy" is . . . apt: that is, some students may remember her with fondness for the entertainment she provided, but they are unlikely to have gained much knowledge from the experience. . . . As I sat in one of her Intermediate Latin classes recently, I noted that she conducted herself more like a teacher of early elementary school children than a college professor. . . . Her manner, in general, was one of condescension towards her students. . . . My impression of her is that she does not hesitate to sacrifice substantive comment for mere entertainment; that she is perhaps not willing (or able?) to make a distinction between that which is trivial and that which is significant. [In a 1974 response to Aya Betensky, Hallett] sets the tone for most of the rest of her writings: her insistence on terminology inappropriate for ancient Rome (e.g. "feminism" . . .), and her use of fashionable jargon (e.g. "personhood"). . . . The closing of the manuscript with the quote from a Cole Porter song is typical of her unenlightened attempts to make scholarly studies somehow more readable by inserting "cute", trivial allusions. On the whole I find her scholarly work shallow; the output, by no means negligible in quantity, contributes very little to our knowledge or understanding.

Her strong points . . . do not justify awarding her tenure. I believe it is just these points – her congeniality, her constant attendance on professional committees (*any* committee), her developing of professional contacts – that have gained her what small reputation she now holds. She seems at every opportunity to try to cloud the intellectual poverty of her work with quantity, or just with names.

Hugh Lloyd-Jones, *Greek in a Cold Climate* (London, 1991: 218–219), (From "A Valedictory Lecture delivered in the Library of Christ Church, Oxford, on 31 May 1989"):

Classical scholarship in the United States has suffered greatly from the failure of most schools to teach languages: it is hard to learn Greek and Latin really well if one starts late, and although America makes a vast contribution to classical scholarship, not many Americans are experts in these languages. One result is that the enemies of exact scholarship can easily find an audience there, and gifted rhetoricians find it possible to set themselves up as local gurus, teaching a method which rapidly produces fashionable results.

E-mail message to members of the University of Pennsylvania Graduate Education in Classics List. Forwarded October 23, 1994:

> I am not going to [the American Philological Association and Archaeological Institute of America meetings in] Atlanta [to find a Greek archaeologist who can teach Latin and Greek], because Grad. Ed. in the US doesn't produce such things. The reason is that the programmes do not seem to exist that force students to know Greek before interpreting Greek vases. I most emphatically believe that programmes are important, and I should be happy to close down about half of the ones in the States tomorrow, because they do not provide or require a coherent education. We produce students who can do archaeology or history and also teach Latin and Greek, why can't everyone? We have hired three US PhDs, and all have been disastrous; in all cases the programme they took was so open-ended that they didn't know anything well, and their thesis was minimal. . . . So a pox on grumbling about Ann. Phil., concentrate on producing decently trained students, and the rest will look after itself.

Response by Daniel Tompkins, October 24, 1994:

> I have to say that the notion that Greek archaeologists can't be found in the US is just wrong, for lack of a stronger term. If this place . . . hires the wrong candidates, then blackens their names as well – not a very nice thing to do – it's got itself to blame. When I make the same mistake three times in a row, I usually see a pattern.

"Doin' What Comes Natur'lly" (Irving Berlin, 1946):
>   Folks are dumb where I come from
>   They ain't had any learnin'
>   Still they're happy as can be
>   Doin' What Comes Natur'lly,
>   Doin' What Comes Natur'lly.
>
>   Folks like us could never fuss

With schools and books and learnin'.
Still we've gone from A to Z
Doin' What Comes Natur'lly,
Doin' What Comes Natur'lly...

Vergilius Reader's Report on "Vergilian Verses on the Inauguration of William Jefferson Clinton," *Vergilius* 39 (1993): 30:

> The author claims to be writing (or assembling) Vergilian verses, but line 11 contains a metrical feature that is never found in Vergil. This has the appearance of the ridiculous. The vowel in the ending -bus is short by nature but it must be scanned as long here because it is followed by two consonants (-s + the "y" sound in i-). Down to the youth of Cicero, however, final -s did not make position. As a result, the metrical feature in line 11 . . . is quite common in Ennius, Lucilius, and even Lucretius. But it occurs only once in Catullus . . . and never in the Augustan poets. Cicero (I believe it is in the Brutus somewhere) says that this weak pronunciation of final -s was once considered chic (*lautum*) but was now regarded as the mark of a bumpkin (*subrusticum*). In short, this should be repaired. There are a lot of mean-spirited British classicists out there who will just take it as one more proof that Americans don't know anything about Classics.

Judith P. Hallett, "The Case of the Missing President: Werner Jaeger and the American Philological Association," in *Werner Jaeger Reconsidered* (ed.) William M. Calder III (Atlanta, 1992), *Illinois Classical Studies*, Supplement 3: especially 41: ("I decided to emulate my [and now my daughter's] childhood literary heroine, Nancy Drew, and investigate the matter further on my own."). Other relevant essays in the volume include Calder, "12 March 1921: The Berlin Appointment," and Alessandra Bertini Malgarini, "Werner Jaeger in the United States: One Among Many Others" (with Jaeger's remark, from the introduction to *Scripta Minora*, vol. I: xxvi [1961]):

> Ohne die dauernde Geltung der antiken Idee des Menschen in der menschlichen Kultur schwebt die klassische Altertumswissenschaft in der Luft. Wer dies nicht sieht, der sollte nach Amerika kommen und sich vom Gang der Entwicklung der klassischen Studien dort belehren lassen/Without the continuing prestige of the ancient idea of Man in human culture, classical scholarship is just a waste of time. Anyone who does not see this ought to come to America and let himself learn from the way classical studies have developed there.

Judith P. Hallett, "*Ubi Fuimus? Quo Vadimus?*: Feminist Challenges and the Profession of Classics," paper presented at the conference on Feminism and the Classics, University of Cincinnati, November 5, 1992:

> Thomas Figueira has recently referred to the "systematic denigration of North American [classical] scholars in favor of European candidates for positions in US graduate departments", to the "re-configuration" of US jobs in classical studies to match specific European talents, and to the application of different expectations and standards to European job candidates. . . . My answer to all of these questions is "I'm not so sure. If we consider how individual European scholars have been involved in the democratic phenomenon of concern to us here – by evincing support for fuller inclusion of women and feminist work in classical studies – a more complex situation emerges. Some classicists of European birth and training have strongly supported women, feminist scholarship and democratic change within our profession generally. . .

Cf. also Thomas Figueira, "Open Letter to American Ancient Historians," May 14, 1992:

> I am not indulging in some crude nativist attack here. . . . But academic friendship, like any other friendship, is based on mutual respect. How can we command others' respect when we are prepared to install [European] redundancies as our leaders? . . . We are seeing an absolutely absurd evaluative context in which the entire academic hierarchy in Britain and Germany (mainly) is thought to lie super-imposed upon all the American practitioners of our discipline.

as well as the *American Philological Association Newsletter* 15, 4 August 1992, 11, candidates' response to the 1992 Election Questionnaire:

> Among the more pervasive and insidious forms of illegal discrimination plaguing us is the systematic denigration of North American scholars in favor of European candidates. What is the point of encouraging an inclusiveness for women, minorities, and the economically disadvantaged when we can only offer inclusion in a body of second-class academic citizens?

Z. Philip Ambrose, review of *Werner Jaeger Reconsidered, New England Classical Newsletter* 20, (May 1993): 41 ff:

> Focusing more particularly on J's *intentions* are the articles by Judith P. Hallett (her explanation of why J never became president of the APA

perhaps overrates how significant he considered the office), Alessandra Bertini Malgarini (a comparison of J with other scholarly emigrants) and William M. Calder III, whose too-intimate narrative of J's appointment to the chair of Wilamowitz in Berlin paints an unattractive portrait of the man, unfortunately coloring, as the keynote article, most of the others.... In his review of this same volume in *BMCR* (3.5.2) Charles Beye properly suggests that J's tendency towards "withdrawal" after leaving Germany may be in part a sign of his discouragement at the "shallowness" (Beye's term) of his American colleagues.... In one matter, lying very close to the heart of this investigation, I would disagree with Beye's excellent and extensive response: he calls for more research on the "possibly negative European influence in [*sic*; "on" would have sounded less sinister] American classical studies" and objects that some of the articles of this volume are in German. Classicists should "write up their material in the one contemporary international language as editors of the honestly international scientific journals try to do." This, not the only expression of xenophobia I have recently heard from American classicists, is a betrayal of a unique resource of our profession: that we have learned not only to study the languages and culture of antiquity, but that we have taught ourselves to do so with an international perspective.

Judith P. Hallett and Lee T. Pearcy, "*Nunc Meminisse Iuvat*: Classics and Classicists Between the World Wars," *Classical World* 85.1, (1991) esp. 21 ff. ("Lee T. Pearcy – Some Final Thoughts"):

Our flight to the frontier struggles against our importation of European manners, European styles and European thoughts.... What we are, what exactly we do, and why we do it are surely basic questions for any group engaged in what it hopes will be a common endeavor. American classicists' reluctance to ground answers to these questions in analysis of our history has made it almost inevitable that classical philology has been driven to its present, marginalized state within our universities. Jaeger's perceptive observation that in America one saw what it was to practice classical scholarship in a country that had never known classical humanism raises an urgent issue for American classical scholars. Our relation to our society cannot be an unimaginative or timid reproduction of European experience. In that sense all American classical scholarship is refugee scholarship, and the experience of the refugee scholars considered by our panel is not only interesting, but also paradigmatic. We must examine our own history to find our place in the American dialectic of emulation and rejection. We must transform American classical philology from refugee into citizen.

Cf. also William M. Calder, III, "Classical Scholarship in the United States : An Introductory Essay," in Ward W. Briggs, Jr (ed.) *Biographical Dictionary of North American Classicists* (Westport, Conn. and London, 1994: xxiii):

> Nationalism plays no role in our classical scholarship. Whether non-Greek blood flowed in Alexander's veins or whether there is Jewish influence on Vergil's *Eclogue* 4, or whether Agricola was French or the Thracians Bulgarians are just scholarly questions of no more emotional import than whether Euripides' *Electra* precedes Sophocles'.

From the questionnaire sent to prospective members of a task force on professional socialization of graduate students in classics (University of Pennsylvania initiative on graduate education in classics):

> We are still living under the European shadow, but I think that secretly everyone (except us) knows that America is the most exciting place to do Classics now!
>
> (Professor, female, at a US liberal arts college)

> I am not sure what an "international perspective" might be or how I would go about recognizing one if I were to encounter it . . . I doubt that most people living in this country do much thinking about classicists at all . . . I think it is more important for us to reestablish contact with intelligent, concerned people outside academe than strive to win some sort of popularity contest within it.
>
> (Associate Professor, male, at a US state university)

(To the question "Were you taught the study of classical antiquity from an international perspective?"):

> Yes, and no. Two of my favorite teachers were uninterested in European scholarship and largely estranged from British scholarship, although the latter clearly had a much greater influence in their teaching. Both were essentially new critics and their major influence on me was as an undergraduate. A third teacher, however, had broad foreign contacts and interests, ranging from Slavic through German to French scholarship. His work was the greatest influence on my own, and it was through him that I discovered modern French work of the Vernant–Detienne school and, even more importantly, the great German scholars of the late nineteenth and early twentieth century.

Without such examples, I don't believe I would have been able to remain a classicist, since American scholars were very much disparaged during that period, and I find much that is repellent in the British classicist mind-set...

Yes, indeed [it is my impression that American classicists are regarded as products of inferior academic training relative to colleagues elsewhere]. One of the causes of this is that we have permitted British classicists to establish the credentials necessary to be a classicist – namely perfect mastery of Greek and Latin grammar and lexicography. We make much of the early training available in their schools (although less and less so nowadays). What we ignore is the ignorance perpetuated by a system of education that treats whole areas of learning, from humanistic philosophy, through literary theory, anthropology, sociology, women's studies and linguistics as "peripheral" and unimportant. This sort of exclusion frees up a lot of time to study grammar.

> (Professor, female, at a US public university
> with a classics PhD program)

I do have a couple of questions or comments for your "internationalist" perspective, which seems to want to articulate a double point, if I understand you, that on the one hand classicists are encouraged to take a dispassionate, professionalized, pan-disciplinary voice (which may, surprise, surprise have something to do with hegemonic values of male, white, upper-class status) and on the other, that Americans are, in ways as yet undefined, disparaged for not living up to that voice, an attack usually made and sometimes internalized in the form of the slur of "poor training"...

There has been since the war or even earlier, I expect, a particular love/hate, envy/disregard for American culture in England, as there is a nostalgia and fantasy about England in many American cultural artefacts (and people: as a student in the States, I was constantly asked to say something "cute and British"). This no doubt informs some classicists' responses to American work. The "poorly trained" slur, however, has an obvious basis if not a reason in precise institutional factors. Because of the vastly different requirements of specialization in the British educational system in comparison to the American, most undergraduates from the States have indeed studied far less than their counterparts – at least, in technical classics. Of course, anyone with any intelligence knows not only that this is a question of a different *timing* of technical knowledge, but also that the broader education brings different benefits. We are delighted to take American students here, but it does upset some of them to realize that in most cases it is necessary to do a second BA (although later they realize that this BA work is much closer to what they would have done in grad school at the beginning in the States). I don't know if this is a reason for "internalized poor self-image." It certainly shouldn't be. . . . Even in England, there is a constant theme among classicists that no-one "these days" could live up to the training of a Fraenkel or a . . . Wilamowitz . . .

I personally try to encourage in all my students the question of why particular scholars ask particular questions, offer particular answers, and write in particular ways. The answer to these questions do include specifically "nationalist" perspectives, not because of any racial essentialism, but because different countries enforce different institutionalizations and police their disciplines in different ways. . . . I've had my say elsewhere about the difficulties of using an identity defined by simple labels as an explanatory concept. Intellectual and social history is too complicated and important to be left to such exchanges of names. . . . I look forward to seeing how nuanced and layered an account of intellectual and social forces on the discipline you produce.

(Faculty member, male, at a British research university)

I would like to know how Professor Ambrose would define "international perspective." In order to get one's doctorate, one must be able to read two modern foreign languages; would this proficiency qualify as having an international perspective? As far as I can tell, my professors always used the best sources available to them, regardless of language, and told us to get through them. . . . Were my professors working from an international perspective? One professor, trained in Europe, once complained of the unnecessarily dense and intellectually shallow nature of most German scholarship.

(Junior faculty member, male, at a US state university)

One of the signal failings of our profession is its so-called internationalism. We Americans are constrained to think as privileged upper middle class Europeans who are the ruling class with minimal upward social mobility and severe racial exclusion while our societal and cultural realities and aspirations are either unknown or judged immaterial to Europeans. It has been the death-knell of classics *here* and abroad as well, as the larger popular cultures of that continent adopt the American view of things.

I have lived abroad on various occasions and I have rarely met a European intellectual trained in the classical tradition who had the least interest in or understanding of America. So I don't think it is fair to say that classicists by virtue of understanding a variety of languages are part of an international scholarly consensus.... [B]ecause [Europeans] don't have general education courses the average European undergraduate is likely to have had less exposure to antiquity than his/her American counterpart.

(Professor, male, at a US public university with a PhD program)

This [international] perspective has both positive and negative aspects. Too much emphasis in Classics on the "superiority" of certain national scholarships (German as opposed to Italian, for example).... It's amazing where this attitude [of American classicists' inferiority] surfaces. I've heard the British complain about the "ruin" of the Cambridge Latin course by American adaptees!!!

(Associate Professor/Administrator, female, at a US state university)

[I agree that an "international perspective" is shared by Americans] ...and not only Americans)....My Oxford DPhil was based in Greece – hence the need first to get into modern Greek as well as German, Italian, French *et al.* I was taught – and teach – that we all belong to one big "happy family" or a community of scholars. True or not, it's a desirable aspiration.... We in the UK tend to think that (i) on the whole our UK students start off a little ahead of your brightest and best on average, technically anyway but that [ii] by the time your US/Canadian graduates achieve their PhDs there's little or nothing to choose, again on average, and [iii] comparisons should probably be quite restricted, as between (e.g.) Oxbridge and London vis à vis Harvard, Princeton, Michigan, Berkeley?

(Faculty member, male, at a British research university)

Does form not influence content? Then does not the language in which ideas about antiquity are expressed not affect an influence upon those ideas? Does the Bible really say the same thing in Hebrew as it does in Greek? Are we not regularly reading about antiquity in German, French, Italian, and even in Greek and Latin? How many of our colleagues in, say, Political Science, can read Thucydides in Greek, or *about* Thucydides in the Pauly–Wissowa? Nasty question? Then why did I have to order the complete Freud for our library? By international perspective I do not refer to some defined "wholesome" global outlook (as promoted by our College of Education). I mean that we expect scholars in our field to feel familiar with the world.... I have heard myself criticize the Oxford approach to the classics; put to Plato and

Thucydides the questions of our own times. Do I have to confess to a Germanic virus by taking a more historical approach?

(Professor, male, at a US state university)

Undergraduates interested in classics often seem to have internalized rigid values by the time they arrive on campus: intellectual excellence consists of translating accurately and nothing else, and approaches that involve more than translating strike many of them as irrelevant or wrong. Does this reflect the profession's sometimes nearly exclusive emphasis on philology, and denigration of approaches that are not exclusively philological? ... On your question about international perspective: In my department it is very common to ridicule American education, but I don't find it convincing. It doesn't necessarily represent an international perspective, but perhaps another version of xenophobia. I'd cast the issue not so much as one of an international perspective as of broad-mindedness: if a classicist will tolerate only one approach to classics and denigrates other approaches, does it make them "international" if they read various international journals?

(Professor, male, at a US liberal arts college)

Of all my teachers, only Bill Calder offered, in those far-off days so innocent of theory, an explicit definition and justification of an international perspective on our subject. His definition can be summarized as "classics = Altertumswissenschaft"; his justification was simply that in order to know what we needed to know, we needed to know what had been and was being done in Germany. I vividly remember an early conference with him ... in which he mapped out a course of study... that was to include time in Italy and England ....
Although only Calder articulated the idea that classics was an international field, my other teachers in school, college, and graduate school were... a remarkably cosmopolitan lot.... In our adult scholarly lives – the last thirty years – a uniquely American way of doing classical scholarship has begun to emerge. Call it the Puritan, Evangelical mode. In contrast to our European colleagues, we are intensely aware of the need to justify and explain what we do, and we debate issues of purity, right thinking and renewal. We see ourselves as a saving remnant, sometimes as a remnant of a remnant, in a hostile wilderness of intellectual danger.... We imagine ourselves as perpetually in crisis, perpetually in struggle for our souls. We are constantly alert to the need to reach out to the unconverted and ignorant. Now that we have a style, we need to become conscious of it. We have spent too much time wondering who will be the Wilamowitz or Nietzsche of

American classics. We need to find our Whitman, and our Henry James. . . . Certainly American BAs were regarded at one time as inferior to Oxbridge BAs. . . . Why we were so regarded is not far to seek. We were in fact less adept linguistically because most of us did not start Latin or Greek until our fourteenth or fifteenth year, and some not until much later. . . . I don't know anyone who labors any longer under an inferiority complex vis-à-vis British or European classics.

(Lee T. Pearcy, The Episcopal Academy)

I am a generation older than you, and I have lived to see American scholarship overtake European, both British and German, in many areas. They may get a better foundation – though that is not so prevalent any more – but their teachers often drown the value of their minute expertise in stodginess, so that Latin means nothing more than word blocks to be moved around with adolescent facility. I think that American women are way ahead of the continent and British Isles, aren't they, on theory and application of the material to Classicists?

(Professor, male, at a US state university with a PhD program)

Leaving aside that I'm not sure what the term means . . . my graduate training with one or two exceptions was entirely determined by men who were not Americans. And it was these men (not the Americans) who offered me the ideals of the field which I continue to espouse. . . . I don't know that any of these men ever thought of their perspective as "international." They rather embodied for me the values of scholarly life in general, a life that was shared by others from this continent. . . . I don't think [our feeling of inferiority is] a matter of training so much as of prejudice, often by those very refugees (political and economic) who came to this country and took positions of importance at major institutions. I think we have a greater sense of humor about ourselves than many of our foreign colleagues have. They tend to regard our refusal of the lofty "Stand" that those foreign colleagues take as a sign of our inferiority. Alas, American social class structure includes those snobs among poor school teachers, and has as little regard for them as they do for anyone who does not earn high six or seven figure salaries. But it's impossible to teach those folks about the nature of American society, since they never really became part of it. I think we have often internalized this feeling of inferiority. I don't think we are regarded abroad the way we regard ourselves. . . . We are better trained in fields other than strict classics than most of our European contemporaries. . . . Still, it holds true that we are weak in our knowledge of foreign languages . . . and few of us can speak or write German in the way many a German scholar can speak or write English. . . . As a result we often overvalue certain kinds of European scholarship and scholars.

(Professor, male, at a US state university with a PhD program)

[I was taught from an international perspective] at Stanford by Toni Raubitschek and his worldwide network of fans, friends, and students and also in Athens. Classics is *world-wide* as a field. . . .Journals, excavations, scholars from many (not all, of course) nations have contributed. I like the Classics in part because of its pre-Christian, pre-modern, pre-national state subject matter.

(Professor, male, at a US liberal arts college)

There are those who would say that American classicists share an "international perspective" because of the large number of classicists from England, and, to a lesser extent, Germany who have been awarded plum positions at so many universities in the United States. Yet this is not the case, since many of those who have come here from overseas represent the most narrow and restrictive part of the profession. As a graduate student . . . I was fortunate in having one or two teachers who encouraged me to go beyond the narrow model advocated by the prevailing Anglo-American establishment. . . . American classicists have been socialized to believe that they are inferior to colleagues from Britain and Germany. Thus the rush to hire people from overseas to fill so many major positions here. In spite of all the self-promoting hype about "excellence" in which so many of our graduates indulge, these same programs never seem to be able to find American scholars who are "good enough" to fill vacancies on their own faculties.

(Professor, male, at a US liberal arts college)

I believe that Classics can offer a unique international perspective, but I do not see why this should be restricted to American classicists. Since my undergraduate teachers were a mixture of English, Canadian and US trained, I think I did receive an "international perspecti-ve". . . . One way classicists can convey an international perspective is by keeping in touch with what classicists in other countries are doing. . . . At the same time there are bound to be and should be regional differences in what is studied and how. . . . [American classi-cists are regarded as products of inferior academic training relative to colleagues elsewhere] to a steadily diminishing extent. . . . [T]his attitude of superiority on the part of countries other than the US stems from the fact that in most European countries (and to some extent in Canada) there has been much more opportunity for secondary school Latin and Greek at a more advanced level. The situation is changing. . . . I don't think that most US classicists buy this view of European superiority. We may lament that Europeans have a big head start on us . . .

(Professor, male, at a US private university with a PhD program)

I don't know if it's unique to classicists, but yes, we are an internationally-minded lot: Oxford in the 1960s: Eduard Fraenkel comparing us unfavorably with Leo's seminar; undergraduate reading lists with items in French, Italian, Spanish and German; all our tutors had friends in other countries, invited them over, just as we do now. . . . I don't know anyone who generalizes about American classicists. There *used* to be a problem because many American graduates learned Greek or Latin in graduate school, but we've got it too!

(Faculty member, female, at a British research university)

On foreign classical scholars in the US, see James Halporn, "Foreign Scholars and American Classical Education." On the plight of classics in Margaret Thatcher's Britain, see Richard Janko, "Dissolution and Diaspora: Ptolemy Physcon and the Future of Classical Scholarship," in Phyllis Culham and Lowell Edmunds (eds) *Classics: A Discipline and Profession in Crisis?* (New York, London, Lanham, 1989).

For the debate within the Modern Language Association on the hiring of foreign-born and trained scholars, see Robert C. Holub (University of California at Berkeley), "Professional Responsibility: On Graduate Education and Hiring Practices," *Profession* 94 (Modern Language Association of America, 1994: 79–86), especially 83–84, in which he – unlike those who respond to this essay – deals briefly with systemic differences:

Let me emphasize that I am not at all against the hiring of foreign-born teacher-scholars who are trained in the United States or who are already teaching in the United States. It seems to me that these people have committed themselves to our educational system and that they have placed themselves in direct competition with our other graduate students. I believe it is unfair, however, to compare one of our graduate students or one of our assistant professors with persons trained abroad. It is unfair because training and opportunities differ so greatly that comparisons are apt to be inaccurate. In Germany young scholars who have written a dissertation and who are trying to complete a second, larger project . . . are often supported liberally by fellowship funds. Sometimes these funds are sustained for as many as six years. Often young scholars in Germany are incorporated into projects sponsored by full professors and in this way enhance their publication records. The comparison between the research produced by a German scholar at age forty-five and that or his or her American counterpart may therefore be unfair. But even if we could factor out all elements of inequality, it seems to me self-defeating and irresponsible in the current employment situation to hire scholars who have no background in and have shown no commitment to higher education in the United States while our own students, who invest many years of their lives and often a good deal of money, end up without a position.

Roy Sellars (University of Geneva), *Profession* 95, 105–106, especially:

> Perhaps it is also "unfair" that some foreign candidates will be better qualified for a position than their American competitors because they have benefited from more rigorous or supportive academic systems in Europe or elsewhere. . . . In that case, though, instead of attacking the appointment of foreign scholars in America, might it not be more productive to examine those systems critically and to determine how their more positive features could be incorporated?

N.B. Sellars does not provide such an examination himself or suggest determining how the more positive features of the American system might be incorporated elsewhere.

Ruth Vanita (University of Delhi), *Profession* 95, 106–107, especially:

> Holub's proposal for indigenousness over excellence as the basis for hiring is right in line with the racist tendencies of some US immigration policy makers . . . ; Holub's example of German versus American scholars makes the latter appear underprivileged. But many scholars from Asian and East European countries are trained in conditions of underprivilege and deprivation that an American scholar would find hard to imagine, and achieve excellence against great odds before applying for jobs in the US. They have a commitment to excellence in the study of a language/literature and expressed this commitment wherever they happened to be born.

And the reply by Holub, *Profession* 95, 107–108:

> Of one thing I am convinced. . . . It is easier to make clichéd accusations of xenophobia and racism than to confront the actual issues. . . . We should stop training so many people, but until we do, the people who are training graduate students for a national labor market, should hire

the people we train for that market before turning to foreign labor markets.

"Is There An Anglo-American Feminist Criticism?", *Tulsa Studies in Women's Literature* 12. 2, (1993).

Special Issue of *Boston Review* 19. 5, October/November 1994, "Patriotism or Cosmopolitanism?": Martha Nussbaum in a debate with Hilary Putnam, Herbert Gintis, Nathan Glazer, Michael Dorris, Amy Gutmann, Michael Walzer, Anthony Appiah, Harvey Mansfield, Benjamin R. Barber, Sissela Bok, Paul Berman, Judith Butler, Charles Beitz, David Strauss, Robert Pinsky, Michael Lerner, Richard Sennett, Sheldon Hackney, Leo Marx, Anne Norton, Rachel Hadas, Charles Taylor, Lloyd Rudolph, Lawrence Blum, George Fletcher, William Connolly, Anthony Kronman, Immanuel Wallerstein, Arthur Schlesinger, Jr. Cf. in particular:

> Let me now return to the defense of shared values in...Sheldon Hackney's project. In these eloquent appeals to the common there is something that makes me very uneasy. On the one hand Rorty and Hackney seem to argue well when they insist on the centrality to democratic deliberation of certain values that bind all citizens together. But why should these values, which instruct us to join hands across boundaries of ethnicity and class and gender and race, lose steam when they get to the borders of the nation?...What is it about the national boundary that magically converts people toward whom our education is both incurious and indifferent into people to whom we have duties of mutual respect? I think, in short, that we undercut the very case for multicultural respect within a nation by failing to make a broader world respect central to education....Rorty's patriotism may be a way of bringing all Americans together; but patriotism is very close to jingoism...I don't see in Rorty's argument any proposal for coping with this very obvious danger.

Frank Gardner Moore, "A History of the American Philological Association," *Transactions of the American Philological Association* 50, (1919): 5 ff, especially:

> The first Washington meeting [1907] had its unique feature in the presentation of the members to President Roosevelt in the East Room of the White House, where the President received us with great cordiality, spoke appreciatively of our studies, commending scholar-

ship and its achievements; also of his recent interest in Victor Bérard's *Les Phéniciens et l'Odyssée*, which he hoped we would all read. Was it imagination, or was there the suspicion of a smile playing about [the Yale Homerist Thomas Day] Seymour's mouth as he heard this recommendation, and then proceeded to present us severally to the President?

Paul Shorey, "Fifty Years of Classical Studies in America," *TAPA* 50, 1919: 33 ff., especially:

A plausible, if partial parallel could be drawn between the history of American scholarship and the history of American literature. In both, the proportion of hope, aspiration and prophecy is excessive. In both, the historian must guard equally against the brag of provincial chauvinism and the undue self-depreciation of what Herbert Spencer calls the anti-patriotic bias. . . . In both, injustice is done to America by comparing her output with that of Europe as a whole or only with that of the leaders, Germany, England, France . . .

[E]xcept in the merest matters of fact, a German philological enquiry is, owing to the abuse of conjecture and the pyramiding of hypothesis, almost never a safe authority about anything. It is at best a stimulating discussion of and a helpful index to the sources, which must always be independently verified. The German philological mind, like the German political mind, is fertile and ingenious in the multi-plication of arguments for a chosen thesis or a foregone conclusion. It cannot be trusted to weigh them. . . . The German–American doctoral dissertation in particular is singled out for reprobation as the culmination of all pedantries and the extinguisher of all genuine human and humanistic and literary interest in classical study. . .

A fling at pedantry always gets a hand or wins a laugh from the audience. But it is also in part an expression of the ungenerous and jealous attitude towards American scholarship which I have already deplored. We may possibly deserve this by our marked inferiority not only to all foreign scholars, but to all intellectuals in America and to all teachers of other subjects – but we can hardly be expected ourselves to favor that explanation. . . . Theodore Roosevelt's name, with two other presidents, heads the Princeton list of tributes to the classics. . . . But when Roosevelt was rough-riding on his own in literature the encouragement he gave us was simply to sneer at the man who spends his youth in a German University and can thenceforth work only in the fields fifty times furrowed by German plows. This was of course a bluff. He had not compared the last twenty volumes of the *AJP* or of *Classical*

Philology or the fifty best American doctoral dissertations with similar products in Germany. But the public takes it as the verdict of a connoisseur.

My space does not allow me to work out such a comparison. I can only suggest it.... Much of the progress recorded [in classical philology by Wilhelm Kroll] is purely illusory – the setting up of theories by one German philologian to be bowled down by another.... Greek metric was taught at Bryn Mawr in 1886 as effectively as Wilamowitz taught it in Berlin in 1913, and I would confidently match the last little Pindar class at Chicago with any seven readers that Germany could produce – professors or students. If you think that unbecoming petulance or American brag let me remind you that Karl Mutzbauer in his *Grundbedeutung des Konjunctivs* quotes *Aen.* VIII, 560 in the form *O si praeteritos Jupiter mihi referat annos*, with short *Jupiter*, that Leo cites Pope's famous line in the form "the proper study of mankind's man," that Ferrero quotes Horace's epistle to Augustus *cum tot sustineas tanta et negotia solus* with long *negotia*, that Christ uses the roughly anapaestic "Erlkönig" as an example of weighty trochees and light tripping dactyls? Why should any American who possesses an ear worry about their theories of metric?

Chapter 8

A response[1]

Charles Rowan Beye

A day spent learning about personal voice theory perhaps calls for an autobiographical note from me. Here's a bit. I started Latin in school over fifty years ago – the world in which I began my studies was positively antediluvian – did classics in college, and got a PhD at Harvard. This last completed my qualifications for that most detested of creatures in contemporary American academia, a WASP male of the monied class with a Harvard PhD. But then at the time I entered the field so was almost everyone else, or at least in the Ivy League which set the tone for the field. Those who were not worked energetically to appear so. Thus, taking one definition of the personal voice as I seem to have heard it today, I would say that for most of us in those days to speak with our personal or individual voice was to speak with the generic voice as well. Conformity is, of course, a characteristic of any group. The WASP male in addition has always practiced anonymity. It is one of the effective WASP strategies for controlling others, for creating and maintaining power. Just as imperson- ality, for instance, was the mode my parents employed in dealing with the servants, it was the mode desired by most academics for the teacher– student relationship, and this extended into scholarly activity. Anonymity and impersonality were emphasized and reinforced in the early years of teaching. I can well remember that academics who might on occasion stop by the office with a child in tow were given the horrified looks one would have thought reserved for lepers. To be a father or a husband other than at the annual departmental picnic simply was not on. Bradford Welles of Yale's Classics Department handled the husband/scholar dichotomy most originally by having hot dogs and the trimmings on the lawn for those junior faculty who were silly enough to bring their wives and children to the annual get-together while martinis and hors d'oeuvres were served to the others in the quiet and dignity of the Welles' home. Years ago when I used to lecture around the country a lot, one of the most frightening and tedious aspects of the visit to other campuses was the obligatory dinner after my talk when, seated male/female, male/female as one was in those days, I found myself between two wives, spouses of my professional colleagues, in those days housewives, usually with unused PhDs and no careers, usually rather drunk, generally quite angry, whose confessional conversations were so much at variance with the performance in social relations effected by their husbands as to make the experience of the evening entirely schizophrenic. Maybe it is this schizophrenia that the adherents of personal voice theory are getting at.

One of my dearest friends from those early days was a Boston-born Irish-American who had survived the condescension and scorn he received from the Harvard Classics Department and had gone on to teach at Yale and Stanford. He was a thoroughly conflicted person. He was an energetic Catholic apologist and devoted to his working-class family, yet on the other hand just as snobbish, elitist, self-effacing Yankee Protestant-seeming as he could manage. He had a marvelous, almost impervious, facade and an accent that was an extraordinary blend of working-class Irish and WASP Beacon Hill. Only when he was drunk did his rage show, rage against such worthies as John Huston Finley, Jr and Brooks Otis, the first an invented Boston Brahmin by way of New York, the second absolutely the real goods, born on Beacon Hill as he never tired of telling us. Ted was obviously the first Irish person they had encountered out of the kitchen. Ted was such a conflicted person that he would have hated the personal voice. I mention him because he is a demonstration of the truth that more than anything else my generation's dislike of the personal voice theory stems, I think, from a profound need to use classics as a place to hide. I might also argue that he hid himself in epigraphy both in graduate school and professionally thereafter because he could never find a voice and manner that reflected his true self in historical and literary studies. That is to say that Ted was trained to repress himself in his writing, that therefore he was required to submit to the assumed identity of the generic voice in classical literary studies of the time, that he had a vigorous and angry sense of the incongruity of this posture but neither the courage nor the avenue to express his distance from the social and economic circumstances of that generic voice. Epigraphical studies were sufficiently neutral as to save him from the conflict. The Ted who argued and reflected brilliantly in his rich Irish, Catholic, and working-class way in the classroom and in my home was never the Ted of his epigraphical studies.

I was saved from too conventional an existence, WASP that I was, by the complicating fact that, on the one hand, I had been openly gay since I was fourteen and, on the other, that in my twenty-first year in a moment of crazy but genuine emotion and physical interest I had married a woman, and we thought it prudent to present ourselves in Cambridge as your typical young academic couple. It was all marvelously ironic, really; in those days graduate students did not marry, yet there was I so thoroughly gay (even if it was only I, my wife, and some very close friends who knew this) and the only married man in all of our circle of friends. So despite my credentials as they appeared to the outside world I was in a very peculiar way marginalized, the outsider looking on at the playing field of power. Since, however, to my colleagues I was in disguise, I could, of course, play on the field as well. In fact I managed to kick all the requisite goals, although I never felt I was doing it legitimately. It perhaps put interesting pressures on me that I have never really been able to acknowledge.

The Harvard classics department in those days was sundered by the personal rivalries of most of the senior faculty. It always struck me that there was a kind of gender tension in the division between the ancient historians, epigraphists, and archeologists and their rivals, the historians and critics of ancient literature. There was one old bird in particular who in his gravel voice, devoid of any inflection that would acknowledge much of the range of human emotion, was forever inveighing against interpretation, arguing for the simple truth of so-called "facts." His condescension directed at the literary figures, the critics, translated the advocacy of interpretation into something feminine, flighty, if not hysterical, and definitely second or third rate and hardly lasting. Whenever I ventured timidly upon interpretation or mildly advanced some idea about any aspect of our subject, his devotees would immediately bark out harshly, gruff as they could be: "What are your refs [references]?" I sometimes found his celebrated lunches at which his favorite graduate students obssessed about fact and still more fact mildly titillating sexually, but most of the time an exercise in S & M that left me trembling. Surprisingly enough I chose to write a dissertation with this man. Over the years I have asked myself more than once whether I was motivated to do this by my sense that the literary people were not keen on me or by my desire to lodge myself securely in the seriously "masculine" side of classical studies, or whether I just had an unacknowledged need for discipline and bondage. More specifically I remember how strange it was at Harvard never to be able to acknowledge myself openly to my favorite Latin professor who was so very gay, while from time to time having the occasion to discuss him with various sexual partners who had also on other occasions shared his bed. But that is the way it was, and of course that was before the days of "gay," so I really would not have known how to identify myself to him in any case.

Do any of these biographical details matter in the arena of scholarship? The papers today on personal voice have made me concede the possibility. I think that it is fair to say that I, as an alienated person, however secretly, had no secure way to establish what I wanted to say about my subject, or what I needed to say, or how I wanted to say it. I allowed myself to speak through other voices. Someone who is despised, vilified, rejected, someone who is made to feel inferior to other males, inadequate as a male, someone who knows himself to be liable to physical assault and battery, someone who whenever he acts upon his natural sexual inclinations is in many states of the Union indulging in criminal behavior punishable by years of imprisonment, or more positively someone who knows himself to be fully a male and relates to other males warmly, passionately, and possessively, such a person brings a special perspective to the human condition. Perhaps if it had been easier to acknowledge my gayness or I could have had a better understanding of what I was acknowledging, then I could have shared my intellectual self with other similarly gay persons so as to establish the possibility of a common point of view. As a young teacher when I made pronouncements about male–female relationships in Greek literature, my students were led to believe that they were coming out of the mouth of a good old, straight old boy. And when I talked about the ancient Greek adulation of the young male body, my students did not necessarily recognize the enthusiasm in my voice that was fueled by my own erotic interest in the subject. Can one imagine how perverse it is to speak in utterly neutral tones with a distanced sensibility about the institution of erotic physical contact between two males when the speaker is himself a veteran of more such encounters than he could possibly count? My initial field of study was Homeric epic; I could never really deal with how much I as a marginalized masculine person was alienated from the Homeric hero. Society had typed me in such a fashion that I was not sure that it gave me permission to understand the Homeric hero. Of course, in my disguised person I could speak with authority, but what authority had I within me? All I could really identify with was the controlling, exploiting behaviors of rulers. It was such a relief to turn to Apollonius in my forties and to find there the conflicts and ambiguities of acculturated gender-defined roles that have always defined my experience of life.

So, although it is a little late in the day for me, I welcome the personal voice in scholarly studies if it will allow teacher and student or writer and reader of a scholarly article to isolate, identify, and clarify more readily the idiosyncratic aspects of interpretation that hitherto may have been concealed. Most of all, and this is to me the really important benefit of personal voice theory, if it will allow a scholar to understand him or herself well enough to recognize the personal element in what may initially have seemed to be an "objective" or value-free criticism of a text. Objectivity is what my generation was taught to value and try for in everything we wrote. Anonymity was my cultural heritage. It surprised me therefore to have a colleague in the profession who knows me well identify me in my writings as a twenty-five year old widower in my portrait of Admetus and Alcestis in an article written about that time; as an academic on the make in my thirties, a wannabe Odysseus in my portrait of that hero in a book I wrote about thirty years ago; as the embittered veteran of a dying marriage in my book on Jason and Medea in the *Argonautica*; and now in what I am writing about the *Aeneid* perhaps as an aging conservative who wants to believe that Virgil applauded what he saw of Mussolini in Augustus, and always, of course, as he never ceases to point out, as a product of America's ruling class in any number of other articles. But in saying what I have I believe that I must distinguish another sense of personal voice, one which is not so much style, vocabulary, diction, but life experience informing that which is said. Naturally the two come together to form any verbal construct we make, but they are perhaps worth considering separately as well.

Speaking of America's ruling class leads me to remark that in so many differentiations of the personal voice – Patricia Moyer speaking, for instance, of the "multiplicity of personal voice" and mentioning gender, race, nationality, age, and so on, there is so little reference to class. It seems to me that, since what remains of classical antiquity and what constitutes the classical tradition which has been so carefully nurtured through the centuries are manifestations, if not justifications, of the ruling, exploiting class, class ought to be one of the more distinctive perspectives of personal voice theory. I would suggest that so much of contemporary hostility or indifference to the classics among students derives from their incapacity to understand what is to them the voice of an entirely alien class, and from their teachers' incapacity to speak of antiquity in any other way than as apologists for the ruling class. In the present crisis of a widening gap between the haves and have-nots, certainly in the USA, if not in the rest of the industrialized nations, it is not clear how relevant to a typical student body is either personal introspection or a literature describing a class who never labored for their own survival. Nothing will make this clearer than to teach classics in an American urban college or university serving the so-called inner city, that is to say, the urban poor. Interestingly enough, as global economics increasingly takes away any control of their destinies from the traditional privileged and ruling classes, their progeny will increasingly fail to identify with the literature and culture of classical antiquity as it has traditionally been taught.

In listening to the talks [at the 1995 meeting of the British Classical Association at St Andrews] I was reminded of a recent article by Arlene Croce in *The New Yorker Magazine* which has created a tremendous stir in the USA. As dance critic of that magazine, Croce wrote an essay defending her decision to refuse to review the recent dance program of the noted choreographer Bill T. Jones who is ill with AIDS and who created a dance peopled with men and women dying from the effects of that syndrome. Croce argued that the desperate circumstances of the performers made criticism impossible, that human sympathy must inevitably deform critical judgement. She inveighed against the parade of victims presented in art works before which her critical faculties shrank. I think of this in reference to Van Nortwick's critique of Odysseus and de Luce's recounting of her acculturated feminine instinct to serve males. Van Nortwick has fought a hard battle to rid himself of the demons that beset the adult children of alcoholics. If he sees in Odysseus all the ugly traits from which he believes that he has freed himself, what is one to say? I personally could argue that as a gay male I much admire Odysseus' capacity for lying, his ever-ready suspicion of all persons, the narrator's revelation that in Odysseus' one moment of trust he was damaged (that is, when he felt safe enough to boast of his name before the Cyclops), no different to my mind from the false moment of safety and confidence before a would-be friend and perhaps lover turns into a gay basher. If Van Nortwick were to counter that my judgements are skewed by my unfortunate life experience, then he would be denying me my own personal voice in which I will call betrayal normal and distrust healthy awareness. My experience of teaching in impoverished neighborhoods of New York City has made me realize as never before how immediately true the story of the *Iliad* can be for some, how a street scene in which rival drug gangs are shooting down male persons in horrifying numbers is reflected in the underlying despair and weariness as well as the exhilaration of killing that characterizes the *Iliad*. Likewise I have found a context in the streets of the Bronx in which the *Odyssey* is a highly successful manual of behavior.

But the fact of the matter is that neither Van Nortwick nor I have any reason to use Odysseus as a model for our own behavior and thus to find fault with him for what he does or does not do. Odysseus is true to the narrative and true to the time in which he lives. We Americans once subscribed to a notion inherited in the nineteenth century from the British and the Germans that classical literature and the ideas found therein could function as a kind of alternative to the Christian religion and as such the memorable figures of myth, story and drama could be presented as so many spiritual templates for the *tabulae rasae* of our students' minds. It seems to me that this lies behind the criticism of de Luce as well as her need to reject the model provided by Ariadne, Medea, and Dido.

Personal voice theory and reader response theory allow de Luce to speculate on her instinct for servitude, culturally determined to be gender bound to women, and clearly a part of the Western tradition since it has been identified by her in Ariadne, Medea, and Dido. If it were not for the weight of their quasi religious status, which endows these stories and the literature in which they are embedded with such authority, de Luce could consider them as so many curiosity pieces. But as a woman, formed in part by the Western literary canon, she must protest. De Luce is using reader response theory as her mode of criticism, and I would analyze her approach in terms of reception theory, that is to say that she looks to the dynamics of these women's relationships in terms of very contemporary modes of personal self-discovery. But let us employ context theory here as well. To do so is to deprive ancient literature of its transcendence and hence higher authority and make it rather a collection of curiosity pieces. As such it is curious that males, who we may assume created, carried, delivered and heard the myths and the art forms in which the helping princesses made their appearance, determined that the stories go in such a way that the males always seem from our contemporary vantage point so ethically bankrupt in their betrayal and desertion. But it may be the case that to males this behavior does not seem morally derelict. Perhaps I as a male will have another personal voice to introduce into the reading of these texts, and that is the male instinct to move on after having taken advantage of a woman. Let us imagine that the various acts of kindness offered by the women of these stories are merely euphemisms for surrendering to sexual intercourse with the males in question. Let us further imagine that the women in question consider that the rendering of the favors entitles them to some commitment from the men, accompanying them on their future voyages obviously being a consideration. But the males seem free to move on after accepting the favors and distinctly do not want the commitments of the women. This seems to be perhaps a basic human truth that has made the relations between the sexes tragic since the beginning of time. This is how I as a male would read these myths. I accept that the men work cruelties upon the women, but only from a woman's point of view.

One has also to distinguish between the myth and the story. Medea may be forsaken in myth, but in the Euripidean version once she is rejected, she manages to murder her children in revenge upon her errant spouse, and then take off for Athens. One might want to read this as a woman who triumphs over the commonplace burden of child-rearing thrust upon her by a husband who deserts her as he goes through the mid-life crisis, ridding herself of the albatross of children for her own new life of freedom. Likewise, the Apollonian Medea who as a teenager maneuvers the simple-minded teenaged Jason into proposing marriage in return for the magic potion, and later is vouchsafed eternal life in the Elysian Fields with no less a celebrity than Achilles is not exactly the deserted helping princess of the myth.

To note how differently Van Nortwick and I read the Odyssey and how we can easily secure both readings in the experience of our lives makes for a richer understanding of the poem, and that is good. I question Van Nortwick when he finds fault with the old rogue for his capacity to reinvent himself in every social situation. Where Van Nortwick attributes contemporary approval of such a conception of character to postmodern-ism I would rather suggest that it is normal human behavior. As a matter of fact one might argue that the behavior strategy Van Nortwick adopted to cope with his alcoholic mother and which he has now shed betokens in each instance a different person rather than the core person initially hidden under layers of maladaptive reactions to impossible situations. The point of these observations is that they represent the merest iceberg tip of speculation in which I could continue endlessly. This is to me the great danger and weakness in the personal voice theoretical approach: that it leads into endless speculation about the critic rather than the text. To the extent that the personal voice theory derives from the feminist movement and to the extent that women (in the USA at least) are acculturated to analyze other persons – what dismissive males call "gossip" – such endless speculation can perhaps please the one sex and repulse the other. One sometimes speaks of the "confessional" when talking of personal voice; this leads me back to Arlene Croce, since it could be argued that the confessional style of personal voice scholarship defends against negative criticism by turning the reader into priest or psychiatrist whose role, as most readers would be acculturated to take on, is to be sympathetic or to absolve.

Personal voice inevitably engenders a species of autobiography. Now, many would argue, myself included, that autobiography in general is perhaps no more than mythmaking. Hence, the danger that the classicist who self-consciously uses the personal voice in the interests of what he or she imagines is greater clarity is in fact obfuscating things all the more if the autobiographical bits and pieces are introduced to shore up self-esteem or provide an apologia or to charm the students. One could probably argue that my own revelations in this essay derive from my desire to appear chic and trendy as only gays can be, at least in contemporary USA.

Medea, Ariadne, and Dido found their males non-committal. I am reminded of the remarks made about the non-committal voice of scholarship so much detested by so many. The non-committal voice is the voice of authority. It is the scholar's voice. Some argue that it is the male's voice, but no, it is the voice of authority. Because authority figures tend to be male, it becomes the male voice, but, be assured, there are great numbers of males who detest that voice as much as women do because of their own struggle with authority. Still, until one can diminish the fear of failure which is so closely related to the fear of being exposed which drives most significant authority figures in the field of classics, it is hard to imagine that any change can occur in the preferred style. The journals are edited by males or their female clones; their editorial standards are arbitrary and cannot be appealed. A decade ago I received a rejection for an article that later, unchanged in any way, enjoyed considerable success. This rejection came from the editor of a journal who said among other things "You achieve results which are either demonstrably wrong or unverifiable if tested by the accepted methods of Homeric scholarship," and "the style of your article is uncommonly careless." No argument for these assertions, just the assertions. This by the way was from a German-born person whose English style to my mind resembles computer-generated translatese. Imagine what he would have done with the impressionistic prose of Hilda Doolittle as she developed her ideas about Greek literature!

I sympathize utterly with Susanna Braund. Articles in classical journals are more often than not dreary, unimportant, and defeating. I feel so lucky to have been able to write two books for Doubleday's Anchor series; my editor in each instance was a person of intelligence, education, and style who encouraged me to write criticism in a manner that was comfortable to me. Later I had the great good fortune to have the literary critic John Gardner as editor on my Apollonius book; he gave me permission to write as I chose, to employ irony and hyperbole, for instance, thus helping me to fashion a fluent prose style that both acknowledged the conventions of scholarship and criticism and yet remained entirely personal. Twenty or thirty years ago Doubleday Anchor was publishing for a presumed audience of educated readers. Sadly enough, no such audience can be presumed today. Books about literature will be read only by students, and usually by compulsion. Or they will be read by colleagues. Here again the academy dominates. How can one create alternative journals? *The Bryn Mawr Classical Review* got off to a good start as an alternative, and remains so in the speed with which they review newly published books. The tone of each review, however, which used to be relatively irreverent, vernacular, and witty – implying, as it should, that opinions offered were nothing more than that – has changed to something far more wooden, nay, lapidary, more suggestive of a *monumentum aere perennius* than a critical take on a new book.

Recently friends have been murmuring about a Festschrift for me, and I have said that the only one I would like would be a collection of articles that their authors had had rejected as being too flaky, too *outré*, too completely unverifiable, and which are all fun to read. Which reminds me of a comment made earlier from someone in the audience at this panel that there is safety in the so-called neutral, impersonal professional style, and that asking scholars to write in a personal style might very likely result in disaster since it would require them to write well. One can only speculate about how learning to couch one's thoughts in the so-called professional style may neutralize and diminish the specifics of a personality; perhaps it is this that makes for the dry-as-dust, boring academic speaker in the classroom or lecture hall of which we all have had in our lives only too many examples.

Personal voice theory is equally relevant to teaching students to write. Recently I have been teaching in an institution that caters to the urban poor. I have students whose education in poor and isolated grade schools has left them utterly ignorant of the writing style that they must adopt if they are ever to try to enter a profession or the upper echelons of American business. As they respond to texts we are reading I feel compelled to shape the response in the language and manner of argument that most approximates the white middle-class, middle American style. Yes, that happens to be male writing. But more than male it is power writing. As I remarked earlier, the essence of power and the holding of power is to have knowledge and the facts and to deny these to the powerless. This is true with a so-called neutral writing style where information is delivered without the context of the writer's personality.

In the essays of younger students in my classes I habitually and ruthlessly root out any suggestion of a personal response in their writing. Whatever my doubts about doing this, I feel compelled to teach them skills that will help them get out of the dead end of the world in which they live. My older students, on the other hand, who, alas, rarely have the chance to move up into better jobs, are left free to write as they choose. Their narratives invariably become autobiographical. They cannot imagine any other way to express themselves than to express themselves. It was illuminating to be reminded of Hilda Doolittle and ironic, too. H.D.'s very personal engagement with the ancient texts, her idiosyncratic prose style and critical manner, are features that would have denied her any hearing by the academy if she were writing in the late twentieth century. Ironically and oddly enough she shares with my middle-aged students, locked into their jobs, this freedom of expression. Doolittle, privileged, financially independent, connected to all the right persons, is freed of the necessity of following the rules, as are my students although for vastly different reasons of social class. Academics have increasingly controlled the language and terms of the criticism of literature. They have denied to lay persons, such as Hilda Doolittle, the right or even the chance to make a reading of ancient literature. The academic importation of French critical theory may raise the final impossible barrier to any lay person who would try to interpret.

The arrival of French critical theory is the latest in American enthusiasms for things trans-Atlantic. Hallett's evocation of the issue of American identity in her appeal to song and costume [see Chapter 7] was a dramatic demonstration to me of the emotional and ideological tensions underlying personal voice theory. Watching her dressed in red, white, and blue, listening to her asking us to sing along with her produced in me such violent negative reactions as to make it very clear upon reflection how much I had been schooled into "proper" behavior in a setting such as a meeting devoted to classics. Hallett's mission was to subvert thinking and speaking on classics, to insist that the discourse was open to an American-izing emphasis upon showbiz, commercialism, feminism, or anything else, for that matter. In short: be yourself. My reaction of fear and disgust showed how close she was to an important truth. In my youth there was the general conviction that the British and the Germans had the only real training and understanding for classical studies. The presence of British and Germans in a classics faculty might signal the prospect of some mightily boring classroom hours but they guaranteed quality. This looming presence seems odd today when other disciplines have more or less shed their insecurities and gone on to hire Americans. Younger classicists more and more tend to make the angry observation that classical studies in the United States more than any other American academic discipline are still largely dictated by the interests and standards of British and European members of the profession. Certainly it is fair to say that proportionally there are more foreign nationals in American classics departments than in any other; the important statistic is that the major American universities have a preponderance of them and so they have an extraordinary power in the profession. It does not seem to be the case that the objections are of the order of, say, an auto mechanic in Los

Angeles who fears his job will be taken by a Mexican wet-back. Yes, the profession is dwindling and there are not enough jobs for Americans. But the resentment grows from the perception that entirely inappropriate teaching on the part of the foreigners has been significant in the decline and now the possible demise of the field.

Many will argue that the damage that foreign classicists have inflicted upon the profession of teaching of classics in America is immense. The culture of the United States of America is so utterly different from anything else in the world that it requires very special knowledge to penetrate its mysteries. Historically, the power elite of the East Coast subscribed to the culture of the aristocratic and clerical elites of Britain and Europe. This imported culture was diluted in the nineteenth century by the increase in wealth and power of the western sections of the country that were populated by immigrant farmers who were divorced from an elite European cultural heritage. On the East Coast itself the late nineteenth and early twentieth century witnessed massive arrivals of Irish and Italian peasants at an even further remove from European Higher Culture. In the 1920s the African-Americans, who for a century and a half had been rigorously denied any participation in Eurocentric culture, began to find their voice in the Harlem Renaissance. After the Second World War the West Coast Japanese who had been interned in the camps found that experience a catalyst to begin the process of finding their own place in American society and helping other Asians to it. Immigration from Southeast Asia has grown immensely during the time of the Vietnam War and afterwards. While Asian bourgeois admire Western technology, Asian peasants have never even heard of Eurocentric culture. Such is the extraordinary upward mobility of American society that representatives of all these groups have found themselves among the present-day elites.

These various groups were aided in their efforts to have an identifiable presence in America by the emergence of the mass consumer society after the Second World War. For the first time in history a very large segment of the population was able to demonstrate what they wanted and needed, intellectually and spiritually as well as materially. In the 1960s American universities, which were now devoted to mass education as never before, switched to consumerism as well. Universities were like department stores in which each academic discipline was a boutique set out on the main floor to sell its wares. Students began to dictate the curriculum. Surprise, surprise, it wasn't classical antiquity that they immediately wanted. To a very large extent this was because they knew nothing about it. Classics departments that survived were those who learned how to sell the product. That is a hateful phrase, I know, but one that there is no escaping in the United States. Like it or not, academics must now justify their discipline, just as Estée Lauder must sell her perfume or General Motors must hawk its cars. I mean academics must make clear why it is that students should study their discipline. This is *essential* to the academic enterprise in the United States of America. This is something that very few foreign academics understand or – more to the point – can tolerate. Since I am old enough to remember the elitist context in which classics once thrived, I am entirely sympathetic. Yes, Tallyrand was right when he said that "it was sweet before the revolution," but as an American classicist of the late twentieth century I am far more concerned about getting salespersons who will move the product. (If we have to have Brits why can't it be Tina Brown editing *The American Journal of Philology?*)

In America a classics program has to be developed in such a fashion that it relates to the polyglot, multi-ethnic, populist truth of American culture. The absolute decline of an elitist insider culture, the so-called Higher Culture of other centuries, and its dilution into the greater Mass Culture means that teachers of classics have to be familiar with an enormous variety of cultures and sub-cultures; they must know, for instance, about the history of slavery in this country, the Reconstruction, and the 1960s liberation movements, they must understand the Holocaust, they must know about Native American religions and customs, not to mention the major Western and Eastern religions, and they must have some superficial knowledge of Ireland, Italy, Germany, and nowadays the Caribbean, Haiti, and all sorts of countries in Asia; they must know about Fred and Ginger, film noir, soap operas, Elvis, Madonna, and Mrs Bobbit.

To my mind the trans-Atlantic import considers classics to be either (1) an end in itself for the obsessive minded – this is called philology; (2) a badge of entry into a class – this is the use to which the nineteenth-century British and German upper classes put it, in other words an adornment to that group; or (3) an alternative to the Christian religion – this is the legacy of the Oxford Movement as well as the ill-defined Third Humanism preached by Werner Jaeger. Because in the 1920s the United States of America ceased to be a colony of Europe, no longer in bondage, as it had been in the nineteenth century, to European culture, the European arguments for the study of antiquity simply do not work here. One remembers Werner Jaeger's strongest objection to the American profession of classics when he first arrived here in the 1930s, that it was devoid of humanism and much too pedantic. Maybe now with historical hindsight that tendency can be analyzed as the transition, the necessary and inevitable shedding of the European ideology with which the study of classics was imbued, as a new generation struggled to make the subject more its own. In the transition, of course, all that would be or could be retained was the pedantry, the obsession with texts and grammars. It was in the 1960s that the discipline had a chance to develop an American ideology.

Americans are not alone in having to deal with European domination. In one way or another it remains the world's problem. Moyer relates an anecdote, for instance, about Frobenius' equation of Olokun with Poseidon. One wonders when the Nigerian Wole Soyinka composes a *Bacchae* whether he is assimilating the Euripidean play or the ancient Greek myth to his own culture or assimilating his own culture to the European experience. Part of the freedom that comes from rejecting our imperial masters is to reject the past which is their past. Frobenius had nothing but contempt for the contemporary African who he considered a degraded heir to a greater past. But his condemnation seems to me to be less racial than it is generational. The same burden of the past rests upon the shoulders of today's Italians and Greeks. One can, for instance, see its workings all too often among classicists whose adulation of ancient Greeks or Romans is balanced by their condescension or contempt for contemporary Greeks or Italians.

America is a culture formed to a large extent by people who left their ancestral homes in dissatisfaction, not to mention those who killed the indigenous population or enslaved an imported one when they arrived on this continent. Understandably they do not want to remember. Theirs is a culture that rejects the past and looks to the future. Only in America can one contemplate a perfectly solid, reasonably attractive, reasonably sized home and say "What a great tear-down!" As the remark will indicate, American culture is also philistine and ignorant; Americans comfortably reject any attempt to stretch their intellects, enlarge their aesthetic sensibilities, engage their souls. The present rise of fundamentalist Christianity is certainly symptomatic of the absolute decay of serious culture in the USA. Classics wilts in an environment such as this, but unending powerful teaching, research, humane understanding and good old academic politics can still work wonders. It is hard to convince the great powerful educational institutions that the foreign nationals on their classics faculties do not help the cause of classics in this country in any way, since these institutions use their humanities programs as they do their brick, ivy, and historic architecture, to project an image nationwide that says "quality education." Most academic imports have not the least clue about American culture, they disdain teaching courses in English translation since they have only the most limited notion about the subject as being part of a larger whole, or their English is so weak that they could not manage to speak it sufficiently fluently on a twice a week basis to make the class go. They rarely if ever make any contact with other departments in their universities and thus reinforce the isolation of the classics department. Their condescension to their American students and easy dismissal of American culture do not help to contextualize classics for an American audience. In sum they have been a disaster, but such is their chic that it is well nigh impossible to turn the tide against them. When I once learned that the discovery of a "controlled substance," as it is called, in the pocket of a foreign national is grounds for instant deportation without a hearing, it took every ounce of Christian forbearance to prevent me from trying to improve the playing field for American classicists with this strategy.

I should not make this condemnation universal. We will always salute the late J. P. Sullivan as one of us. Maybe in part because he was the son of a stevedore in Liverpool. And let me close with a remark of the eternally wonderful Hermann Fränkel who was my colleague at Stanford University. He had left Stanford after the war to return to Germany from which he had fled in the 1930s. But then he returned to Stanford after five years. His colleagues were surprised since in those days Stanford was even more of a backwater than it is today, but in reply to their questioning he always said: "American students ask the right questions." I think that somewhere in this remark is the binding thread to everything that has been said today [at the St Andrews meeting]. The speakers want to find a new voice for classics, they want to penetrate and go beyond or to demolish the voice of establishment classics. They want to get away from the preconceptions that make questions clever, they want to return to an innocence that frees one for asking the right questions. They want to find their own voice.

NOTE

1 Although these are substantially the remarks made at St Andrews, reflecting their oral delivery, I have after the fashion of Cicero reshaped and amplified them somewhat for publication.

Chapter 9

The authority of experience

Susan Ford Wiltshire

A few minutes before the library was to close at midnight on a mild mid-October evening in 1987, I wrote the last words of the manuscript, stacked my books, stood up, and walked out of my carrel toward the elevator. I stopped, smiled, and with the clarity of an epiphany thought to myself: "I am ready to do this again." I had finished my first book. I had found my voice, assumed my authority, and discovered that I loved the work.

Two questions about this moment bear comment before I turn to the matter of authority. First: how could I have been tenured at a research university for a number of years by that time without already having published a book? When I was appointed with tenure, over twenty years ago, such a thing was possible at my university. It never would be now. I am grateful to have had the time to write my way into the book that I wanted deeply to write *because* I had the time to live my way into the depth of questions central to Vergil's *Aeneid* as well as to my life. Any earlier, I could not have written a book about that poem in a way that matters to me. In this case at least, scholarship depended on *skole*, on leisure and the passing of time.

More to the point: why did this occasion take so long to come about? Very simply, for many of my forty-six years I did not think I *could* write a book. The causes for my diffidence, of course, are rooted in time and place and life story. I grew up in the Texas Panhandle where I attended high school in the late 1950s. I was drawn to Latin because of a rigorous teacher who took us seriously. In our third year she gave our class, all seven of us, the choice of reading Cicero or Vergil. We chose Vergil. I was also encouraged by the example of my mother, who had studied Latin for nine years – from the beginning of high school through her graduate study for an MA in English literature. I do not recall being prodded by her toward classics, but always I was supported in my interests. As many students of Greek and Latin know, this is no small gift from a parent.

I inhabited, nevertheless, a male-defined world. At the University of Texas in Austin I never had a female professor in any subject, although Harry Leon and John P. Sullivan did encourage me to continue in classics. For that matter, I never had a female professor in four years at Columbia University either. On one occasion, Howard Porter invited Helen Bacon from Barnard to join him in the teaching of one of his courses. To watch Professor Bacon's brilliant mind at work widened my horizons, but I still held the notion that scholarship was the purview of men.

Charles Beye speaks elsewhere in this volume of his Irish friend who coped with the ethnic idiosyncrasies of the Ivy League by hiding behind epigraphical studies and who was "trained to repress himself in his writing" and to "submit to the assumed identity of the generic voice" in classical literary studies of the time. That may be. I know only second-hand how restrictive that particular tradition of the Ivy League can be for individuals who do not fit the mold – which, one way or another, is probably every individual involved.

I know this second-hand because the only students in my graduate cohort who had mentors among the faculty were young men. Perhaps by their mentors they were "trained to repress themselves" in their writing. I do not know. Since no one who taught me, so far as I could tell, assumed that I would be an active scholar or set about training me to be one, I was spared that particular form of repression. (My perceptions of the negative effects of my southern accent were another matter altogether!)

After two years of teaching at the University of Illinois and two more directing the Honors Program at Fisk University, I came to Vanderbilt University in the fall of 1971. I continued to love teaching, and I conceived the plan of writing an article about every author I teach. That plan took me through the 1970s, with more and more emphasis on Vergil.

But I was one of a tiny handful of faculty women in yet another university that was almost completely male-defined, and by this time, history was catching up with Vanderbilt. I assisted in developing the Women's Studies program and participated in various efforts to promote equity for female faculty and staff. In 1981 I became deeply involved in a supportive role in a sex discrimination lawsuit brought by a superb young English professor whose pioneering work in Women's Studies was discounted when the tenure recommendation of her department was overturned unilaterally by the college dean.

By this time I knew I could be a teacher and, when necessary, an activist. But even though I had published a dozen articles by then, the old belief system persisted: scholarship was the purview of men. Then, in a moment, something happened that crumbled and swept clean that obsolete, self-limiting supposition. The evening before the lawsuit was to be heard in Federal Court, the English professor, Elizabeth Langland, and I went for a leisurely run. We talked about various matters – my fond memory is that among other things we exchanged recipes. Then at one point Elizabeth said to me, "We must never assume positions of authority until we gain genuine authority ourselves. For me, that authority will come through reading and writing about literature."

"Yes," I knew instantly, "that's it." I reminded my friend that "authority" is derived from *augeo*, which has to do with increase or enlargement rather than hierarchy. In that moment I understood for the first time that when we "author," we are assuming the authority of our own voice. By bringing everything we know to what we write, by assuming the authority of our experience, we are not attempting to enter into or create a niche for ourselves in a pre-existing scheme. Rather, we are enlarging the range and nuance of the human response to literature and ideas. True authority is spacious, not restrictive. It is hospitable, not hostile to different voices and ideas.

The next day I began writing the Vergil book in earnest, no longer constrained, no longer afraid.

What is important in this narrative is not the particular details but the fact that each of us has a story. It is out of our stories that our authority as scholars comes. In that sense, all scholarship is personal, no matter how we go about it. After arguing the case for that claim and offering examples, I will propose some caveats and then conclude by suggesting reasons why an understanding of the personal voice in scholarship is beneficial both for scholarship and for our lives together.

ALL WRITING IS PERSONAL.

All scholars are poets, fashioning the work we do and the ways we do it out of the matter at hand. Chemists and mathematicians no less than professors of literature choose their subjects according to the instincts, training, and accidents of their lives. I will focus on studies of literature, the classical tradition, and the history of ideas, the areas within our discipline I know best. My hunch, however, is that finally all of us – historians, scientists, social scientists, humanists alike – write out of who we are.

In our writing we are always making choices about our subjects. Those choices are personal choices, no matter how strongly they are defined by others. Further, the nature of our scholarship is affected not only by our choice of subjects, but also by the ways we have seen it done by others, including our teachers. The friends with whom we share ideas, those we choose (or are chosen for us) to read and comment on our work, the phone call or letter of support – all these shape our writing.[1] Where we have lived and where we have traveled inform us, too, as do the places we teach – as Professor Beye points out with some poignancy in his chapter. The other books we are reading at the time we are writing influence us, as do the seasons of our private lives and the character of the public times in which we work.

All of these conditions make our response to literature and to ideas as personal as a fingerprint – responses that change and grow as we change and grow. In a fine *praeteritio* Doris Grumbach observes: "I refrain from saying that there are as many plots as there are writers narrating them, that the voice telling the story is what matters" (Grumbach, 1991: 250). Our subjects are in the air like lyrics all around us. How we apprehend them will be fashioned by our habits of being, habits unique to each of us.

We write for all sorts of reasons. Some years ago I proposed five reasons why we write at all. Now I see more clearly how rooted these reasons are in time and place:

First, we write because we can. Society has afforded us the training, the resources, and the time to write. Some go so far as to say that because of these advantages, we have a moral obligation to write.

Second, we write out of gratitude. We write a review or an article or a book because of all the books and articles and reviews we have read. Our writing is a recognition of the efforts of all of those who have brought us this far. It is a return on their investment.

Third, we write as an act of hospitality to strangers. In an earlier period of my life I thought of writing as the most private of acts, the work of seclusion far from the claims of the public realm. Now I see writing as the most public thing I can do because it touches people I will never meet, some of whom will come after me. Writing is meeting. We are hosts, inviting a company of strangers to gather around the words we offer in hospitality.

Fourth, we write to persuade, because we care about something passionately, because we are committed enough to grind ourselves up and do it again and again until we get it right, as right as we can get it. The very best writing in our disciplines does not cover up this passion. The very worst writing in our professions does, pretending a false authority of objectivity. The Nobel Prize-winning scientist Isidor Isaac Rabi urges, "Take your profession personally."

Finally – and I do not know how to say this except directly – we write for the joy of it. I do not say the pleasure. For me, writing is usually much too hard to be fun. But I know that it is the most creative thing I can do and that the joy when the idea first comes and then when the argument comes together at the end more than compensates for the anxiety of the waiting and the burden of the work.

(Wiltshire, 1987: 233–234)

What follows are accounts of how one classicist apprehended her subjects and how her experience shaped the way she wrote about them. Every book has a biography.

THREE BOOKS AND THE AUTHORITY OF EXPERIENCE

My first sustained work was on the themes of public and private in Vergil's *Aeneid*. The origins of that book lay in my increasing awareness of the theme of grieving mothers in the *Aeneid*, a motif that appears in every one of the twelve books of the poem either in the narrative or in similes. I have heard colleagues say that they never really understood the *Aeneid* until they had lost a father or had a son. Surely I became more sensitive to the theme of mothers in the *Aeneid* because I had two small children during the time I was writing *Public and Private in Vergil's Aeneid*.

Also formative was the fact that history had changed and by now it was not only respectable but encouraged to attend to the traditionally female, usually private, realm in texts and other evidence from classical antiquity as well as the traditionally male, usually public, world. Now I was free, because of the times in which I lived, to see what was already there in the *Aeneid*. I was not inventing a new poem. Rather, I had new eyes with which to see the existing poem whole instead of being confined by pre-conceived notions of proper topics for scholarship. I speak with authority on this subject, because I blush to confess thinking to myself in graduate school: "I would never write on the female characters of Euripides. I want to be a *real* scholar."

Once I had seen the persistence of the theme of grieving mothers in the *Aeneid*, I began to see that this was only one subset of a larger concern for the private world in this most public of poems. A related theme was the yearning for home in the *Aeneid*, the relentless longing for a home lost in the past or forever receding into the future. Still another was the various forms of personal love in the poem as they conflict with public obligations. Each of these three subjects in turn became scholarly papers, then eventually chapters for a book.

At the same time that I was learning to appreciate Vergil's embrace of the private world, I became more curious about how he mediated between the two realms that often seem so irreconcilable. This query led to a study of self-distancing in the poem, the strategy of relating to the public world in a way that does not impose on it at every moment one's personal circumstances. I came to see this as a kind of courtesy that permits community with others whose situations are different from one's own. It is the capacity Aeneas demonstrates when he speaks words of encouragement to his comrades, fixing hope on his face while pressing pain deep in his heart (*Aen.* 1.209).

This capacity for self-distancing was also illustrated by an event I witnessed at the time I was writing the chapter on that subject. At a small campaign gathering for Albert Gore, Jr, who had recently announced his bid for the US Senate, I noticed that Gore seemed somewhat distracted even though he conducted the meeting skillfully. The following morning I read in the newspaper that his beloved only sister had died of cancer the previous night. In the published version of the Vergil book I began the chapter on self-distancing with a list of examples, which indirectly included this one.

Another form of mediation between the public and private realms elaborated by Vergil is hospitality, but hospitality in the ancient rather than the modern sense. Modern hospitality is typically a transaction among friends, while ancient hospitality is typically a transaction among strangers. Ancient hospitality – *xenia* in the Greek tradition and *hospitium* or *ius hospitii* in the Roman – provides a meeting place between personal and political interests in ways that often transform both. Acestes, Evander, and Diomedes provide instances of such hospitality in the *Aeneid*.

Here, too, a personal experience during the time of writing the book confirmed for me this sort of transforming hospitality. I had gotten from a friend the name of a welder in a small town near the farm where my family and I have lived and worked on weekends for the last twenty-two years. When I went to call on this gentleman for a small job I needed, he invited me to join him and his family for lunch. After some hesitation I did so. As we ate, I was asked many questions – where I was from, who my people were, almost everything except how old I was when the Medes came. It was not until dessert, however, that I was asked my name.

I was tempted to include this example in my book but chose not to do so. The details were too tied to my own story to be appropriate for an illustration in the kind of book I was writing. Nevertheless, the authority of my experience in this case braced my critical analysis. I was writing in the personal voice, even if at one remove.

In the final chapter I suggested that *labor*, which Vergil defines in a variety of ways that cover the lifespan from birth to death and all the work in between, is the primary means by which an individual bridges the gap between private and public life. The social motive that sustains such labor, however, is *pietas*, the communal quality that guards various forms of relatedness subsumed under the term "loyalty." That kind of loyalty includes obligation to the generations yet to come, a constant theme in Vergil's *Aeneid*.

I had learned about these forms of work and loyalty long before I studied Vergil, because from early childhood I had had occasion to observe among the farmers in and near my family these same habits of work and faithfulness to the land and future generations. The personal voice I brought to this argument in the book, however, was not directly my own but that of Wendell Berry, the most Vergilian of contemporary American writers. In *A Place on Earth*, Berry's character Mat Feltner, whose only son Virgil has been lost in World War II, contemplates his responsibility for a parcel of land left by a dead relative:

> But now Virgil is missing, and Mat needs no more land for himself. He is too old now to need it – if he ever did. This new work must be done for the sake of the land itself – for the sake of no one he can foresee, someone who will come later, who will depend then on what is done now.

> (Berry, 1983: 150)

In addition to an introductory chapter on the problem of time in the *Aeneid*, I now had three chapters on the private realm of the epic and three on the ways Vergil mediates between public and private. I could not, however, figure out how to arrange the chapters. As so often happens in creative work, the solution came unexpectedly and in a quite different context. I finally gave up puzzling over the proper arrangement of the book and took some time off. As I sat in a rocking chair on a porch by a creek, thinking about something else altogether, I thought of the *pas de deux* in ballet. In that dance the movement of one partner seems necessarily to cause the corresponding movement of the other. That is when I knew that I would alternate the private and mediating chapters.

My conclusion at the end of the long labor of conceiving and writing *Public and Private in Vergil's Aeneid* was that if either the public or the private realm is collapsed into the other, it means the death of both. I argued further that Vergil knew this, which in part explains the shadows over the conclusion of the epic with the killing of Turnus, and that it is this awareness that makes Vergil a truly modern poet for our times as well as his own. I concluded the book with these words:

The separation of public and private life, caused in part by the bureaucratization originating in the Roman Empire created by Augustus, can be countered by the epic poem the same emperor commissioned. What bureaucracy has sundered, Vergil can help put back together. The power of the *Aeneid* is Vergil's insistence on honoring the claims of both the public and the private worlds, together with the possibilities he offers of mediating between the two.

To live and work in any age with care for both the public and private realms requires a tremendous courage. That Vergil accomplished such a task for his own times can give us courage for ours.

(Wiltshire, 1989: 143)

Over the years of writing the Vergil book, the understandings I was reaching about the dilemmas and queries of my own life were as much formed by reading the *Aeneid* as my personal experience was shaping my reading of the poem. The conclusions I reached in the book addressed and in important ways resolved both my intellectual concern about the *Aeneid* and my personal values for living a life. Such readings – always given the caveats I will detail later – bear an inner authority that can withstand the scrutiny of the most rigorous scholarly standards. That same authority underlay two more recent books, which I will address much more briefly.

The origins of *Greece, Rome, and the Bill of Rights*, a study of the history of the idea of rights and of the classical antecedents of the first ten amendments to the US Constitution, are precisely identifiable. They also demonstrate the effects of accident and *amicitia* on the ways our interests and voices are shaped.

During my first days in graduate school I was wandering in the depths of Butler Library looking for the section on Horace. Somehow my eyes fell on Lester Cappon's two-volume edition of the correspondence between Thomas Jefferson and John Adams. I was fascinated to discover the extent of their interest in classical subjects, a discovery that led to my first published article.

My interest in the classical tradition in America continued as an avocation ("Sunday afternoon work," as a friend called it), until the American Philological Association received a grant from the National Endowment for the Humanities in observation of the nation's bicentennial celebration in 1976. On the basis of the Jefferson–Adams article, I was invited to join the committee that administered the grant and its activities, and eventually I edited a volume of papers that came out of the project. Over the years I continued to publish in this field, with emphasis on the classical tradition in the South. I also wrote a long paper on the history of the idea of separation of powers in the US Constitution.

Then *amicitia* took a hand. Invited to give a paper in honor of my friend Meyer Reinhold on his eightieth birthday at a Boston University colloquium on the classics and the US Constitution, I was at a loss for a subject because I had already delivered the separation of powers paper elsewhere. Recalling the events of Meyer's life and the lives of others in our profession at a critical time in the nation's history, I realized again the importance of the Bill of Rights to us all. I knew then that I would write on its classical antecedents.

While the personal voice is muted in that volume, my personal concerns about the quality of public life very much underlay its argument. These extracts contain some of those concerns:

> For individuals to live together happily in communities requires a compromise between freedom and order. The Bill of Rights achieved this balance because of the two intellectual traditions that combined to give it birth: the natural law tradition, with its earliest origins among the Greeks, and the positive rule of law that is the gift of Rome.

> An understanding of the long heritage of the Bill of Rights helps us realize that in terms of its defining documents, the United States is founded on traditions stretching back to Greece and Rome rather than to Jerusalem. In our civic infrastructure we are a secular nation.

> The Constitution is the glue that holds American society together. It is the only defining document that applies to everyone and to which, by virtue of citizenship, the assent of everyone is implied. It provides the foundation for what has been called "constitutional faith," that is, an attachment to the Constitution as the basis of political life for both individuals and the nation. In an odd way, Homer's poetry provided a similar glue for the diverse communities of ancient Greece. It provided a common frame of reference for diverse peoples and communities without requiring conformity.

> In a liberal democracy, where freedom of thought is valued, attitudes toward any issue may vary widely with impunity. The Bill of Rights preserves the possibility that we do not all have to be the same to get along.

> (Wiltshire, 1992: 184–186)

The last phrase of the preceding passage first appeared to me on a postcard from China where my younger brother John Ford had led a trade delegation in 1984 as an undersecretary of Agriculture in the Reagan administration. John had gone by himself at 2.00 a.m. to Tiananmen Square (well before the terrible events that occurred there five years later). He wrote that as he sat in that vast place alone, two thoughts became clear: conditions change rapidly, and we do not all have to be the same to get along.

The former of those observations brings hope.or fear, depending on one's point of view. The latter saves lives. It was this latter nation that continued to motivate my work on the book on the Bill of Rights, the assumptions of which are crucial to the healthy survival of pluralistic societies.

My close relationship with my brother John led to my next book, one that I would wish dearly not to have written. Sometime in the 1980s John became HIV-positive. In 1985 he resigned from his position in government, came out as a gay man, and spent his remaining years championing the survival of the family farm in American agriculture as well as the need for education on gay and AIDS-related issues, especially in rural areas. John died of AIDS on April 3, 1993.

The day my brother's condition became AIDS-defined in January 1990, I began writing the book that became *Seasons of Grief and Grace: A Sister's Story of AIDS.* It is a personal book and the details of it are not important here, except in two regards.

First, I wrote it always with the "good case of one" maxim in mind, namely, that any story can have a wide reach if it is written well enough. I brought to this book the finest writing I could because I wanted to address not only one family's experience with AIDS but also wider issues of sibling relationships within the family drama. I wrote it out of the conviction, too, that telling our stories can help heal horrible rents in the social fabric. The hospitality of all literature is that it creates a sense of community among us. I harbor a hope that this is the way we read and teach – and when we can, write about – our classical texts as well.

Second, to the personal voice in which I wrote this book I frequently brought the authority of classical literature, rather than the other way around. I called on Homer, Aeschylus, Vergil, and Catullus in various contexts. It was Sophocles, however, who helped me most. The following passage illustrates one way this was so:

Sophocles' Oedipus plays provide an analogy for this epidemic. It was a social ill – a plague – that brought Oedipus into Thebes when he solved the riddle of the Sphinx. It was another kind of social ill – fear of pollution – that drove him out. Oedipus's suffering was never merely individual; it was always also political. Like AIDS.

(Wiltshire, 1994: 107)

Sophocles' *Oedipus at Colonus* helped me through my brother's pain also with its luminous hospitality and grace at the end of a life that included immense suffering. The night before John died I thought of the play again. I arrived at his home about 10.00 p.m. from Nashville, with tales of a recent controversy at my university. Like the old and ragged Oedipus at Colonus, John was capable to the end of wondrous outrage at injustice of every kind. It was a fine thing to behold. I knew from Sophocles' last play, too, as well as from my own experience, that deaths sometimes occur with serious family problems left unresolved. In the case of the play, the father was never reconciled with his warring sons. Finally, Sophocles provided the epigraph for my final chapter with Oedipus' last words to his daughters:

I know it was hard, my children, but one word makes all those difficulties disappear. That word is love.

(Wiltshire, 1994: 181)

CAVEATS CONCERNING THE PERSONAL VOICE

Having argued that all writing is personal, I offer these few cautions concerning the use of the personal voice. The first is that we will want to avoid intruding ourselves carelessly into our writing. References particular only to ourselves can be distracting to readers and, worse, lacking in tact. The purpose always is to call attention to our subject, not to ourselves. The goal is communication, not solipsism. Stories bring us together.

The use of the first person pronoun itself will depend on the circumstances of our writing. Sometimes it will be appropriate, sometimes not. It may be that we become more comfortable with using it as we become older. Often, however, the most effective expression of our personal experience is to distill from it a more general point for the passage or problem we are addressing. This is a habit of mind we learn partly through the experience of teaching, where it is often better to use our lived experience to help us frame the best questions to put to our students rather than offering our own experiences unmediated. (This is made easier by the fact that our students, like our children, rarely believe us anyway when we share our personal experiences directly. Our lives, they are sure, could never be like theirs – and they are right.) Through a subtle subordination of the details of personal experience to the larger concerns of our texts, we widen the range of the personal voice.

It is important, too, to remember that no personal experience privileges us absolutely – not the death of a father, not the bearing of children, not having read a thousand books, not a position of great influence, not the possession of an ideology. The amplifying rather than hierarchical understanding of authority brings with it a certain humility about our claims even as it enables us to make them with authenticity.

It is appropriate here to address one further question: if we admit the validity of the personal voice in our scholarship, how can we exercise rigorous judgment regarding our own work and that of others? What then is the grounding of our critical assessments?

I would argue that our grounding is the same as it has always been. In literary studies at least, this includes how well we situate our subject in a context and muster around it all the "correlative knowledge" we have of that context and related texts. It means how well we place our work in the larger scholarly tradition, whereby we pay tribute to those who went before, argue respectfully with those who think differently, and address as honestly as possible those positions opposing our own. It includes how well we pay attention to the "surrounding atmosphere," to the larger questions in other fields and in the culture to which the subject might offer some insight or perspective. It means, finally, how well the work is conceived and written. When we pay attention to these things, we may rely confidently on our own authority as we assess the authority of others.

ADVANTAGES OF THE PERSONAL VOICE

A certain courage is required to trust in the personal voice as a reliable ally of our scholarship. The costs of muting that voice, however, are perilous. Film director Roland Joffe says to aspiring directors: "There's nothing worse for human beings than to lose their voice. Don't be afraid. Don't give up" (Joffe, 1995: 11).

The advantages of the personal voice in scholarship for ourselves, our work, and our communities are numerous and significant. One advantage of the personal voice is that it helps us avoid abstractions. Assuming the authority of experience helps keep us connected in ways that make our writing more pointed and vibrant. At the very least, personal experience helps us sort out which issues are appropriate for abstraction and which are not. In his memoirs Nobel laureate Pablo Neruda says, "I harbor a natural indifference toward people who are theorists about poetry, politics, or sex" (Neruda, 1977: 345).

A related benefit is that the personal voice will help us follow Sander Gilman's succinct advice to younger scholars: "Write accessibly" (Gilman, 1995: 4). The more we assume our own authority, the less likely we are to hide behind the pseudo-authority of specialized jargon.

Another advantage of relying on our experience is that it keeps us aware of the complexity of all the issues we face in our writing and other work. Each one of us is composed of thousands of fragments of lived experience. How infinitely more complex, then, is the whole profession to which each of us brings what we know.

One of the most compelling arguments for recognizing and appreciating the personal voice in classical scholarship is that it keeps us from attacking personally others who do their work differently. Ours is a spacious discipline, with ample room for many different approaches. Once we become conscious of that, our field becomes more hospitable. Recognizing and assuming our voice makes us more magnanimous toward our colleagues because we are able to appreciate the fact that unique factors have also shaped their voices. When our own work is close to the heart, we are less defensive about the work of others.

Finally, respect for the personal voice can help us communicate better with others outside classics, both those in other fields and those in the larger community. Classics is far too rich a field to be hoarded merely among ourselves. Assuming the authority of our personal voices helps us connect with issues that matter also to other people.

Once we are conscious of ways in which the personal voice works, it is as if we have gained the vision of our other eye. We can see perfectly well with one eye only, even write whole dictionaries with one if it lasts long enough. But with the second eye, we gain two critical abilities: peripheral vision and depth perception. With peripheral vision, we embrace more fully the multiple possibilities for seeing evidence and bringing various kinds of authority to our work. With depth perception we realize more accurately how personal in origin and execution are all the texts that have come under our care.

When we read and write with this authority, our work is enriched, our communities are enhanced, and we become aware of the threads of warp and woof that bind our knowledge with our lives.

NOTE

1   I am grateful to Nancy Felson, Stephanie Quinn, and Thomas Van Nortwick for their helpful comments on this chapter.

REFERENCES

Berry, Wendell (1983) *A Place on Earth*, San Francisco, CA: North Point Press.

Gilman, Sander (1995) "What Should Scholarly Publication in the Humanities Be?" President's Column, *MLA Newsletter* Fall: 4.

Grumbach, Doris (1991) *Coming Into The Endzone*, New York: Norton.

Joffe, Roland (1995)*The Killing Fields; The Mission*, Interview with Denise Abbott in *On Production and Post-Production* September: 11.

Neruda, Pablo (1977) *Memoirs*, trans. Hardie St Martin, New York: Farrar, Straus, and Giroux.

Wiltshire, Susan Ford (1987) "On Authoring and Authority," *Southern Humanities Review* 21.3: 233–234.

—— (1989) *Public and Private In Vergil's Aeneid*, Amherst, MA: University of Massachusetts Press.

——(1992) *Greece, Rome, and the Bill of Rights*, Norman, OK and London: University of Oklahoma Press.

—— (1994) *Seasons of Grief and Grace: A Sister's Story of AIDs*, Nashville, TN and London: Vanderbilt University Press.

Chapter 10

Conclusion
What is classical scholarship for?

Thomas Van Nortwick

> What the past and future have in common is our imagination, which conjures them.
>
> Joseph Brodsky

I never write alone. Scholarship is often said to be a solitary occupation, but when I sit down in front of the keyboard, I never lack for company. Looking over my shoulder, whispering or shouting red-faced in my ear, imaginary companions are always with me. They may nod approvingly, exclaim over my insights, pat me on the back. More often, though, they complain: Who does he think he is? How can he say that? He obviously hasn't read/doesn't understand (insert name of prominent theorist). He doesn't know Greek! The voices babble and roar as I write this sentence ("Trying to take the rhetorical high ground, are we?"), prompting pre-emptive revisions. Recording the approving voices might seem a trifle, well, *self-serving* – leave them to their tasteful musings, then. What about the rest? Can I answer them?

When I write in a "personal voice" about classical literature, the noise level soars. Am I not imposing my own subjective interpretations on works of art from a distant time and place, distorting the truth to suit my own personal agenda? Who says Homer's audience would have had the same preoccupations I do? Who cares how Achilles makes me think about my mother's death? A more polite version of this voice would say: "It's all very interesting, but it's not scholarship." Or, "This tells me a lot about the scholar, but not much about the work of art." The issue here is not whether what I say is interesting or convincing, or provokes further thought about a poem. Rather, there seems to be a dispute over definitions: this is scholarship, that is not; scholarship is about the text, not the scholar. The authority for such pronouncements is largely historical: this is what we have called scholarship in the past. And not the distant past: the notion of objectivity as an ideal in scholarship does not pre-date the nineteenth century, when the "Science of History" came into being in Germany and then elsewhere, reflecting the anxieties of scholars not working in the so-called "hard sciences." Still, that objectivity is a relatively new ideal does not mean it is not a good one. Some may see this emphasis as a sign of progress – we are getting better at being scholars. I wonder, though, whether arguments over definitions do not sometimes cover over prior assumptions that go unexamined. What if I were to rephrase the question: instead of asking what classical scholarship is, maybe we should ask what classical scholarship is for.

For those who practiced textual criticism in its heyday (1875–1950, picking round numbers), the purpose of classical scholarship may have seemed easier to define: we studied the manuscripts in order to establish as best we could what the authors actually said. There was no sense in going on about motifs and structures when we didn't know whether the texts were accurate. There were also, of course, brilliant classical scholars in that period who did other kinds of work, historical research, interpretive studies of literature, stylistic analyses. But running underneath all of this scholarship was a fundamental assumption: there is something of the world of antiquity which has survived through the vehicle of its artifacts, which can be known directly. Thus the imperative of re-creating the closest possible approximations of the "original texts"; thus the contagious excitement of Milman Parry, who was sure he and Albert Lord had discovered a way to listen to Homer himself; thus the wonderful pictures of Sophie Schliemann in her jewels.

Notice the effect of this assumption. Because our goal was to uncover the world of Greece and Rome undistorted by intervening events and preoccupations, we focused on those aspects of classical civilizations and their artifacts that seemed to have been important and valuable then. So epic poetry carried more weight than romances when we were looking for the defining ideals of ancient cultures; the public world of politics, largely the domain of males, was more significant than what little we might discover about private life; Greek art was more profound than Roman, Virgil better than Lucan, and so forth.

The practical effect of these attitudes was – and is – profound. In comes an article to be considered for publication in a journal, on, say, how studying the poetry of Sulpicia can teach us something about Roman sexuality; in the same pile of mail there arrives a study of Horace's Roman Odes as evidence for the political significance of Augustan literature. Both manuscripts go out for a reading, both reviewers admire the tight structure of the arguments, careful documentation, and felicitous expression of their respective articles. But finally, the reviewer of the Sulpicia study says, "This is all very well done, but Sulpicia just isn't a very important author." When the time comes to decide what to print in a journal with limited space, the Horace article, other things being equal, goes ahead in the line.

I am not saying that these priorities are necessarily wrong – certainly some thoughtful people still honor them. The point is that we have tended to see the hierarchies implicit in such choices as part of the "truth" we look for when studying ancient civilizations, not as the product of our own preoccupations. We have been reluctant to examine our priorities, to ask "Important to whom?" "Better for what purpose?" And most significantly for the present essay, we have not often asked ourselves, "Why is this work of art important to *me,* in my own time and place?" By adopting the role of objective scholars, unearthing a lost culture that we can "see" as we see a red light at the intersection, we have been leading an unexamined life.

In the last fifty years or so, under the influence of Freud, Marxism, structuralism, feminism, postmodernism, and other paradigms of thought, the study of classical antiquity has become more varied in its methods, and certainty – or maybe I should say consensus – about the goals of classical scholarship has become much harder to achieve. The effect of all these approaches has been, one way or another, to draw attention to the context within which a work of art is created. The "discovery" of the unconscious piques our interest in the murky depths of the author's mind, and plants seeds of doubt about the intentional design of a work of art. The social and political matrix from which a poem arises suggests aims for the work that lie outside its "artistic" themes, while the polarities of Lévi-Strauss cut across traditional modes of analysis in other ways. Finally, the very boundaries of the literary text melt under the postmodernist gaze, as the whole world becomes one gigantic text, to be read by the deconstructionist.

In this perspective, the New Criticism, my mother's milk as a graduate student, looks like a rearguard action, trying to hold the textual fort against the forces of disintegration. The brilliance, as teachers and writers, of Brooks, Wimsatt, and others gave weight to a mode of thought that in many ways ran against dominant trends of twentieth-century intellectual life in Europe and America. As readers of literature, we were forbidden to discuss either the author's intentions or the audience's frame of mind. To commit fallacies, either "intentional" or "affective," spelled doom for the apprentice professor. This way of talking about literature was alluring, because it seemed to excuse us from knowing or acknowledging anything much about the historical context within which a work of art arose.

Indeed, even to think very much about such things was to put one foot on the fallacious slope. At the same time, by elevating the text to the status of timeless icon, New Critics also endorsed the assumption that the poetry and prose of antiquity carries in itself some kind of unchanging truth, available to anyone who reads the text with appropriate care and sophistication.

These distinctions aside, however, all the paradigms for reading and interpreting texts of any kind in the first three quarters of this century still finally shared the fundamental modernist assumption that there was such a thing as objective truth, however obscured by the circumstances of those who search for it. To put it another way, there is a world to be known by a detached knower. Freud's unconscious leads to Jung's archetypes; the "laws" of Marxism point toward universalizing notions of human behavior; the deep structures of a culture exist outside of human interpretation. Our ability to recover the lost civilizations of Greece and Rome, though challenged by new models of analysis, could survive in this intellectual climate.

The appearance of what we have come to call postmodernism, and its more specifically academic branches, semiotics and deconstruction, marks a major departure. Now the idea that there exists any kind of objective truth comes into question. Because there is always finally a "difference" between the thing known and a culture's linguistic signs for marking it, direct apprehension of the world, unmediated by signs, can never occur. The radical subjectivity that inevitably follows from postmodernist paradigms undermines any search for the "real" antiquity. Once we accept its central premises, postmodernist thought contextualizes all knowledge and collapses the gap between the "objective" world and its formulation in the mind of the knower. In one sense this shift only brings into a more common parlance the startling findings of quantum physics, which have been with us (or some of us) for eighty years. The idea that by looking at something we determine its position has been under consideration by physicists on the sub-atomic level for decades. But the Newtonian physics has still seemed to serve us well enough in the world we can see without powerful microscopes, and the paradigms of Heisenberg and others have, until recently, remained relatively arcane to the non-specialist.

The great divide, in the particular intellectual evolution we have been tracing here, comes, then, at the epistemological crisis brought on by postmodernist perspective. As long as we could feel confident about our ability to know the world as apart from ourselves, then the ideal of objective scholarship remained viable. We might need to recognize that our apprehension of the truth is informed by psychological, political, or social circumstances, but once acknowledged, these veils could be drawn aside to reveal the "real" world out there. Classical scholarship could still aim at uncovering antiquity and bringing it back to the present. But once the separation between knower and known comes into question, the goal of objectivity becomes elusive and problematic.

Another set of companions is talking to me insistently now. All this epistemological stuff is fine, but let's get real: scholarship may be driven in part by a selfless desire to learn the truth, but we also have to publish or we may not keep our jobs; once we have tenure, low productivity means we lose ground in the race to bigger salaries and more prestige. Once I start listening to this chorus, a decidedly dark tonality creeps in: the whole enterprise of graduate programs is just a way of supporting in-bred cliques, bent on reproducing themselves and so cranking out clones to feed the Dean's relentless bottom line. What does knowing the metrics of Plautus contribute to the overall health of the nation? This voice, I hasten to say, sounds peculiarly American to me, echoing a virulent strain of anti-intellectualism in my own country, and becoming frighteningly loud at present. If we cannot answer, the whole question of why we pursue classical scholarship may well become moot. But any response we give must finally emerge from some kind of consensus about the intellectual goals of classical scholarship – arguing for the need to preserve classics departments in our colleges and universities will not get us far if we cannot decide what it is we do and why we do it. And answering these questions for ourselves, in the current intellectual climate, means checking our motives: why do *I* think classical scholarship should take one path and not another? What is there to be learned from examining my particular priorities in the light of my present circumstances?

Much of what I've been saying here might apply to any discipline in the humanities or social sciences. Thinking about classics in particular takes us to another set of issues, ones reflecting the place of classical antiquity in the cultural histories of various nations. The Renaissance rediscovery of Greco-Roman civilization both nurtured and was driven by the excitement of seeing Western European culture – particularly in Italy and France – as an extension of Roman civilization; German Romanticism seized on the Greeks as a paradigm, and elevated Homer over Virgil; in late Victorian England, the identification of the new nation of Germany with Sparta, England with Athens, seemed natural, and British soldiers went to war with Homer in their rucksacks. All these countries enshrined the study of Latin and Greek as the centerpiece of the gentleman's education in the eighteenth and nineteenth centuries. In the United

States, all of the above became to one degree or another part of the justification for elevating classics to a special place in the liberal arts curriculum. At the same time, influenced by the spirit of the French Revolution, we also saw the founding fathers as reflections of a new kind of classical humanism, Jeffersonian democracy as the latest realization of the great heritage of Greco-Roman civilization.

Running alongside the desire to know the civilizations of classical antiquity as they were, honoring the unique qualities of each, was, then, a competing desire to see the continuities between ancient and modern societies and their works of art. The specialized knowledge of texts and physical sites produced by scholars could trickle down to a wider audience, whose appetites were whetted by various forms of national identification with classical antiquity. All of this became problematical, however, after the First World War. The horrors of Verdun and elsewhere seemed to sever the connections between Roman and European culture, plunging us in the aftermath into a frightening new world, estranged from the values of classical civilization. Now the need for a classical education seemed less obvious. In the intervening seventy-five years, the study of ancient Greek and Roman civilizations has been declining, further imperiling consensus about the place of classical learning in our various cultures.

A somber picture. But if we are loathe automatically to give the study of classical civilizations a special place in a liberal arts education, we also have the opportunity to look again at our field, and think about what it offers to its students at the turn of the millennium. Where I teach, the great majority of students in classics courses, especially in the original languages, are encountering classical civilization in a systematic way for the first time. Arriving unburdened by the onus of having to crawl like snails unwillingly through Caesar, they see the material through fresh eyes, and evaluate it alongside other literatures and disciplines. The result is that though the numbers in language courses remain lower than we would like (this has to do in large part with language study in general in the United States, a subject for another essay), overall enthusiasm for knowing about Homeric epic or Thucydides can run high. Those of us who have devoted our lives to studying the ancient civilizations needn't be told that the material is intrinsically rich and interesting, that if we teach it well, students will come to learn it.

The clean slate approach can have other benefits for us as scholars and teachers. In the midst of a fractious faculty debate about multiculturalism and course requirements, I was puzzled to learn that many of my colleagues refused to grant that studying, say, Aristotle, could help students to learn about misogyny or racism. They seemed to assume that when we in the Classics department teach Aristotle, we must endorse his views on women and slavery, and so proselytize innocent minds. How could intelligent people hold such a naïve view of teaching? Do early modern historians endorse the Inquisition? Were Hitler's biographers all Nazis? What better place to begin thinking about the background for modern theories about the "natural" place of women in society than with an extraordinarily articulate and forceful proponent of these ideas? The reason for my colleagues' obtuseness about these issues was, I believe, a residual effect of the traditional aristocratic elevation of classics to a special place in the curriculum: studying classics made you a better person, and proved you were worthy of a special place in the nation's business; conversely – and here we come to the nub of the matter – studying Latin and Greek was in itself a sign of one's superiority. The narrow-mindedness of such views still dogs those of us who teach classical civilizations, whatever our own circumstances and attitudes might be. I was told in my youth that privilege brings responsibilities. It can also bring cultural baggage we do not want to carry.

Where does scholarship in a personal voice fit in this picture? Clearly the subjective aspects of such a perspective have become less worrisome in the wake of postmodernism. If finding objective truth seems increasingly problematical, then being open about a personal agenda is only honest. Some might say, indeed, that the mask of objectivity has allowed scholars to voice personal opinions with impunity. Insofar as we accept that all subject positions are inevitably informed by the author's circumstances, by just so much are we obliged, one might say, to come clean about our own subjective agency in establishing what is important, interesting, valuable. (I would leave out of this discussion the many engaging personal memoirs written by classicists over the years. Though these works often deliver insights into classical antiquity, their authors never saw them as scholarship, as contributions to the knowledge of Greek and Roman culture.)

My *consilium* when I write personally about classical texts is, then, a modernist gang, recruited for the most part in my graduate school days. They yell at me for anachronism, for distorting the societies of the ancient world to fit my own time and place. Students can never achieve any kind of detached perspective on their own world if they are given an Athens that sounds like late twentieth-century Oberlin. It's the *differences* between Rome and the United States that must be emphasized. Well, yes, if in fact we can apprehend Athens directly, but that kind of knowing has become suspect. In any event, is it not the case that choosing to study one set of differences rather than another reflects our own time and place? In his great book on the Greeks, an open attempt to see that civilization in the light of modern psychological preoccupations, Dodds had no interest in exposing the differences between Athenian and modern British attitudes toward women (Dodds, 1951).

Which brings me to my next point. I have not said much so far about the significant impact of feminism on classical scholarship. In one sense, this (increasingly diversified) set of voices fits with other perspectives calling for us to acknowledge the cultural context for our work – the patriarchal biases of modern societies are reflected in how we see antiquity; indeed, ancient Mediterranean cultures are an important source for modern misogyny. But gender issues intrude on the issue of personal voice scholarship in another way. Looking at the assumptions about gender that underlie Greek and Roman thought has shown us that the very idea of objectivity is to some extent "gendered." In the Greek paradigm for how civilization is formed, it is the imposition of masculine reason on the rhythms of nature that produces human culture. And women, in this view, occupy at best a marginal position between nature and culture, always ready to overflow the bounds that define the meaning of human life, needing to be controlled. The illusion fostered by this model has been alluring and tenacious, forming the underpinnings of heroic cosmogonies and persisting well into the twentieth century in the myths of heroic scientists and doctors, conquering nature for the benefit of humans.

So it is no surprise that feminist scholars were among the first to urge us to acknowledge our subjectivity in writing about classical antiquity. To insist on maintaining a detached position from which to analyze the raw material of scholarship has always been a masculine position; the very autonomy of the individual who would make that inquiry has been seen as masculine: masculinity is defined as separation from the rest of the world, femininity by connection. We may go further. One strain in the objections to personal voice scholarship has been that to speak of one's own life is somehow undignified, not befitting the modesty and maturity of the scholar. We can hear now the echoes of the aristocratic aversion to public exposure, to putting oneself forward. At the same time, the public world in Western societies has been until recently a masculine preserve. To control this arena requires patrolling the boundaries against the intrusion of a private, feminine, world – the colorless phrase *res publica* deflects interest in the workings of an oligarchy.

What, then, is classical scholarship for in the gloaming of the twentieth century? Uncovering the objective truth about antiquity, unfiltered by distortions from the present, seems increasingly problematical. Documenting the classical heritage of our social and political systems continues to be important, but not from the privileged position classical learning once had. Rather, we see the legacy of Greece and Rome in our own time increasingly as one among many cultural traditions, models to consider in our own search for a more viable society in the post-industrial West. Nor can we take for granted, as we have done, the sanctity of the canon of ancient writers. Acknowledging the subjective, contextualized nature of value judgments about quality means rethinking the list of texts we rank as essential reading for the educated citizen. The scholarly chorus too is less harmonious at present than it may once have been, more polyphonous, reflecting the fragmenting of Western social fabric – writing in a personal voice or from a more detached position becomes a matter of choice, each with its own opportunities and dangers. But finally, we circle back to the familiar reasons, the compelling depth and complexity of the issues raised by the texts themselves. The allure of classical antiquity has always been as a mirror for our own struggles to define what it is to be human, to live a good life, to die a good death. That we are lately more inclined to acknowledge that we see ourselves when looking does not diminish the power of the material to shape our lives, for better or worse.

REFERENCES

Dodds, E. R. (1951) *The Greeks and the Irrational,* Berkeley and Los Angeles, CA: University of California Press.

Index